DATE DUE			

MEADE'S HEADQUARTERS
1863-1865

Col. Theodore Lyman

MEADE'S HEADQUARTERS
1863-1865

Letters of
COLONEL THEODORE LYMAN
FROM
The Wilderness to Appomattox

SELECTED AND EDITED BY
GEORGE R. AGASSIZ

BOOKS FOR LIBRARIES PRESS
FREEPORT, NEW YORK

First Published 1922
Reprinted 1970

INTERNATIONAL STANDARD BOOK NUMBER:

0-8369-5582-X

LIBRARY OF CONGRESS CATALOG CARD NUMBER:

71-137381

PRINTED IN THE UNITED STATES OF AMERICA

To
ELIZABETH RUSSELL LYMAN
and the Inspiring Influence
of her Beloved Memory

Introduction

Theodore Lyman — man of science — soldier — and man of the world — touched life at many points. He could draw easily on his varied experience, from a well-trained and well-stored mind. This, added to good looks, charm, and good humor, a ready wit and great tact, made him a striking and telling personality, whether in the camp, a scientific meeting, or social gathering.

Among his many activities, he served, from 1883 to 1885, as a member of the House of Representatives at Washington, being elected on an independent ticket from his Massachusetts district. As he was the only independent member then in Congress, he held there a position of unusual influence. At that time the Harvard Club of Washington celebrated its birth by having a dinner. The first two speakers, a member of the cabinet and a senator, indulged in dry and inappropriate political harangues; and the event threatened to be *un dîner manqué*. The chairman next called on Lyman, who regretted that the previous proceedings had been tinged with a levity unworthy of so serious an occasion, proposed to do something solemn, sang a comic song, and saved the day.

The Lyman family of New England is of old English stock. Its founder, one Richard Lyman, came to America in 1631, on the good ship Lyon, which among its sixty odd passengers included John Eliot, and the wife of Governor Winthrop and her children. The first Theodore Lyman, a direct descendant of Richard in the fifth generation, was the son of the pastor of Old York in the District of Maine.[1]

[1] Maine was then a part of Massachusetts.

Toward the end of the eighteenth century Theodore left York, and came to Massachusetts Bay, where he settled in Boston. There he became a successful man of business, and laid the foundation of the family fortunes.

The second Theodore (1792–1849) was born in Boston, and graduated from Harvard in 1810. He was a man of note in the community of his time; had studied abroad and travelled in Eastern Europe, an unusual circumstance in his day; and was Mayor of Boston in 1834 and 1835. In 1820 he married "the beautiful and accomplished" Mary Henderson of New York.

Their only son, Theodore Lyman, the third of that name, and author of the present letters, was born on August 23, 1833, in the well-known family homestead at Waltham, Massachusetts. But almost his whole life was passed in Brookline, where his father afterwards built a house, a pleasant and spacious dwelling, set in ample lawns and spreading elms.

Young Theodore received his early education from private tutors, and spent the years 1848 and 1849 in Europe. His mother died when he was three years old, and the year of his return from abroad he lost his father. This left him at sixteen an orphan, heir to an independent fortune and the Brookline estate. Two years later he entered Harvard with the Class of '55. It was natural that one so charming, high-spirited, and companionable should feel himself warmly drawn toward the social side of college life. In his studies, for the first two years, he hovered about the middle of his class. It was not till his junior year that his intellectual ambitions were aroused, and in his senior year his true abilities asserted themselves. For in that year he received the highest marks in the class, and graduated fourth. After leaving college, he turned his attention to

Natural History, and worked under Louis Agassiz. Devoting himself to the study of Ophiurans while maintaining a broad interest in the outside world, Lyman became the authority of his day on that group.

In 1858 he married Elizabeth Russell, daughter of George R. Russell, an East India merchant of Boston. Lyman took his bride home to his Brookline house, where they lived some two years, before starting to travel in Europe. There a daughter was born, and there they remained until she was old enough to be brought safely home.

In the winter of 1856, the year after he graduated, Lyman was sent by Agassiz on a scientific pilgrimage to Florida waters. In Key West he ran across Captain George Gordon Meade of the Engineers, who was superintending the construction of lighthouses in that district. In those days a traveller was a *rara avis* in Florida, and a lonely wanderer found but scant accommodation. Captain Meade had a ship at his disposal, and was delighted to have the chance of offering Lyman the hospitalities of his floating home, for a far less agreeable man would have been a godsend in the wilderness. The Engineer Officer was eighteen years the senior of the Roving Naturalist, but they proved congenial companions, and the intimacy so formed was afterwards maintained.

And thus it chanced that, on his return from Europe Lyman, from September 1863, until the end of the Civil War, was a member of the staff of General Meade, commanding the Army of the Potomac. The present volume is composed of a selection of Colonel Lyman's letters to his wife from the front. His vivid picture of the life and actions of that army has an added interest from the contrast that it offers to the late World War. Still, the con-

test was titanic for the times; and during the four years of
the Civil War there were mustered under the Union Flag
over two and three quarter millions[1] of men. This was a
far greater proportional drain on the American youth of
that day than the drafts for our recent armies. Nevertheless, in no battle of that war was an army of much over
100,000 men engaged. But one must remember that
Napoleon had less than 75,000 men at Waterloo, and that
the eighteen miles or so of intrenched line before Petersburg could, in 1865, justly be considered vast.

Five years later the Franco-Prussian War taught us to
think of battles on a larger scale; while the opening of the
century saw Russia and Japan fighting along battle-lines
of sixty miles, with armies of half a million. To-day the
white races of the world lie panting from a struggle in
which armies of millions have wrestled along battle-lines
stretching across the Continent of Europe.

Small as they were in the light of our recent experiences,
the battles of our fathers might have furnished valuable
military instruction for Europe. As Lyman says, it was
shown that an army could dig itself in in a few hours, and
completely intrench itself in three days. Had the French
war office profited by this lesson, and, instead of building what proved useless fortifications, established an intrenched line along the Belgium frontier, there would be
to-day, in all probability, no devastated France.

GEORGE R. AGASSIZ

BOSTON, MASSACHUSETTS
September 15, 1922

[1] This includes re-enlistments and 90-day men.

CONTENTS

ILLUSTRATIONS

MAPS

[Drawn by Colonel Lyman]

MEADE'S HEADQUARTERS
1863–1865

I

FIRST MONTHS

THEODORE LYMAN reached Boston early in June 1863, hoping to obtain a Staff appointment. His first weeks were spent in settling his little family in Brookline, adjusting his private affairs, and sorting the collections of his beloved Ophiurans that had accumulated during his absence in Louis Agassiz's newly built museum.

Many of Lyman's friends thought that his desire to join the army was quixotic and unnecessary. Meanwhile Lee's advanced guard had crossed the upper Potomac, and Hooker had moved on Centreville from Falmouth. "There will be stirring times ahead," writes Lyman in his journal. "Every one takes the matter with great calmness; we are too dead!" Soon came Gettysburg; and shortly afterward Mrs. Lyman's cousin, Robert Shaw, fell at the head of his negro regiment in the assault of Fort Wagner. Again Lyman writes: "Bob was a shining example of great development of character under pressing circumstances. In peace times he would have lived and died a quiet, manly, happy-tempered fellow; but the peril forced his true spirit into action, and now his name stands as that of one who gave up a life spotless of low ambition, of cowardice, of immorality; a life torn from all that is attractive and agreeable and devoted to the cause of Eternal Right."

An entry in his journal says of a shooting-trip of his on some old haunts among the marshes of Cape Cod: "As I walked about this beautiful old place, with the clear air and the fine breeze, the idea of going to war struck me with a ten-fold disagreeable contrast. N—— B—— was quite eloquent on the topic and strongly urged against it. But what's the use? A man must march when it is his plain duty; and all the more if he has had, in this world, more than his slice of cake!"

On August 10th Lyman wrote the following letter to General Meade, in command of the Army of the Potomac:—

As your time is valuable I will write in few words. I arrived here from Europe, with my family, some few weeks since; all well. In your letter to me, dated, Camp opposite Fredericksburg, December 22, 1862, you were kind enough to say: "I shall be delighted to have you on my staff"; and you go on to suggest that I should come as "Volunteer Aide" with a commission from the Governor of the state, and getting no pay; only forage for my horses. I clearly understand that this is *no promise*, only an expression of good will. Therefore I ask you frankly if you are now able and willing to take me as a Volunteer Aide? I am assured that Governor Andrew would, for his part, give me a commission. My military accomplishments are most scanty. I can ride, shoot and fence tolerably, speak French fluently and German a little, have seen many thousands of troops of most nations of Central Europe, and have read two or three elementary books. After all, I fear my sole recommendation is my wish to do something for the Cause. I will take anything you have to offer. If you have nothing, perhaps one of your generals would take me on his staff.

[To this General Meade promptly replied from the Headquarters of the Army of the Potomac.]

George Gordon Meade

Your note of the 10th inst. is received. I continue in the same disposition as when I wrote you on the 22d of last December. If you are anxious to see service or think your duty requires you to do so, I shall be very glad to avail myself of your services, and the best position for you is the one I indicated — that of Volunteer Aide. This will leave you free and independent; and enable you, whenever you have seen the elephant, or have satisfied the demands of duty, to return to your family without embarrassment. If the Governor will confer on you the commission of Lieutenant-Colonel, it will give you the right to wear the uniform and bear the title, and I can arrange here for the position you will occupy. You will require two good horses, a competent man to take care of them, and the smallest outfit that you can well get along with, as our transportation is limited. You can take your own time in joining, as you come in an independent position. Now I beg you will let Mrs. Lyman understand that this is all *your doings;* and that she must not hold me responsible for anything beyond not throwing obstacles in your way, which, in view of your very agreeable company, she could hardly expect me to do.

[Armed with this letter Lyman was soon in the possession of his commission as Lieutenant-Colonel in the Massachusetts Militia, and received a special order giving him a furlough for a year, and detailing him to serve on the staff of General Meade. "God give me," he writes, "proper qualities to discharge my duties."

A few hurried days busy in buying horses and equipment, and he was ready to start. His journal closes with these words before leaving for the front: "A most splendid day. Mimi went with me a pleasant walk in the woods, and we picked flowers. It will be hard to part — harder than we think for! How many a brave man has never come back! The retribution of Sin descends with compound force on the generations that come after. To-morrow I leave for the army. May I do my full duty; without that there can be nothing worthy."

He left New York for Washington the next night, "getting a sleeping-car at Philadelphia." In Washington he saw "the streets full of soldiers, many slouchy, some dirty; but nearly all tough and strong looking," and he characteristically remarks of the Capitol, "The interior is an incongruous mixture of fine marbles, common plaster and tobacco juice."

The following day found him about three miles from Warrington Junction, at the]

HEADQUARTERS, ARMY OF THE POTOMAC
September 3, 1863

Behold me, installed in solemn state! having thus far lost no limb. Betimes, at seven this morning, I was duly at the Alexandria ferryboat with horses, Silas and Albert. Having shown my pass, I assured the worthy corporal on guard that there was no liquor in the saddle-box, and was allowed to go on board, and twenty minutes took us to Alexandria, a town in no wise remarkable except for an antique pavement, much resembling that of Pompeii and of the Via Appia at Rome, in respect to deep holes and ruts. Here I was driven to the "Depot," which consisted in one wooden counting-room, closely beset on all sides by puffing engines and innumerable freight cars. Having, at great risk, got into the shanty, I of course found a Marbleheader at the head of all affairs, viz., Colonel Devereux. He received me with tenderness, my horses were put in the best car and I was placed in a state chair until the train was ready, when the conductor solemnly took me and placed me first in the only passenger car. Shoulder-straps *is* shoulder-straps down here, and folks is obleeged to stand round. The conductor (the dirtiest mortal I ever saw, but extremely energetic and capable) said we should have no trouble with guerillas, as they had a very nice colonel in command near there, who had taken the wise precaution to seize the father and brother of the chief guerilla and then to send a civil message to him stating that, if any trains were fired into, it would be his (the Colonel's) painful duty to tie said relations on the track and run an engine over them! This had an excellent effect. I have only time to-night to say that we got down all safe. . . . You may rest easy on my account for the present. There is about as much appearance of an enemy near at hand, as there would be on Boston Common. The nearest of them (except a few guerillas) are many miles from here.

September 5, 1863

Our train consisted in a large number of freight cars, all marked "U. S. Military Railroads," and of one passenger car containing its precious freight of officers, not to speak of the female doctor who knocked Zacksnifska out of all sight and knowledge. She was going down to get the son of an old lady, who (the said son) had had a sunstroke, and this female doctor had great confidence she could cure him. She was attired in a small straw hat with a cockade in front, a pair of blue pantaloons and a long frock coat, or sack. Over all she had a linen "duster"; and this, coupled with the fact that she had rips in her boots, gave her a trig appearance. She was liberal in her advice to all comers and especially exhorted two newspaper boys to immediately wash their faces, in which remark she was clearly correct.[1] . . .

. . . At Warrenton Junction there was luckily an ambulance from headquarters; and as its owner was only a diminutive captain, I had no hesitation in asking him to carry me up, with my traps. . . . So off we set, on a road which went sometimes over stumps and sometimes through "runs" two or three feet deep. We passed any quantity of pickets and negroes and dragoons in twos and threes; till at last, looking off to the left (or rather right), I beheld what seemed a preparation for a gigantic picnic: a great number of side-tents, pitched along regular lines, or streets, and over them all a continuous bower of pine boughs. These were "Headquarters." I put my best foot forward and advanced to the tent of the Commander-in-Chief, in front of which waved a big flag on a high staff. In my advance I was waylaid by a lieutenant, the officer of the day, who with much politeness said General Meade was out for a ride, but would I not walk into a tent and take some whiskey; which I accepted, all but the whiskey. He turned out to be a Swede, one Rosencrantz, and I rejoiced his soul by speaking of Stockholm. Presently there arrived the General himself, who cried out, "Hulloo, Lyman! how are you?" just as he used to. He was as kind as possible, and presently informed me I was to mess with him. As the Chief-of-Staff is the only other man who is allowed to do this, you may concede that my lines have fallen in pleasant places! The said Chief-of-Staff is General Humphreys, a very eminent engineer. He is an extremely neat man, and is continually washing himself and putting on paper dickeys. He has a great deal of knowl-

[1] Dr. Mary E. Walker (1832–1919).

edge, beyond his profession, and is an extremely gentlemanly man. As to the Assistant Adjutant-General, S.
Barstow, he was most hospitable, and looked out for
getting me a tent, etc. He really has a laborious and difficult position, the duties of which he seems to discharge
with the offhand way of an old workman.

Now I will pull up. As to my riding forth yesterday and
to-day, in martial array, beside the General, and with
dragoons clattering behind, shall not the glories thereof be
told in a future letter? Meanwhile, if you want to feel as
if nobody ever was or could be killed, just come here!
This is the effect, strange as it may seem. For your assur-
ance I will state, that we yesterday rode seven miles
directly towards the enemy, before we got to a spot
whence their pickets may sometimes be seen! . . .

[A few words will recall the position of the Army of the
Potomac at that time. Halleck was virtually in command
of the Union armies. In June, Lee turned the right wing
of the Union Army, crossed the Potomac, and entered
Pennsylvania. Hooker, then in command of the Army of
the Potomac, followed on Lee's right flank, covered Washington, and crossed the Potomac. On June 27, Lincoln
relieved Hooker and appointed Meade, who was then in
command of the Fifth Corps. Four days later, Meade
got in touch with the Confederate Army, and placed his
forces in such a position, on the heights of Gettysburg,
that Lee was forced to attack him. After three days' stub-
born fighting, which culminated in the repulse of the
magnificent Confederate charge under Pickett, Lee was
forced to retreat. Meade followed him, but Lee succeeded
in recrossing the Potomac before the former considered
himself in position to attack him. Meade also crossed the

river into Virginia. Lyman joined the army in the midst
of the manœuvres that ensued. It was a campaign of
skirmishes and combats, but with no general battle before
both armies went into winter quarters in December.]

September 6th, 1863

I promised to tell you how I invited General Meade to
go with me and see General Sykes. If I didn't know anything, I *looked* like a Commander-in-Chief, for I had the
best horse and the best accoutrements, and as for clothes,
General Meade was nowhere; besides which, he had no
sword, while I had. The cavalry escort reminded me
exactly of the Guides that go with the little Prince along
the rue de Rivoli. No two of them had caps alike, none
had their jackets buttoned; all were covered with half an
inch of dust, and all eschewed straps to their pantaloons.
Nevertheless, had the Rebs appeared, I should have pre-
ferred these informal cavaliers to the Guides. Each man
had a sabre with a rusty scabbard, and a revolver hung at
his belt. They all ride well, and would be handsome
horsemen, if "got up."

General Humphreys, with his usual bland smile, appeared on a small gray, which was of a contrary and rear-
ing disposition; but the General remarked, with the air of
an injured man, that he had had three valuable horses
killed under him in battle, and *now* he should only get
cheap ones. General Meade, whose saddle-flap was ornamented with a bullet-hole within an inch of his leg, was
mounted on a small bay. And so we jingled off; sometimes
in the road, sometimes in the open fields, sometimes in
the woods and sometimes through creeks and mudholes.
The Chief rides in a most aggravating way, neither at a
walk nor a gallop, but at a sort of amble, which bumps

you and makes you very uncomfortable. . . . In due
season we got to the 5th Corps Headquarters, near the
Rappahannock, which is a very narrow affair at this
point, and not over four feet deep on the shallowest fords.
General Sykes looks a little like the photograph of General
Lyon and has a very thick head of hair, which stands up
like Traddles's. He is a mild, steady man, and very polite,
like all the officers I have seen down here. Indeed, a more
courteous set of men it would be hard to find. I have yet
to meet a single gruffy one. They are of all sorts, some well
educated, others highly Bowery, but all entirely civil. . . .

The astute Sykes talked some time with the Chief, and
then we rode to the Headquarters of General Newton, who
commands the 1st Corps, hard by. This chieftain had a
very gorgeous tent, erected for the express accommodation
of Mrs. Newton, who, however, was soon driven forth by
the general order excluding all ladies from the lines; and
the tent was all that remained to remind one of her presence. General Newton also has a thick head of hair, and is
a tall and finely built man and "light complected." He
was in great glee over a *tête-de-pont* he had erected, and
hoped to decoy some unfortunate Rebels to within range of
it. He produced a huge variety of liquids which I had to
refuse. The drinks I have refused will be a burden on my
conscience in time to come. They come from all sides and
in great variety, even champagne! . . .

HEADQUARTERS, ARMY OF POTOMAC
September 9, 1863

In my last I forwarded a landscape with Headquarters
of the 3d Corps in the verdant background. In this, I will
describe the Review, at which, as the Gauls say, "I
assisted." . . . Everybody got himself up in all available

splendor. Those that had scarfs put them on, and those
that had none, tried to make up in the shine of their boots
and newness of their coats. General Meade burst forth in
the glory of a new saddle-cloth, which the expressman had,
in the nick of time, brought fresh from Washington. As
for myself, did I not put on the Brimmer scarf, and white
gloves, and patent-leather boots; whereby, shining like a
lily of the field, was I not promoted to ride immediately
behind the Chief, thereby happily avoiding the dust?
Heure militaire, we all mounted, the escort presented arms,
and the cavalcade jogged off, *en route* for the parade
ground, six miles distant. The road lay through pine woods,
and barren fields, and all sorts of places like most roads
hereabouts, and the cloud of dust we raised must have
been extremely pleasant to the escort in the rear! At
length we got in sight of a big U. S. flag, and, immediately
after, beheld a long slope of clear ground, quite black with
the lines of infantry, while long artillery trains were moving across the fields to get into position. It looked very
handsome and warlike, and the muskets, which had received an extra burnish, were flashing away at a great
rate. The procession rode up to the house and dismounted
midst great cries of "Orderly!" to come and hold their
horses. Then advanced convenient Contrabands and
dusted us down; which improved our aspect not a little.
After which the Corps Commander, General French, came
forth, with proper greetings. He looks precisely like one of
those plethoric French colonels, who are so stout, and who
look so red in the face, that one would suppose some one
had tied a cord tightly round their necks. Mounted on a
large and fine horse, his whole aspect was martial, not to
say fierce. In a few minutes we again got on, and moved
towards the field; whereupon there arose a great and dis-

tant shouting of "Bat-tal-ion! Shoulder! Her-r-rms!"
and the long lines suddenly became very straight and
stiff, and up went the muskets to a shoulder. We rode
down the front and up the rear of each line (of which there
were three, each of a division with the artillery on the left
flank) amid a tremendous rolling of drums and presenting
of arms and dropping flags; the bands playing "Hail to
the Chief." Miss Sturgis's mare behaved very nicely and
galloped along with her neck arched, minding nothing except the flags, and those not much. Even the cannon did
not disturb her behaviour. . . .

After the artillery had in like manner been reviewed, the
General took a station by a little flag, and then all three
divisions marched past, followed by the artillery. It was
a somewhat sad sight to look at these veterans, with their
travel-stained uniforms and their battered canteens; many
of the regiments had no more than 200 men, and their
flags were so tattered that you could barely read such
names as Fair Oaks, and Williamsburg, where so many of
the missing 800 now lie. The men looked spare and brown
and in good health; and also as if they would then and
there fight French Zouaves or anybody else you chose to
bring on. . . . Some divisions at Gettysburg marched
thirty-six miles in one day; and then fought for two days
after that, with scarcely anything to eat or to drink.
Among the troops were the 11th and 16th Massachusetts
regiments and the 10th battery, and certainly none of the
soldiers looked better. . . . The artillery looked even
more serviceable than the infantry; and, independent
of the large number of guns, was well horsed and well
manned. As a rule I am much pleased with the aspect of our
officers, high and low. They are cleanly and have a firm,
quiet bearing. You can often pick out those who have been

through the thick of it, by their subdued and steady look. The dress of the soldiers is highly practical, more so even than the French. The knapsack is baggy and of a poor pattern, however. It is curious how everything has, by sheer hard service and necessity, been brought down to the lowest point of weight and complication. A dragoon tucks his trousers inside his boots, buckles on a belt, from which hang a sabre and revolver, gets on a horse with a McClellan saddle and curb bridle, and there he is, ready to ride fifty miles in one day and fight on top of it. . . . After the Review the generals were entertained in a bower, with champagne and other delicacies, while we of the Staff meekly had big sandwiches and buckets of punch. I tried a sandwich, but found it rather salt eating, and so confined myself to iced water, wherein I got ahead of wine-bibbers who arrived at home very cross and hot. The General, who is very moderate in his conviviality, soon broke up the meeting, and, amidst a most terrible clicking of spurs and rattling of sabres, we all mounted, and so home by a *short cut* which one of General French's aides was kind enough to show us, and which entailed a considerable amount of rough riding; so that, with Mause Headrigg, I had occasion to remark, "By the help of the Lord I have luppen a ditch!"

HEADQUARTERS, ARMY OF POTOMAC
September 11, 1863

The last two days have been most unusually quiet. I read a little in military books, write a few letters, look over the newspapers a little, talk to the Staff officers, and go to bed early. The conversation of the officers is extremely entertaining, as most of them have been in a good many battles. They say that General Meade is an extremely cool man. At Gettysburg he was in a little wooden house, when the hot fire began. The shells flew very thick and close, and his Staff, who were outside, got under the lee of the house and sat down on the grass. As they sat there, out came General Meade, who, seeing them under such a slender protection against cannon-balls, began to laugh, and said: "That now reminds me of a feller at the Battle of Buena Vista, who, having got behind a wagon, during a severe cannonade, was there found by General Taylor. 'Wall Gin'ral,' said he, looking rather sheepish, 'this ain't much protection, but it *kinder feels as it was.*'" As a point to the Chief's anecdote, a spherical case came through the house at that instant, exploded in their circle and wounded Colonel Dickinson. . . .

I walked over and saw the Provost prisoners, the other evening. If you want to see degraded human nature, there was the chance. There was a bough covering, about forty feet square, guarded by sentries, and under it were grouped some fifty of the most miserable and depraved human beings I ever saw—deserters, stray Rebel soldiers, "bushwhackers" and camp-followers. They sleep on the bare ground with such covering as they may have, and get a ration of pork and biscuit every day. This is only a sort of temporary guardhouse, where they are put as they come in. War is a hard thing. This country, just here, was once all fenced in and planted; now there isn't a rail left and the land is either covered with dried weeds or is turned into a dusty plain by the innumerable trains of horses, mules and waggons.

[That evening there was a report that Lee was falling back. The cavalry were gathered for a reconnaissance in force. And Lyman was detailed to Pleasonton's Staff, to give him his first experience of actual fighting.]

HEADQUARTERS ARMY OF POTOMAC
BETWEEN THE RAPPAHANNOCK AND RAPIDAN
September 17, 1863

Having again got "home," I find leisure and paper to write you a rather longer letter than you have got of late. Perhaps you would like to hear about our little cavalry performance. Of course there was not hard fighting, and a hundred or so will cover all the killed and wounded; nevertheless, as the whole was new to me and as the operations covered a good deal of country, they were interesting and instructive both. The whole Cavalry Corps (a good many thousand men) had been massed the day before, and had orders to cross the Rappahannock early next morning. I was to ride down in time to join General Pleasonton. The distance to the river is some eight miles, so I was up at 4.30 — rain pitchforks! dark as a box — thunder and lightning — everything but "enter three witches." However, in my india-rubber coat and much-insulted large boots, much of the water could be kept out, and, by the time we were saddled and had had some tea, behold it stopped raining and away I went, quite thankful, and with a tail of six orderlies and a corporal. The ground was very wet, and we went slipping and sliding, in the red mud, till we drew near the river, when, behold, the whole country alive with train-waggons, columns of infantry, batteries, and ambulances; the latter with the stretchers fastened outside disagreeably suggestive of casualties. The rear of the cavalry had just crossed, when I got there; and General Pleasonton was on the opposite bank, where I presently joined him, crossing by the railroad bridge. He had with him a good many aides, besides orderlies and escort. Just at this point we held the southern, as well as the northern, bank and the pickets were some two miles out.

The country is rolling, but not quite hilly; there are very large open fields (now filled mostly with weeds) and again, considerable woods. In these last our cavalry were hidden, so that you would have said there were not 300 of them all together. This I found, presently, was a great point, to conceal men, behind woods and ridges, as much as possible.

We all now rode to our extreme picket line and took a view; and there, sure enough, was Mr. Reb with *his* picket line, about one third of a mile off. We could see a chain of mounted videttes, and, behind these, on a little knoll, a picket reserve, with their horses tied to trees. We waited some time to give a chance to General Gregg who had crossed on our right, and General Kilpatrick on our left, to get into the proper positions. Then General Pleasonton ordered an advance, and, in a few moments, quite as if by magic, the open country was alive with horsemen; first came columns of skirmishers who immediately deployed and went forward, at a brisk trot, or canter, making a connected line, as far as the eye could reach, right and left. Then followed the supports, in close order, and with and behind them came the field batteries, all trooping along as fast as they could scramble. It was now between eight and nine and the sun was bright, so that the whole spectacle was, to a greenhorn like me, one of the most picturesque possible. Not the least remarkable feature was the coolness of Mr. Reb under these trying circumstances. Their videttes stared a few moments, apparently without much curiosity, then turned tail and moved off, first at a walk, then at a trot, and finally disappeared over the ridge at a gallop. We rode on about a mile, keeping a little behind the skirmishers; General Buford and his Staff being just ahead and to the left. To the left we could hear cannon, General Kilpatrick having got into a skirmish there.

Presently I saw a puff of smoke, on a ridge in front of us, and then *hm-m-why-z-z-z, bang!* went the shell, right by General Buford's Staff, taking the leg off a poor orderly. Much pleased with their good shot, they proceeded to give our Staff a taste; and missiles of various kinds (but all disagreeable) began to skip and buzz round us. It was to me extraordinary to see the precision with which they fired. All the shot flew near us, and, while I had gone forward to the crest of the ridge to get a better view, a shell exploded directly in the midst of the Staff, wounding an orderly and very neatly shaving a patch of hair off the horse of Captain Hutchins. However, two could play at that game, and Captain Graham soon made the obnoxious guns limber up and depart to the next ridge, where they would again open and stay as long as they could. By the time we had got a few miles further, the enemy had brought forward all his cavalry and began firing with rifles, to which our men replied with their carbines.

We now entered a wooded tract, interspersed with mud-holes and springy ground, and here the enemy made quite a hard stand, for the town of Culpeper lay a couple of miles beyond and they wished to gain time to get off their stores by the railroad. The advanced regiments were therefore dismounted and sent into the woods, while the artillery tried to find some place whence the guns could be used. It was at this place that I first heard the yells, for which the Rebels are noted. They were the other side of a high bank, covered with bushes, and they yelled to keep their spirits up as long as possible. But they were soon driven through the woods and then we came on an open country, in full view of Culpeper. This was a very interesting sight. The hills are, hereabout, quite large, and on the one opposite us stood Culpeper, very prettily situated,

the railroad running through the lower part of the town.
Just in the outskirts the Rebels had planted two batteries,
as a last check, and behind were drawn up their supports
of cavalry. Our cavalry were coming out of the woods, on
all sides, moving on the town in form of a semi-circle,
while the guns were pelting those of the enemy with might
and main. Suddenly we were aware of a railroad train
slowly leaving the depot, and immediately several guns
were turned on it; but it went off, despite the shells that
burst over it. Then there suddenly appeared a body of
our cavalry, quite on the left of the town, who made a rush,
at full speed, on three cannon there stationed, and took
the whole of them with their caissons. This was a really
handsome charge and was led by General Custer, who had
his horse shot under him. This officer is one of the funniest-
looking beings you ever saw, and looks like a circus rider
gone mad! He wears a huzzar jacket and tight trousers, of
faded black velvet trimmed with tarnished gold lace. His
head is decked with a little, gray felt hat; high boots and
gilt spurs complete the costume, which is enhanced by the
General's coiffure, consisting in short, dry, flaxen ringlets!
His aspect, though highly amusing, is also pleasing, as he
has a very merry blue eye, and a devil-may-care style.
His first greeting to General Pleasonton, as he rode up,
was: "How are you, fifteen-days'-leave-of-absence? They
have spoiled my boots but they didn't gain much there,
for I stole 'em from a Reb." And certainly, there was one
boot torn by a piece of shell and the leg hurt also, so the
warlike ringlets got not only fifteen, but twelve [additional]
days' leave of absence, and have retreated to their native
Michigan!

The Rebels now retreated in all haste, and we rode at
once in, and found a good many supplies at the depot with

3

a number of rifles and saddles. As we rode up, the building was beset with grinning dragoons, each munching, with great content, a large apple, whereof they found several barrels which had been intended for the comfort of Mr. Stuart's dashing knights. I was surprised at the good conduct of the gypsy-looking men. They insulted no one, broke nothing, and only took a few green peaches, which, I fancy, amply revenged themselves. Culpeper is a really decent place, with a brick hotel, and a number of good houses, in front of which were little gardens. I send you a rosebud, which I picked as we rode through the town; there were plenty of them, looking rather out of place there, in the midst of muddy batteries and splattered cavalrymen! A queer thing happened in the taking of the three guns. An officer was made prisoner with them, and, as he was marched to the rear, Lieutenant Counselman of our side cried out, "Hullo, Uncle Harry!" "Hullo!" replied the captain uncle. "Is that you? How are you?" And there these two had been unwittingly shelling each other all the morning!

After resting the horses we pushed on to the south, towards what is called Pong Mountain, for you must know that this region is more hilly, and Pong Mountain is about comparable to the Blue Hills (not quite so high, perhaps). . . . We drove the enemy five miles beyond Culpeper, making fifteen miles, in all, and there a halt was ordered and pickets thrown out. Our Headquarters were a wretched house, of two rooms, inhabited by two old women. We gave them one room and took the other ourselves. And now I loomed out! The Staff had, in the way of creature comforts, nothing but sabres and revolvers. It was dark and raining guns, and the Chief-of-Staff had the stomach-ache! I took from my saddle-bags a candle and lighted the

same, prepared tea from my canteen, and produced a loaf
of bread and a Bologna sausage, to the astonishment of
the old campaigners, who enquired, "Whether I had a
pontoon bridge about me?" Then I rolled myself in my
coat and took a good night's sleep on the floor.

The next morning we started for Raccoon Ford, on the
Rapidan, five miles distant. The enemy were mostly
across and only opposed us with a few skirmishers. As we
got in sight of it, the prospect was not cheering. The opposite bank, partly wooded and partly covered with cul-
tivation, rose in steep, high hills, which completely commanded our side of the river. It was a fine sight to see the
column splashing along the wood road, lying between fine
oak trees; but the fine sight was presently interrupted by
a shell, which exploded about 100 yards ahead of me and
right among the horses' legs, without touching me! The
General rode into the open field to reconnoitre the position,
and I with him, because he wanted my glass; but Mr.
Secesh has a sharp eye for gold cords round hats, and, in a
minute, *wh-n-n-g, flup! wh-z-z-z!* a solid shot struck just
in front of us, and bounced over our heads. The General
ordered us to disperse about the field, so as not to make a
mark; but, as I rode off, they sent a shell so near me that
a facetious officer called out: "I guess they think you're
somebody pretty distinguished, Kun'l." However, there
may be a good deal of cannon shooting, without many hits;
in proof of which I will say that we had a brisk fire of
artillery from 10.30 to 2.30, together with a sharp spattering of rifles and carbines, and that our loss was five killed
and fifteen wounded! Shells do not sound so badly as I
expected; nor did I feel as I expected on the occasion.
There is a certain sense of discipline and necessity that bears
you up; and the only shell I "ducked" was the first one.

After some difficulty we got some guns in position and drove off those opposed. Then General Kilpatrick's division went to a better ford below, and tried to get over there; but the Rebels opened on him with fourteen cannon and silenced his guns after a hard fire. So we concluded the fords were not practicable for cavalry, which I think might have been apparent from the outset. Whereupon both parties stopped and stared at each other; and we heroes of the Staff went to a house (much better than that of last night) and partook of mutton which, during the day, we had valiantly made the prey of our bow and our spear. On our right General Gregg had driven the enemy beyond Cedar Mountain and nearly to the river, but was there brought up by a heavy force of artillery in position. All day Tuesday we lay doing nothing. I rode over with the General to Cedar Mountain, passing close to the battle-field, and ascended, thus getting a fine view of the Rapidan valley, which is very beautiful and would, in the hands of good farmers, yield a thousandfold. . . . We have taken on our reconnaissance in force about 150 prisoners, three guns, and five caissons. Yesterday the entire army crossed the Rappahannock, and I got orders to return to Headquarters, which I did.

HEADQUARTERS ARMY OF POTOMAC
September 22, 1863

We have had an Austrian officer, awfully arrayed, making a visit to see the telegraphs and the signal corps. He looked so natural with his sprig little bob-tail coat and his orange sash, and presented a funny contrast to our officers, who with their great boots and weather-beaten slouched hats looked as if they could swallow him and not know it. Captain Boleslaski (such was his name) was selected probably for two reasons, in this military mission: 1st, because

he could speak no word of English; and 2d, because he was
very deaf. Notwithstanding which little drawbacks, he
ran about very briskly, from morn to eve, and really saw
a great deal. I roared French in his ear, till I nearly had
the bronchitis, but succeeded in imparting to him such
information as I had. He addressed me as "Mon Colonel"
and looked upon me as the hero of a hundred campaigns;
though he *did* rather stick me, when he asked me whether
our pontoons were constructed on the system of Peterhoff
or of Smolenski! He was much pleased with the attention
he got, and was extremely surprised when he beheld the
soldiers all running to buy newspapers.

Yesterday came General Buford, commander of the
second Cavalry Division, and held a pow-wow. He is one
of the best of the officers of that arm and is a singular-look-
ing party. Figurez-vous a compactly built man of middle
height, with a tawny moustache and a little, triangular
gray eye, whose expression is determined, not to say sin-
ister. His ancient corduroys are tucked into a pair of
ordinary cowhide boots, and his blue blouse is ornamented
with holes; from one pocket thereof peeps a huge pipe,
while the other is fat with a tobacco pouch. Notwithstanding this get-up he is a very soldierly looking man.
He is of a good-natured disposition, but not to be trifled
with. Caught a notorious spy last winter and hung him to
the next tree, with this inscription: "This man to hang
three days: he who cuts him down before shall hang the
remaining time."

September 24, 1863

Yesterday we were favored with the presence of Sir
Henry Holland, the Queen's physician, who is one of the
liveliest old birds for one of seventy-five that ever was
seen. He travels two months every year, and has already

been four or five times in these United States. Dr. Letter-
man, the Medical Director, put him in an ambulance, and
Colonel Townsend and myself completed the party. What
pains wounded people may suffer in ambulances, I know
not; but I do know that, when driven at a trot, over open
fields and through little ditches, the jolting is not to be
expressed in words. But the royal medical person maintained his equanimity wonderfully and continued to smile,
as if he were having a nice drive over a turnpike. First he
was halted on a rising spot, when he could see four batteries of horse artillery, which did defile before him, to his
great admiration. Then we bumped him six miles farther,
to the Headquarters of the 12th Corps, close to the river.
Here he hobnobbed with General Slocum, and then got
on a horse and rode about the camps. After which he was
taken to a safe spot, whence he could behold the Rebels
and their earthworks. He returned quite fresh and departed in a most amiable mood.

There seems to me no particular prospect of a battle. I
thought this morning, that we should have a great fight
within a couple of days; but movements, which I dare say
you will read of in the papers before this letter reaches you,
have just knocked it. *Entre nous*, I believe in my heart
that at this moment there is no reason why the whole of
Lee's army should not be either cut to pieces, or in precipi-
tate flight on Richmond. In saying this to you, I accuse
nobody and betray no secrets, but merely state my opinion. Your bricks and mortar may be of the best; but, if
there are three or four chief architects, none of whom can
agree where to lay the first brick, the house will rise
slowly.

HEADQUARTERS, ARMY OF THE POTOMAC
September 29, 1863

I see such flocks of generals now, that I do not always take the pains to describe them. On Sunday there arrived General Benham, one of the dirtiest and most ramshackle parties I ever saw. Behind him walked his Adjutant-General, a great contrast, in all respects, being a trig, broad-shouldered officer, with a fierce moustache and imperial and a big clanking sabre. I gazed at this Adjutant-General and he at me, and gradually, through the military fierceness, there peeped forth the formerly pacific expression of Channing Clapp![1] There never was such a change, Achilles and all other warlike persons; and is much improved withal. That same evening enter another general (distinguished foreigner this time), El General José Cortez, chevalier of some sort of red ribbon and possessor of a bad hat. He was accompanied by two eminent Señors, Mexicans and patriotic exiles. We were out riding when they came; but, after our return, and in the midst of dinner, there comes an orderly with a big official envelope, proving to be a recommendation from Mr. Seward. "Oh," says the General, "another lot, hey? Well, I suppose they will be along to-morrow"; and went on quietly eating dinner. Afterwards I went into the office of General Williams (or "Seth" as they call him here) and there beheld, sitting in a corner, three forlorn figures. Nobody seemed to know who they were, but the opinion prevailed that they were a deputation of sutlers, who were expected about that time! But I, hearing certain tones of melancholy Spanish, did presently infer that they were the parties mentioned in the big, official envelope, and so it proved! They were speedily entered into the General's presence and, after a

[1] A classmate at Harvard.

few compliments, anxiously asked when the *next train left for Washington;* for it appears that they had supposed Culpeper was a pleasant jaunt of about fifteen minutes from the Capitol, and was furnished with elegant hotels and other conveniences; consequently they had brought no *sac de nuit,* and had had nothing to eat since early morning, it being then dark! Their surprise was considerable, after a weary ride of some hours, to be dumped in a third-rate village, deserted by its inhabitants and swarming with dusty infantry. John made ready with speed, and, after a meal and a bottle of champagne, it was surprising to see how their barometers rose, especially that of small Señor, No. 2, who launched forth in a flood of eulogium on the state of civil liberty in the United States. Our next care was to provide them sleeping-accommodations; no easy matter in the presence of the fact that each has barely enough for himself down here. But I succeeded in getting two stretchers from the hospital (such as are used to bring in the wounded from the field) and a cot from Major Biddle; three pillows (two india-rubber and one feather) were then discovered, and these, with blankets, one tin basin, one bucket, and one towel, made them entirely happy. Really, how they looked so fresh next morning was quite a marvel. Then, after a good breakfast, we put them all on horseback (to the great uneasiness of the two Señors) and followed by a great crowd of a Staff (who never *can* be made to ride, except in the higglety-pigglety style in which "Napoléon et ses Maréchaux" are always represented in the common engravings), we jogged off, raising clouds of red dust, to take a look at some soldiers. . . . El General was highly pleased and kept taking off his bad hat and waving it about. Also he expressed an intense desire that we should send 50,000 men and immediately wipe out the French in Mexico.

"Why doesn't Meade attack Lee?" Ah, I have already thrown out a hint on the methods of military plans in these regions. But, despite the delays, I should have witnessed a great battle before this; if, IF, IF, at the very moment the order had not come to fill up the gap that the poltroonery of two of Rosecrans' Corps has made in the western armies. I do believe that we should have beaten them (that's no matter *now*), for my Chief, though he expressly declares that he is *not* Napoleon, is a thorough soldier, and a mighty clear-headed man; and one who does not move unless he knows where and how many his men are; where and how many his enemy's men are; and what sort of country he has to go through. I never saw a man in my life who was so characterized by straightforward truthfulness as he is. He will pitch into himself in a moment, if he thinks he has done wrong; and woe to those, no matter who they are, who do not do right! "Sir, it was your duty and you haven't done it; now go back and do it at once," he will suddenly remark to some astonished general, who thinks himself no small beer. Still I *do* wish he would order the Provost-Marshal to have a few more of the deceased horses buried. The weather here is perfect — could not be finer.

HEADQUARTERS, ARMY OF POTOMAC
October 1, '63

Yesterday we had a sword presentation (nothing else to do now, you know). It would appear that General Warren is a native of Cold Spring, near West Point; whereupon it did occur to the natives of his mother town to buy a sword for him in token of their, etc., etc., etc. The weapon was duly entrusted to the safe keeping of a certain Dr. Young, and of another certain Mr. Spaulding, both of whom arrived, a day or two since, with the precious casket. Early in the morning came an orderly with a notice, saying that the Staff officers were respectfully invited to, etc., etc., etc. We persuaded the Quartermaster to give us a car (which turned out to be a grain car with a few chairs), and, by this means, we were enabled to go from Culpeper in about twenty minutes, the General leading the crowd. General Warren was lodged in Spartan simplicity, in a third-rate farmhouse. His dress was even more Spartan than his lodgment. Did I ever describe him to you? Fancy a small, slender man, with a sun-burnt face, two piercing black eyes, and withal bearing a most ludicrous resemblance to cousin Mary Pratt! He was dressed in a double-breasted blouse, buttoned awry, a pair of soldier's pantaloons, rather too short, and a very old little straw hat, of the kind called "chip." Such is the *personnel* of one of the very best generals in the Army of the Potomac! He is a most kind man, and always taking care of hysterical old Secesh ladies and giving them coffee and sugar. As to Secesh *males*, in the army, he is a standing terror to them. This valiant warrior, who don't care a button for missiles, was extremely nervous at the idea of the sword presentation, and went trotting about the house consulting with Dr. Young. There soon arrived sundry other generals, each with a longer or shorter tail. General French, the pattern of the Gallic colonel; General Griffin, whose face is after the manner of his name; and quite a bushel-basketfull of brigadiers. Then the band arrived; and, by that time, there was a house filled with shoulder-straps of all sorts (I certainly knocked the crowd by having a pair of cotton gloves). Thereupon we formed a semi-circle round the porch, where was deposited, on an old pine·table, the elegant rosewood case. General Warren stood up, looking much as if about to be married, and Dr. Young, standing opposite with a paper in his hand, so resembled a clergyman, that I fully expected him to say, "Warren, will you have this sword to be your lawful, wedded wife?" But instead, he only read how the citizens of Cold Spring, desirous of showing their appreciation of the patriotism, etc., had procured this sword, etc., in token of, etc., etc. To which the General, looking, if possible, still more as if in the agonies of the altar, replied from a scrap of note-paper, the writing whereof he could not easily read. The whole took about five minutes, at the end of which he drew a breath of great relief, and remarked, "The execution is over; now won't you come in and eat something?" The spread consisted of roast beef, baked ham, bread, assorted pickles, laid out on a table with newspapers for a cloth. The generals fed first and were accommodated partly with chairs and partly with a pine bench, borrowed from a neighboring deserted schoolhouse. While some ate, the rest were regaled with a horse-bucketfull of whiskey punch, whereof two or three of the younger lieutenants got too much, for which I warrant they paid dear; for the "Commissary" whiskey is shocking and the water, down near the river, still worse. All this took place in full view of the hills, across the river, on and behind which were camped the Rebels; and I could not help laughing to think what a scattering there would be if they should pitch over a 20-pound Parrott shell, in the midst of the address! But they are very pleasant now, and the pickets walk up and down and talk across the river. And so we got in our grain car and all came home. . . .

HEADQUARTERS ARMY OF POTOMAC
October 4, '63

We have sad cases come here sometimes. Yesterday
there was a poor farmer, that filled me with admiration.
He had travelled a thousand miles from his place in Indiana
to get the body of his only son, killed in our cavalry skirmish of the 13th September. "I am most wore out," said
he, "runnin' round; but the ambulance has gone over to
that piece of woods, after him. And that old hoss, that
was *his;* the one he was sitting on, when he was shot; she
ain't worth more than fifty dollars, but I wouldn't take a
thousand for her, and I am going to take her home to
Indiana." So you see that bullets fired here may hit poor
folks away in the West. To-day is a Sunday, which is
marked by General "Seth" shutting up shop and obstinately refusing to talk with sundry officers who deem it a
good leisure day to go over and consult on their private
interests. "Sir!" says "Seth" (who cuts off his words and
lisps them, and swallows them, and has the true Yankee
accent into the bargain), "Sir! The Pres'dent of these
'Nited States has issued a procl'mation, saying nothing
should be done Sundays; and Gen'l Merklellan did the
same, and so did Gen'l Hooker; and you wanter talk
business, you've got er come week days." "The Father of
the Army" is also much exercised with people who want
leaves of absence. "Now here's a feller," he cries ("feller"
means officer), "here's a feller that wants to go because
he wants to git married; and here's another who wants to
go because he has just *been* married; and here's a feller
asks for three days to go to Washington and buy a pair of
spectacles!" Notwithstanding his trials, he gets quite
stout on it, and preserves the same unruffled countenance.

HEADQUARTERS ARMY OF POTOMAC
October 11, '63

As all is packed, I take to pencil correspondence. Uncle Lee has concluded that we have stared long enough at each other, and so is performing some fancy antics, though whether he means to fight, or retreat after a feint, or merely take a walk, I know not. He is now paddling along, in the general direction of Warrenton, between us and the Blue Ridge; and so has entirely left his station on the other bank of the river. . . . Last night I, being of a foxy disposition, turned in at an early hour, so that I was fresh and fine at four this morning, when we were routed out, and assisted to coffee and bread and cold ham. It was a Murillo-esque (!) sight to behold the officers, in big coats and bigger sabres, standing with the bright light of the camp-fire on their faces. The cavalry cloaks, slouched hats, and great boots, though, as Co[1] says, "drunk"-looking, are much more suited to a painter than the trig uniforms of the Europeans. So here we are, with horses saddled, waiting to see what is what. You understand that Mr. Reb is not very near us, in fact further off than before, but he is moving, and so we, too, are *"en garde."* Our army, I say with emphasis, *ought* to be able to whip the gentlemen.

Down comes General Meade; I clap the pencil in my pocket, and in two minutes we are off, escort, orderlies, Staff and all, winding our way midst miles of baggage and ammunition waggons and slow columns of moving infantry. Ha, ha, ha! They don't look much like the "Cadets," these old sojers on the march. There is their well-stuffed knapsack, surmounted by a rolled gray blanket, the worse for wear; from their belt is slung a big cartridge-box, with

[1] His sister.

forty rounds, and at their side hangs a haversack (satchel you would call it) quite bursting with three days' rations. Hullo! what has that man, dangling at the end of his musket? A coffee-pot! an immense tin coffee-pot! and there is another with a small frying-pan — more precious to them than gold. And there goes a squad of cavalry, the riders almost obscured by the bags of oats and the blankets and coats piled on pommel and crupper; their carbine hangs on one side and their sabre clatters from the other. And then behold a train of artillery (the best-looking arm of the service), each gun drawn by six or eight horses, and the caissons covered with bags of forage. And so the face of the country is covered, when an army is on the march, the waggons keeping the road, the infantry winding through the open land. It is singular, in regard to the latter, that, however dirty or slovenly the men may be, their muskets always shine like silver; they know it is an important member. Well, you perceive I have leisure to get a pen-full of ink, to continue the letter, begun this morning. In fact we have done our day's march and our movable houses are all up at a new "Headquarters." We hear nothing much of the *Insurgés*, but are all ready to pitch into them if we find them in a soft spot. . . .

[At this time Meade's main line was from Rapidan Station, where the railroad from Alexandria to Charlottesville crosses the river, to Raccoon Ford, some seven miles down the Rapidan. During the following days there was a series of minor engagements, Lee endeavoring to turn Meade's right flank, and get between him and Washington. But Meade, outmarching Lee, kept between him and Washington, finally bringing the Headquarters to Centreville about twenty-four miles west of Alexandria.

Meanwhile, it appears to have been extremely difficult to locate the enemy. "It is quite extraordinary," writes Lyman, "what little information is to be had. The idea of the enemy, 50,000 or 60,000 strong, marching about, and we not knowing whether they are going one way or another, seems incredible; but then it is to be observed that, 1st, the woods and hills greatly conceal distant moves; and, 2d, by an outlying cavalry, a move may be either covered or simulated."]

HEADQUARTERS ARMY OF POTOMAC
October 12, 1863

You will probably have all sorts of rumors of defeats, or victories, or something. The facts are very simple: as our great object is Uncle Lee's army (one might properly say our *only* object), we have to watch and follow his movements, so as, 1st, to catch him if possible in a good corner; or, 2d, to prevent his catching us in a bad corner; also 3d, to cover Washington and Maryland, which, for us, is more important than for him to come to Richmond. Thus we have to watch him and shift as he shifts, like two fencers. One may say, pitch into him! But do you think he is so soft as to give us any decent chance, if he knows it? Not he! Meanwhile Meade knows what hangs on this army, and how easy it is to talk about raising 3,000,000 men and how hard it is to raise 30,000. He said yesterday: "If Bob Lee will go into those fields there and fight me, man for man, I will do it this afternoon." But "Bob" doesn't see it. Sharp chaps those Rebs. . . . I do hope that no great battle will be fought unless we can really deal a staggering blow to the enemy. The great fault of the Potomac campaign has been the fighting without any due prospect of profit. This will be found, I think, a good trait in our General, that he will hold his forces in hand for a proper occasion. Meanwhile the papers say, "The fine autumn weather is slipping away." Certainly; and shall we add, as a corollary, "Therefore let another Fredericksburg be fought!" Put some flesh on our skeleton regiments, and there is no difficulty; but if, instead of ten conscripts, only one is sent, *que voulez vous!*

HEADQUARTERS ARMY OF POTOMAC
IN THE FIELD, *October* 16, 1863

Contrary to expectation to-day has been a quiet one for us; and I have not left camp. The Rebels toward evening went feeling along our line about three miles from here with cavalry and artillery, and kept up a desultory cannonade, which, I believe, hurt nobody. Early this morning two batches of prisoners, some 600 in all, were marched past, on their way to Washington. They looked gaunt and weary, and had, for the most part, a dogged air. Many were mere boys and these were mostly hollow-cheeked and pale, as if the march were too much for them. Their clothes were poor, some of a dust-color, and others dirty brown, while here and there was a U.S. jacket or a pair of trousers, the trophies of some successful fight. Some were wittily disposed. One soldier of ours cried out: "Broad Run is a bad place for you, bóys." "Ya-as," said a cheery man in gray, "but it's puty rare you get such a chance." An hour before daylight came General Warren, exhausted with two nights' marching, and a day's fight, but springy and stout to the last. "We whipped the Rebs right out," he said. "I ran my men, on the double-quick, into the railroad cut and then just swept them down with musketry." I got up and gave him a little brandy that was left in my flask; he then lay down and was fast asleep in about a minute. To-day they brought here the five cannon he took;

they got the horses of only one piece, four miserable thin animals, that had once been large and good. I ought to say there are two very distinct classes among the prisoners. Yesterday they brought in a splendid-looking Virginian, a cavalry man. He was but poorly clad and was an uneducated person, but I never saw any one more at ease, while, at the same time, perfectly innocent and natural. "You fellers" was the way in which he designated General Meade and two other major-generals. When asked where Zeb Stuart was, he replied, with a high degree of vagueness: "Somewheres back here, along with the boys." . . .

HEADQUARTERS ARMY OF POTOMAC
October 19, 1863

It seems to me I had got to Sunday morning, the 11th, when we began to march back. We started from Headquarters and passed through Brandy Station, forded the Rappahannock, close to the railroad, and took up our camp near the railroad and about two miles from the river. . . . This move, though in the wrong direction, was, without question, a good one, as it bothered the enemy and caused them to hesitate. . . . In the morning we got off about ten (for the General does not mount till he has heard that the army is properly under way) and rode along the north side of the railroad, past the camp I first came to (H.Q. near Warrenton Junction), and so to Catlett's Station, where we found the 1st Corps taking their noon rest; also their chief, General Newton, and General (Professor) Eustis, partaking from a big basket. A spy came in also, who gave such information as showed that the Rebels had made less rapid progress than we supposed. Going a mile or two on, we saw a spectacle such as few even of the old officers had ever beheld; namely, 2500 wag-

4

gons, all parked on a great, open, prairie-like piece of ground, hundreds of acres in extent. I can compare it to nothing but the camp of Attila, where he retreated after the "Hun Schlacht," which we saw at the Berlin Museum. They were here got together, to be sent off to the right, by Brentsville, to Fairfax Station, under escort of General Buford's division. How these huge trains are moved over roads not fit for a light buggy, is a mystery known only to General Rufus Ingalls, who treats them as if they were so many perambulators on a smooth sidewalk! We turned off to a house, two miles from Catlett's, and again pitched our movable houses, on a rocky bit of a field. . . .

At daylight next morning, every corps was in motion, tramping diligently in the direction of the heights of Centreville, *via* Manassas Junction. We of the Staff had hardly dressed, when there was a great cracking of carbines. in the woods, not a mile off, and we discovered that a Rebel regiment of horse had coolly camped there during the night, and were now engaged with our cavalry, who soon drove them away. Pretty soon the sound of cannon, in the direction of Auburn, announced that the Rebels, marching down from Warrenton, had attacked General Warren's rear. He, however, held them in check easily with one division, while the other two marched along, passing our Headquarters at 9.30 A.M. As they went on, I recognized the Massachusetts 20th, poor Paul Revere's regiment. And so we jogged, General Meade (who has many a little streak of gunpowder in his disposition) continually bursting out against his great bugbear, the *waggons;* and sending me, at full gallop, after General Sykes, who was a hundred miles, or so, ahead, to tell him that the rear of his ambulance train was quite unprotected. . . . The 15th was employed in feeling the intentions of the enemy and resting the exhausted men. On the 16th came on a deluge of rain which spoiled our contemplated move next day. On the 18th, yesterday, we got some information of reliable character for the first time, viz: that they had torn up the railroad and were falling back on Warrenton. Before that there was every kind of report: that they were going up the Shenandoah Valley; marching on Washington, and falling back on Richmond; and they keep so covered by cavalry, that it is most difficult to probe them. Thus far in the move they have picked up about as many prisoners as we, say 700; but we have the five guns and two colors, they having none. To-day we all marched out at daylight, and are now hard after them, the General praying for a battle. Our cavalry has been heavily engaged this afternoon, and they may make a stand, *or* indeed, they may not. I think I was never so well and strong in my life. General Buford came in to-day, cold and tired and wet; "Oh!" said he to me, "do you know what I would do if I were a volunteer aide? I would just run home as fast as I could, and never come back again!" The General takes his hardships good-naturedly.

[The result of the manœuvres brought the army toward Washington, which caused uneasiness and dissatisfaction at the Capitol. "At Centreville," writes Lyman, "we had a set-to between Meade and Halleck. Meade had asked, by telegraph, for some advice, and stated that he was not sufficiently assured of the enemy's position to risk an advance; so conflicting were the reports. Halleck, apparently after dinner, replied in substance, 'Lee is plainly bullying you. If you can't find him, I can't. If you go and fight him, you will probably find him!' General Meade, much offended, prepared a reply in some such words as these: 'If you have any orders, I am ready to obey them; but I must insist on being spared the infliction of such truisms in guise of opinions as I have recently been favored with. If my course is not satisfactory, I ought to be and I desire to be relieved.' He had written 'bunsby opinions,' and consulted me as to whether it would do; to which I replied that the joke was capital, but not in accordance with the etiquette of a commander-in-chief; so he substituted the other. Poor General Meade! Said he, 'I used to think how nice it would be to be Commander-in-Chief; now, at this moment, I would sooner go, with a division, under the heaviest musketry fire, than hold my place!'" Lee, finding that he could not outflank Meade, fell back, and Halleck apologized.]

HEADQUARTERS ARMY OF POTOMAC
October 23, 1863

And where do you think I was all yesterday? I will tell you. Early, the orderly, poked his head into the tent saying: "Colonel Lyman, the General will have breakfast at seven" (which was an hour earlier than he had said the night before). As soon as I sat down, says the General: "I am going to Washington; would you like to go?" . . . Major-General Humphreys said he too would go, and the General's son George completed the party. In much haste I ran, and crammed my best coat, pantaloons, shoes, sash, gauntlets, and brushes into my big saddle-bags, the which I entrusted to a mounted orderly. Thereupon we speedily got on horseback, and first rode to General Sedgwick (familiarly called "Uncle John"), to whom General Meade handed over the command, in his absence at Washington, to consult about the late moves and those consequent on

GEORGE MEADE
Aide-de-Camp

them. Uncle John received the heavy honors in a smiling
and broad-shouldered style, and wished us all a good
journey, for he is a cheery soul. With little delay, we again
mounted and rode twelve miles, briskly, to Gainesville,
whither the railroad comes. The Chief stepped into a little
room, used as a telegraph-office, and, quicker than wink-
ing, he stood, arrayed only in his undergarments; then,
before, almost, I could get my coat off, he had put on a
pair of shoes, a new coat, and an elegant pair of trousers!
"Now then, Lyman, are you ready? Where's Humphreys?
Humphreys is always late! Come, come along, the train is
going to start!" You should have seen the unfortunate
Aide — his coat unbuttoned, his shoestrings loose; on one
arm the saddle-bags, on the other, his sword, sash, etc.,
etc., and he hastening after the steam-engine Meade!
However I completed my toilette in the car, which was
all to ourselves; and flatter myself that my appearance
was considerably peacock. We went rattling and bumping
over a railroad that reminded me of the one from Civita
Vecchia, to Manassas Junction, and thence to Washington,
over a route I have already described to you when I came
down. Only this time we came through Alexandria, and,
instead of taking there a boat, kept on and went across
the long bridge, going thus into the very city by the rail.
There was a carriage from Willard's awaiting us; the guard-
post near by turned out in our honor, and we drove
in great state to General Halleck's office; where General
Meade went in and held a solemn pow-wow; the two came
forth presently and walked over to the White-House,
where they held another pow-wow with the President.
Captain George and I, meanwhile, studied the exterior
architecture, and I observed a blind had been blown off

and broken and allowed to lie outside. In fact they have a nigger negligence, to a considerable extent, in this half-cooked capital.

October 24, 1863

We went to Willard's after the pow-pow and got a very good dinner; only poor General Meade was bored to death and driven out of all peace of mind, by dirty politicians who kept coming up and saying: "Ah, General Meade, I believe; perhaps you do not recollect meeting me in the year 1831, on a Mississippi steamboat? How do you do, sir? What move do you propose to execute next? Have you men enough, sir? What are the intentions of Lee, sir? How are the prospects of the rebellion, sir? Do you look upon it as essentially crushed, sir? Or do you think it may still rear its head against our noble Union, sir?" etc., etc. All of which the poor Chief (endeavoring to snatch a mouthful of chicken, the while) would answer with plaintive courtesy; while the obscure aides-de-camp were piling in all kinds of delicacies. . . . The papers say General Meade received imperative orders to give Lee battle; not a word of truth in it! You might as well give imperative orders to catch a sea-gull with a pinch of salt. Lee would perhaps have given us a chance; but the same storm that prevented our advance carried away the Rapidan bridge, and he could get nothing to eat. His forces were, I think, larger than supposed, especially in cavalry, which was very numerous.

HEADQUARTERS ARMY OF POTOMAC
October 26, 1863

Ah! we are a doleful set of papas here. Said General Meade: "I do wish the Administration would get mad with me, and relieve me; I am sure I keep telling them, if they don't feel satisfied with me, to relieve me; then I

could go home and see my family in Philadelphia." I believe there never was a man so utterly without common
ambition and, at the same time, so Spartan and conscientious in everything he does. He is always stirring up somebody. This morning it was the cavalry picket line, which
extends for miles, and which he declared was ridiculously
placed. But, by worrying, and flaring out unexpectedly
on various officers, he does manage to have things pretty
ship-shape; so that an officer of Lee's Staff, when here the
other day, said: "Meade's move can't be beat." Did I tell
you that Lee passed through Warrenton and passed a
night. He was received with bouquets and great joy. . . .
The last three nights have been cool, almost cold, with
some wind, so that they have been piling up the biggest
kind of camp-fires. You would laugh to see me in bed!
First, I spread an india-rubber blanket on the ground, on
which is laid a cork mattress, which is a sort of pad, about
an inch thick, which you can roll up small for packing. On
this comes a big coat, and then I retire, in flannel shirt and
drawers, and cover myself, head and all, with three blankets, laying my pate on a greatcoat folded, with a little
india-rubber pillow on top; and so I sleep very well,
though the surface is rather hard and lumpy. I have not
much to tell you of yesterday, which was a quiet Sunday.
Many officers went to hear the Rebs preach, but I don't
believe in the varmint. They ingeniously prayed for "all
established magistrates"; though, had we not been there,
they would have roared for the safety of Jeff Davis and
Bob Lee! . . .

                                        October 28, 1863

. . . The guerillas are extremely saucy of late, and, in a
small way, annoying. Night before last they dashed at a
waggon train and cut loose upwards of a hundred mules and

horses, which they made off with, teamsters and all, leaving the waggons untouched. These men are regularly enlisted, but have no pay, getting, in lieu thereof, all the booty they can take, except horses, which they must sell to the Rebels at a fixed rate. They have taken several officers who, from carelessness, or losing their way, have gone alone beyond the lines. Prisoners are treated with consideration, but I fancy that, from all accounts, Libby Prison is pretty dirty and crowded. When some of our officers were taken through Warrenton, on the retreat of Lee, the inhabitants gave them supper; for the 6th Corps were long quartered there and treated the people kindly. When you are here you see how foolish and blind is the clamor raised by some people, to have all property destroyed by the army in the Rebel states, as the troops passed. There was, you know, a great talk about putting guards over houses of Rebels; but, 1st, it is very wrong to punish a people *en masse*, without regard to their degree of guilt and without properly measuring the punishment; and, 2d, nothing so utterly and speedily demoralizes an army as permission to plunder. It is our custom to put guards over the houses that are inhabited; but, despite that, the cavalry and advanced guard take a good slice of the live-stock; forage, and vegetables. . . .

HEADQUARTERS ARMY OF THE POTOMAC
November 1, 1863

Buford was here last night, and said he thought he could just "boolge" across the river and scare the Rebels to death; which would certainly be a highly desirable event, for we should have quite a chance of a visit home. As it is, no resignations are accepted and scarcely a soul is allowed to go home, even for a visit of two or three days. The life here is miserably lazy; hardly an order to carry, and the horses all eating their heads off. The weather is fine, to be sure, and everybody, nearly, is well; but that is all the more reason for wishing something done. I do not even have the drudgery of drill and parade and inspection, that the infantrymen have. If one could only be at home, till one was *wanted*, and then be on the spot; but this is everywhere the way of war; lie still and lie still; then up and manœuvre and march hard; then a big battle; and then a lot more lie still.

HEADQUARTERS ARMY OF POTOMAC
November 3, 1863

Did I mention that, since Centreville, some two weeks, I have had a tent-mate, a Swede, one of those regular Europeans, who have been forever in the army, and who know no more about campaigning than a young child. After staying five months in this country, he got, at last, a commission as 2d Lieutenant of cavalry; and came down to study our system of artillery. He appeared with a large stock of cigars and hair-brushes, but without bedding, of any sort whatsoever. I gave him, *pro tem*, a buffalo, rubber blanket, etc., and, with these, and a borrowed cot, he has gone on since, apparently thinking that a kind Providence will ever care for his wants. He hasn't got mustered in yet, and seems to suppose that the officers will come to Headquarters and remove all the trouble in his commission. Now he is going to Washington about it; or rather has *said* he was going, for the last three days. *Au reste*, he is a quiet, polite man, who, I think, will not do much to improve the Swedish artillery. He has obtained a nigger boy, whose name is Burgess, but whom he calls "Booyus," remarking to me that it was a singular name, in which I fully agreed! . . .

HEADQUARTERS ARMY OF POTOMAC
(NOT FAR FROM RAPPAHANNOCK RIVER)
November 7, 1863

. . . This morning, forward march! horse, foot, and artillery, all streaming towards Dixie; weather fresh and fine, nothing to mar but a high wind, and, in some places, clouds of dust. Everyone was hearty; there was General Hays, in bed with rheumatism, but he hopped up, and got on his horse, remarking that, "if there were any Rebs to catch, he was all well." Our last Headquarters were on the Warrenton branch railroad, half a mile north of it and three miles from Warrenton Junction. This morning, about 8.30, when all the troops were reported under way, the General started and rode, first to Warrenton Junction, and then down the railroad, towards the Rappahannock. At a rising ground, where a smoke-stained chimney marked the ruins of "Bealton," we halted. Hence we could see a considerable distance, in both directions, and here was canny Warren, waiting while his corps filed past, his little black eyes open to everything, from the grand movements of the entire army down to the inscription on my sword-guard, which he immediately detected, and read with much gravity. The last I saw of him he climbed on his big white horse and remarked with a wink: "As soon as I get there, I shall bring on a general action, right off." It was here that I had quite a surprise. Looking through my glass at General Webb's division, I detected two civilians, in English-looking clothes, riding with the Staff. As they approached, it seemed to me that the face of one was familiar; and as they rode up, behold, to be sure, the Hon. Mr. Yorke, who was our fellow passenger and played on the fiddle and admired the baby! He was in the Royal Artillery, you know, and had come down to see what he could. And there he was, much covered with dust, but cheerful and pleasant to the last.

It was a fine sight to see the great, black columns of infantry, moving steadily along, their muskets glittering in the sun (for the day was quite perfect as to clearness), and then the batteries on the flank, and, in the rear, the train of ambulances preceded by their yellow flag. As the masses drew near, they resolved themselves, first into brigades, then into regiments, and then you could distinguish the individual soldiers, covered with dust and bending under their heavy packs, but trudging manfully along, with the patient air of old sojers. And so we kept on to these Headquarters; but we were only half way (at 1.30), when *bang! bang!* we heard the cannon, in the direction of Rappahannock station. It was General Sedgwick attacking the enemy's works on this side of the river. We had not got a mile, when *whang! whang!* in another direction, announced General French preparing to force Kelly's Ford. For, at these two points, among others, we proposed to cross and wake up our Uncle Lee. The gallant General did not wait to play long shots or throw pontoon bridges. An entire division took to the water, forded the river, in face of the enemy, and, charging up the opposite bank, took 300 prisoners. The Rebs threw forward a supporting division, but the crafty French had established guns on this side of the river, that suddenly opened on them and drove them back. All the afternoon Sedgwick has been engaged against the rifle-pits and a redoubt, that the enemy held on *this* side of the river. Quite late, we got a despatch that he had driven them from their rifle-pits, and we thought he had done pretty well for an afternoon. But, just at dusk, the distant roll of musketry indicated that he was assaulting; and a telegraph has just come, that he has taken the redoubt with four cannon, and some prisoners; I do not yet know how many. So we go to sleep, encouraged and hopeful. Our losses I do not know, but they can hardly be much, as but a portion has been engaged. . . .

HEADQUARTERS ARMY OF POTOMAC
November 9, 1863

We have once more moved our Headquarters. . . . Reveille was beaten so early that, when I popped my sleepy head out of the tent, there were the stars, most magnificent, especially Venus who sat above the moon and looked like a fire-ball. The moon was but a little one, but her circle was completed by that kind of image you often see, only the figure of the Man-in-the-Moon was plainly reflected on this image, a thing I never noticed before. These were the astronomical observations of Lyman, as he stood in the sharp air, clad in a flannel shirt and drawers. A sense of coldness about the legs roused me to a sense of my position, and I speedily added more warm garments. Breakfast was ready by the time it was light; and, every mouthful of beef I stowed away, I expected to hear the cannon that would announce the opening of the great battle. The General was confident of a battle and remarked cheerfully that "he meant to pitch right into them." The idea was that they would take a chosen position, near Brandy Station, and there await our attack, for which they would not have been obliged to wait long. The bulk of the army was therefore crossed at Kelly's Ford, so as to advance with undivided force; General Sedgwick, however, with nearly his whole corps, held the redoubt he had taken on the north side, and, at the proper moment, was ready to throw his bridges, cross the river and take them in the flank. An hour wore away, and there

was no sound of battle; so we all mounted, and rode to a
small house on Mt. Holly. This is a low, steep hill, close to
Kelly's Ford and commanding it. . . . Presently there
appeared a couple of dragoons, with five fresh prisoners.
. . . "How were you taken?" quoth the Provost-Marshal.
"Well, we were on guard and we went to sleep, and, when
we woke up, the first thing we seed was your skirmish
line" (which was only a roundabout way of saying they
were common stragglers). "Where is the rest of your
army?" "All gone last night to the breastworks behind
the Rapidan!" And this was the gist of the matter. We
passed Ewell's Headquarters, a little while after, and there
I learned that, when news of the capture of the redoubt
was brought him, he exclaimed with some profanity,
"Then it's time we were out of this!" and immediately
issued orders to fall back, along the whole line, after dark.
There we crossed on a pontoon bridge, and found the 5th
Corps massed, on the other side. As the cavalcade trotted
by, the men all ran to the road and cheered and yelled
most vociferously for General Meade. Soon we came up
with General Warren. He looked like a man of disappointed hopes, as he gazed round the country and said,
"There's nobody here—*nobody!*" And so we passed on, and
beheld our English friends, with the Staff of General Webb.
They had a very bewildered air, which seemed to say:
"Oh, ah, where are these Rebel persons? pray could you
tell me where they are?" Near Brandy Station we met
good "Uncle John" Sedgwick, who said it was a cool day,
as if there was nothing particular on hand, and he hadn't
been doing anything for a week or two. It was now late on
this Sunday afternoon and the troops were massing, to
bivouac. There seemed really no end of them; though but
part of the army was there; yet I never saw it look so big,

which is accounted for by the fact that the country is very
open and rolling and we could see the whole of it quite
swarming with blue coats. . . . We recrossed the Rappahannock at the railroad, and saw the fresh graves of the
poor fellows who fell in the assault of the redoubt. The
Rebel officers said it was the most gallant thing they had
seen. Two regiments, the 6th Maine and 7th Wisconsin,
just at sundown, as the light was fading, charged up a long,
naked slope, in face of the fire of a brigade and of four
cannon, and carried the works at the point of the bayonet.
. . . I think it no small praise to General Meade to say
that his plans were so well laid out that our loss in all is
but about 400. No useless slaughter, you see, though
there was plenty of room for a blunder, as you would have
known had you seen the lines of breastworks the fellows
had; but we took part of them and scared them out of the
rest.

HEADQUARTERS ARMY OF POTOMAC
November 13, 1863

Here we continue to dwell in our pine wood, in grave
content, consuming herds of cattle and car-loads of bread
with much regularity. Yesterday, who should turn up but
John Minor Botts,[1] the tough and unterrified. The Rebs
treated him pretty badly this time, because he invited
General Meade to dine; burnt his fences, shot his cattle
and took all his corn and provisions, and finally arrested
him and took him as far as Culpeper, but there concluded
he was a hot potato and set him free. He was inclined to
pitch into us, for not following sharper after the Rebs on
Sunday morning, that is, the day after we forced the river.
He said the first of their waggons did not pass his house
till two at night and the rear of the column not till ten

[1] A Northern sympathizer, who had a plantation in those parts.

next morning; that the roads were choked with footmen, guns, cavalry and ambulances, all hurrying for the Rapid Ann. In good sooth I suppose that a shade more mercury in the feet of some of our officers might do no harm; but, on the other hand, it is to be noticed that we had excellent reason to expect, and believe, that they would not *run*, but only retire to the ridges near Brandy Station and there offer battle. In this case, the premature hurrying forward of a portion of the troops might well have ruined the day. All of which reminds me of Colonel Locke's remark: "If we were omniscient, omnipresent, and omnipotent, we might, with care, get a very pretty fight out of the Rebs!" As it was, what we did do was done as scientifically as any army in the world could have done it, and with a minimum loss of life. I do assure you that Rappahannock station was a position where thousands of men might have been destroyed, with no gain whatsoever, if managed by unskilful officers; and even Kelly's Ford was not without serious difficulties. I don't recollect whether I told you that the enemy had made preparations for nice winter quarters, and were hutting themselves and had made some capital corduroy roads against the mud season. In one hut was found a half-finished letter, from an officer to his wife, in which he said that the Yanks had gone into winter quarters, and that they were doing the same, so that he expected a nice quiet time for some months. Poor man! The Yanks made themselves very comfortable that same evening in his new cabin. Our future movements, or standing still, lie between the General and the weather. Meantime we have to pause a little, for there isn't a thing to eat in this broad land, and every pound of meat and quart of oats for tens of thousands of men and animals must come by a broken railroad from Alexandria. . . .

The Palatinate, during the wars of Louis XIV, could scarcely have looked so desolate as this country. The houses that have not been actually burnt usually look almost worse than those that have: so dreary are they with their windows without sashes, and their open doors, and their walls half stripped of boards. Hundreds of acres of stumps show where once good timber stood, and the arable fields are covered with weeds and blackberry vines, or with the desolate marks of old camps — the burnt spots, where the fires were, the trenches cut round the tents, and the poles, and old bones and tin pots that invariably lie about. . . .

As you walk about the country, you often see fragments of shell scattered around; for all this country has been fought over, back and forth, either in skirmishes or battles; and here and there, you come on a little ridge of earth, marked by a bit of board, on which is scrawled the name of the soldier, who lies where he fell, in this desert region. Our people are very different from the Europeans in their care for the dead, and mark each grave with its name; even in the heat of battle.

HEADQUARTERS ARMY OF POTOMAC
November 15, 1863

Yesterday the General made a start at six A.M. for Washington, taking with him Major Biddle, Captain Meade, and Captain Mitchell, and suppose he will perhaps get back to-morrow. A little before one o'clock came a telegraph that four officers of the "Ghords" were coming in the train, and that we were to send an officer, with ten men, also four led horses, to bring them up. So Major Barstow asked if I would go, whereat, there being nothing to do, I said I would. It is about eight miles to Bealton,

the nearest place the railroad runs to, and, by making
haste a little, we got there by two o'clock, and the train
came a few minutes after. And there, sure enough, were
four gents, much braided and striped, who were the parties
in question: viz., Lieutenant-Colonel Earle, and Lord
Castle Cuff (Grenadier Guards), Captain Peel and Captain Stephenson (Scotch Fusiliers). This was the best lot
of Bulls I have seen for a long time. The nobile Lord is, I
should say, about sixteen, and, with his cap off, is as perfect
a specimen of a Pat as you ever saw; but he is manly,
and not so green as many I have seen of double his age.
Colonel Earle is extremely quiet and well mannered, and
was down here in Burnside's time. Captain Stephenson is
in the beefy style, and Captain Peel (son of Sir Robert) is
of the black order; but both have free use of their legs and
tongues, a remarkable phenomenon in a Bull. We put
them on horses, where they were well at home, except they
would persist in trying to rise to the trot in a McClellan
saddle, which is next to impossible. We had to cross the
river, close to the railroad, where I showed them the work
they took last Saturday; at which they remarked: "Oh!
Ah! A nasty place, a *very* nasty place!" Then we rode to
Headquarters, just in time to avoid a heavy rain, which
continued much of the night. To-day we have lain quiet;
but this evening we took them over to see Captain Sleeper,
9th Massachusetts Battery. The Colonel was very inquisitive about artillery, whereupon the enthusiastic
Sleeper had a newly contrived shell, which was loaded,
suddenly brought into the tent! The great improvement
in the shell seemed to be that it was bound to go off, somehow; so that there was a marked nervousness about him of
the Guards, as the Captain poked and twisted the projectile, to illustrate its manifold virtues! . . .

5

HEADQUARTERS ARMY OF POTOMAC
November 19, '63

The Britons still continue with us. Yesterday we took them, with a small escort, to Buford's Headquarters beyond Culpeper. By Brandy Station we came across a line of rifle-pits that the Rebs had thrown up, probably on the Saturday night of their retreat, so as to cover the trains falling back on the Rapid Ann. We found the cavalry Chief afflicted with rheumatism, which he bore with his usual philosophy. Hence we made haste, across the country, to General Warren's, where he had prepared some manœuvres of infantry for us. This was one of the finest sights I have seen in the army. There were some 6000 or 7000 men on the plain, and we stood on a little hill to look. The evolutions ended by drawing up the force in two lines, one about 300 yards in rear of the other; and each perhaps a mile long. Then they advanced steadily a short distance, when the order was given to charge, and, as if they were one man, both lines broke into a run and came up the hill, shouting and yelling. I never saw so fine a military spectacle. The sun made the bayonets look like a straight hedge of bright silver, which moved rapidly toward you. But the great fun was when part of the line came to a stone wall, over which they hopped with such agility as to take Colonel Earle prisoner, while Captain Stephenson's horse, which was rather slow, received an encouraging prod from a bayonet. Which events put us in great good humor, and we rode merrily home.

HEADQUARTERS ARMY OF POTOMAC
November 25, 1863

I write a line, merely to say that the entire army is under marching orders, for daylight to-morrow; the men in high spirits. As to the officers, you would suppose they

were all going on a merrymaking, to hear them when the
order was issued. Our object is to fight the enemy, which
I pray we may do, and with success, but *Dieu dispose.*

Our stopper·has been the weather, which to-night promises to be set fair, and the roads are passable, though not
good. I wish some critics, who complain of our inactivity,
could be compelled to take a soldier's load and march
twenty miles through this mud. Their next article would,
I think, clearly set forth the necessity of doing nothing till
the driest of weather.

HEADQUARTERS ARMY OF POTOMAC
November 27, '63

Here we are, camped south of the Rapid Ann, and I find
a leisure moment to write you a letter, or rather to begin
one. My last formal note, I believe, informed you we were
to move "to-morrow" (26th). And, sure enough, yesterday we kept our Thanksgiving by marching, horse, foot,
and artillery, as hard as we could paddle towards Germanna Ford.

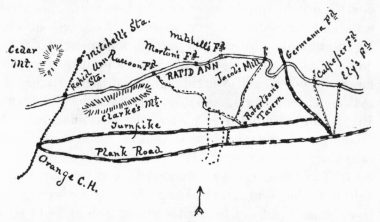

The above rough map, with the other I sent when I wrote
at Centreville, will sufficiently explain our moves. From

Rapid Ann Station to Morton's Ford, the Rebels have a strong line of entrenchments, but, beyond that, it is practicable to force a crossing, because the north bank commands the south. Our forces were encamped in a sort of semi-circle, of which one end rested on Kelly's Ford on the Rappahannock, and the other (at the north) on a tributary of the same river; the centre being about at Brandy Station. . . . The artillery officers had placed two masked batteries, ready to open on the south bank. On the other side of the river there were extensive breastworks, which, however, seemed not occupied. Nevertheless, we could not tell that the woods were not full of them. As the main resistance might be offered here, it was necessary that all the corps should force the passage at the same time, if possible. It so happened that General French was much delayed by heavy roads and other causes, so we had to wait till past twelve before throwing the pontoons. When this was done, there was no opposition whatsoever; but the engineers were stupid enough not to have enough boats, and this made more delay. However, about two P.M. the troops and artillery began to cross, one division having already forded. The solemn and punctual Sykes crossed below, at twelve. But the 3d and 6th, being very large, did not all get over till night, and their artillery, by reason of bad roads, had to come over by Germanna Bridge, and was not over till five the next morning. We (Headquarters) camped on the north bank of the river, near the reserve artillery. It was a magnificent night, but cold. The trains came in after dark, and we had quite a time in finding tents and bedding. Everything is comparative: when I got my tent pitched, my roll of bedding in position, and a little end of a candle lighted, I felt as comfortable as if I came home to a nicely furnished house,

George Sykes

with a good fire burning and the tea-table just set! I was
up this morning a good deal before daylight. The moon
shone very bright and the hoar frost glittered on the
tents. . . . At an early hour the Staff crossed, passing on
the steep bank crowds of ambulances and waggons, which
of course made the General very mad. . . . Do you know
the scrub oak woods above Hammond's Pond, a sort of
growth that is hard for even a single man to force his way
through for any great distance? That is the growth of
most of this country, minus the stones, and plus a great
many "runs" and clay holes, where, in bad weather, vehicles sink to their axles. Along this region there are only
two or three roads that can be counted on. These are the
turnpike, the plank road south of it, and the plank road
that runs from Germanna Ford. There are many narrow
roads, winding and little known, that in good weather may
serve· for the slow passage of columns (though they are
mere farmers' or woodcutters' thoroughfares); but a day's
rain will render them impassable for waggons and artillery.
This whole region (which includes the field of Chancellorsville, a little to the east) is known as the "Wilderness."
Over much of it there is no chance to deploy troops,
scarcely skirmishers, and no place for artillery. . . .

Somewhere about 10.30 we got to the turnpike and
halted, say a mile before Robertson's Tavern; where the
2d Corps had arrived and found the enemy in front; about
eleven they had heavy skirmishing and drove the enemy
back, getting also a few prisoners. They then formed line
of battle and waited news from French on the right, and
Sykes on the left, coming on the plank road. The day was
raw and we stood near the road, over some fires we had
built, waiting for news of French, to form a junction and attack at once; for Warren alone formed a weak centre and

could not risk an engagement. Officer after officer was despatched to him, piloted by niggers who said they knew the country. The indefatigable Ludlow went in the opposite direction, and reported Sykes coming along all right. . . . At 12.30 we heard cannon on our extreme right, which seemed to announce French; still no authentic news, and the precious minutes fled rapidly. At last, late in the afternoon, came authentic despatches that General French's advance had had a heavy fight with the Rebels, in force, and had driven them from the field; but had thus been greatly delayed, and besides had found no roads, or bad roads, and could not effect a junction that evening. And so there was Sedgwick's Corps jammed up in the woods behind, and kept back also! So we pitched camp and waited for morning.

November 28

I thought that our wedding day would be celebrated by a great battle, but so it was not fated. Let us see, a year ago, we were in Paris; and *this* year, behold me no longer ornamenting the Boulevards but booted and spurred, and covered with an india-rubber coat, standing in the mud, midst a soft, driving rain, among the dreary hills of Old Virginny. It was early in the morning, and we were on the crest, near Robertson's Tavern. On either side, the infantry, in line of battle, was advancing, and a close chain of skirmishers was just going into the woods; while close in the rear followed the batteries, laboriously moving over the soft ground. The enemy had fallen back during the night, and we were following. When the troops had got well under way, the General took shelter in the old tavern, to wait for the development. He had not to wait long, before a brisk skirmish fire, followed by the light batteries, announced that we had come on them. Immediately we mounted and rode rapidly towards the front, slop, slop, slop, through the red mud, and amid ambulances and artillery and columns, all struggling forward. We had come on them sure enough, and on their line of works into the bargain, whereof we had notice beforehand, by spies. A halt was therefore ordered and the different corps ordered into position. This was a tremendous job, in the narrow wood-roads, deep with mud; and occupied fully the whole day. If you consider that the men must often move by fours, then a division of 4000 men, closed up, would occupy in marching some 1000 yards, and, by adding the space for pack horses, and the usual gaps and intervals, it would be nearer a mile; so you see how an army would string out, even with no artillery. You must remember also that these long columns cannot move over two miles in an hour; often not so much. . . .

November 29

I rode to and along our front to see the enemy's position, which is a fearfully strong one. Within about a mile of our position, there runs a high, gradually sloping ridge, which trends in a northerly and southerly direction, and crosses the turnpike at right angles, where it is naked, though to the right and left it is wooded in some parts. Between this and a parallel high ground, occupied by us, is a shallow ravine, in which was a small stream, Mine Run. Along their ridge the Rebels have thrown up a heavy and continuous breastwork, supported by entrenched batteries; and, in some places at least, they probably have a second line. Any troops, advancing to the assault, would be exposed to a heavy artillery fire from the very outset, over the space of a mile, besides having to encounter the still worse musketry at the end. At daylight this morning, General

Warren, with his own corps and a division of the 6th, marched towards our extreme left, where, it was understood, the right of the enemy could be turned. His attack was to be a signal for attacking in other places on the line. However, despite that the rain had ceased, the bad roads delayed a good deal, and a false report of entrenchments delayed more; so that, when he got there, after driving in an outlying force, the day was too far advanced for an attack. Major Ludlow, however, came back with a fine account from General Warren of the prospects, and all things were made ready for an assault, next day. . . .

November 30

Almost before daylight our waggons were loaded and away, for the Headquarters are only a few hundred yards in the rear of our heavy guns and directly on the road, so that we expected a nice lot of shells, say at 8.10 A.M. A little before that the General mounted and rode towards General Newton's quarters, and, while near there, *bang!* went a cannon on the right; then *boom! boom!* from the 32-pounders, and then, *bang, boom, bang,* pretty generally. In all the woods the troops were massed for the attack, waiting orders. We rode back to Headquarters, and, a moment after, Captain Roebling from General Warren's Staff, galloped up. He is the most immovable of men, but had, at that moment, rather a troubled air. He handed a scrap of paper. General Meade opened it and his face changed. "My God!" he said, "General Warren has half my army at his disposition!" Roebling shrugged his shoulders. The note was to the effect that General Warren had made a careful examination of the enemy's works, had altered his opinion of last evening, and considered an assault hopeless!!! Orders were at once issued to cease firing. We tried to take it all philosophically, but it was hard, very hard. Most of all to General Meade and General Humphreys, who really took it admirably, for both of them have excellent tempers of their own, which, on occasions, burst forth, like twelve-pounder spherical case. In a little while the General again rode away; this time to see General Warren, some four miles off. Two aides, besides myself, went with him. We rode along the rear of our batteries, which were still, from time to time, exchanging shots with those opposite; though not when I chanced to be passing, I am happy to say. General Warren had a sad face, as well he might. He drew aside, with the two other generals, and there they stood, in long consultation, over a fire which had been made for them, for the air was sharp. Then we started back again, stopping half-way at General French's, whom we found in a fuming passion, partly because two of his divisions had been, in some way, put under guidance of General Warren, and partly because he was all ready for the assault and had pushed his skirmish line to within 300 yards of the Rebel works, while the storming parties were in a great rage at not being led on. Alas! it was of no use; General Humphreys, with a heavy sigh, pronounced the opportunity (if it had ever existed) now past; and, when *he* cries no fight, you may be sure there is not much chance. At a meeting that evening, the other generals concurred. It was physically impossible to flank any more on either side, and the only thing that remained was:

> The King of France with forty thousand men,
> Marched up a hill; and then marched down again.

Wherever the fault lies, I shall always be astonished at the extraordinary moral courage of General Meade, which enabled him to order a retreat, when his knowledge, as an engineer and a soldier, showed that an attack would be a blunder. The men and guns stood ready: he had only to snap his fingers, and that night would probably have seen ten thousand wretched, mangled creatures, lying on those long slopes, exposed to the bitter cold, and out of reach of all help! Then people would have said: "He was unsuccessful; but then he tried hard, and did not get out."

December 1

As I put my head out of my tent this morning, I beheld the heavy guns going to the rear, and I thought, well, we shall follow to-night. And so we did. The 1st Corps marched, in the afternoon, to Germanna Ford and halted, to hold the crossing. At dark the 5th marched, by the turnpike, followed by the 6th; and the 3d, followed by the 2d, took the plank road to Culpeper Ford. There was a piercing cold wind, the roads were frozen, and ice was on the pools; but the night was beautiful, with a lovely moon, that rose over the pine trees, and really seemed to me to be laughing derisively at our poor doughboys, tramping slowly along the road. Just at sunset I rode to the front and took a last look at the Rebels. Through my glass they looked almost near enough to speak to, as they stood, in groups of a dozen, and twenty, on the parapet of their breastworks. Some were on the glacis, seeking, I suppose, for firewood for their camps, whose smoke rose in a thin line, as far as the eye could reach, on either side. The Headquarters waited for some time at Robertson's Tavern, till the 5th Corps had passed, and then followed on. The road was horribly rough, full of great holes and big stones. We crawled, at a snail's pace, till we got clear of the troops, and then the General slammed ahead at a rate that threatened the legs of all our horses; and which gave two or three officers most awful falls on the frozen ground. At 2 oclock this morning (*December 2*) we crossed the Rapid Ann, and were glad to roll ourselves in our blankets in the same camp we had the night of the 26th. And so ends what I think I shall call the Great Seven-days' Flank. If you ask what were the causes of failure, they lie in a nut-shell — *Slowness* and want of *Detail*. We have fought for two years and a half, but it takes no wiseacre to see that we yet have much to learn. Were it not for the remarkable intelligence of the men, we could not do even as well as we do. . . .

HEADQUARTERS ARMY OF POTOMAC
December 10, '63

All the officers are inclined to be petulant and touchy, for they think that winter quarters are coming and are all stretching out for "leaves," which they know only a part can get. Major Biddle becomes quite irate over the subject. "Now there is General Webb has a ten-day leave," says B. petulantly; "every corps is to give one general a ten-day leave. I don't want any little ten-day leave; I want a decent leave; a sixty-day leave. I have been two years and a half in this army, and never had but seven days' leave, except once when I was sick; and it isn't any fun to be sick. If we are going into winter quarters, one third of this army can do what is necessary, just as well as the whole; and they might as well be liberal to us. It is too bad! really too bad!" Such discoveries of patriotic services as the officers now make, to back up their applications, are miraculous. They have all been in service since the First Bull Run (the Genesis of the Potomac Army); they have all been wounded six times; they have never been absent a single day; their wives are very sick; their mothers are not expected to live; and they can easily bring back fifty volunteers with them, to fill up their regiment! All of which General Williams receives with the blandest smile, as if he had never before heard of so strong a case, and promises to refer it to General Meade, which indeed he does. Meanwhile the rattling of axes is heard on all sides, and villages of little log huts, with canvas roofs, spring into existence in a single night. General Ingalls asked if the troops could have permission to build huts: to which the Major-General commanding replied, with charming non-committal. "Build huts; certainly; why not? They can move from huts as well as from tents, can't they?" I observe the papers continue to discuss the succession of the General. He himself thinks he will be relieved, but I doubt it. If for no other reason, because it is hard to find anyone for the post. General Sedgwick would, I think, refuse; General Warren is very young, and is, besides, under a cloud about his movement on our left. General Sickles, people would say, is too much of a Bowery boy. Generals French, Newton, and Sykes are out of the question. General Humphreys has no influence strong enough to put him up. Any subordinate general would have to be of great note to be lifted thus high; there is no such one. I think they would not try a western general, after Pope's experience. The only one I can think of is Hancock, for a long while laid up by his Gettysburg wound, and not yet in the field. He belongs in this army, is popular, and has an excellent name. The New York *Herald* insists on General Pleasonton, which *is* an original idea. I heard of an officer who asserted that he had seen the order putting him in command; a rather unlikely assertion.

HEADQUARTERS ARMY OF POTOMAC
December 12, 1863

I still think, and more strongly than ever, that no change will be made in our chief command; and those who have been to Washington think the same. I am more and more struck, on reflection, with General Meade's consistency and self-control in refusing to attack. His plan was a definite one; from fault of his inferiors it did not work fast enough to be a success; and he had firmness to say, the blow has simply failed and we shall only add disaster to failure by persisting. By this time the officers here know just about how well the Rebels fight, and what we have a reasonable expectation of taking, and what not. It should be remembered, also, as a fundamental fact, that this line is *not* approved as a line of operations, and *never has been;* but we are forced to work on it. Those who think that (according to the Hon. Kellogg) "it would be better to strew the road to Richmond with the dead bodies of our soldiers rather than that there should nothing be done!" may not be content; but those who believe it best to fight when you want to, and not when your enemy wants to, will say simply they are sorry nothing could be effected, but glad that there was no profitless slaughter of troops that cannot be replaced.

HEADQUARTERS ARMY OF POTOMAC
December 16, '63

Yesterday we had one of the funniest exhibitions that the Army has been favored with in a long while. The peaceful *dolce far niente* of the forenoon was suddenly broken by a telegraph, announcing a Russian invasion — nothing less than a legion of Muscovite naval officers pouring down, to the number of twenty-four, in a special train, on our devoted heads! And they were to come in a couple

of hours! Would they pass the night? if so, where put
them, in a camp where two or three guests make a crowd?
Would they be fed? Even this was a problem, unless we
ordered the Commissary to open a dozen boxes of the best
stearine candles. However, General Meade at once orders
the 6th Corps to parade, and gets hold of all the ambulances of the Staff, which are forthwith sent to the depot,
after the serene Bears. And soon the vehicles returned,
with flat caps hanging out of all the openings. Then the
thing was to put them on horseback, as soon as possible,
for it grew late in the day, already. You have heard of
"Jack on horseback," and this was a most striking instance. Each one sat on his McClellan saddle, as if double-
reefing a topsail in a gale of wind. Their pantaloons got
up, and their flat caps shook over their ears; and they kept
nearly tumbling off on one side and hoisting themselves
up again by means of the pommel. Meanwhile they were
very merry and kept up a running fire of French, English
and Russian. The extraordinary cavalcade having reached
a hill, near the ground, there was found an ambulance,
which had brought such as did not wish to ride, including
the Captain, Bootekoff, who was the head feller. He,
however, was persuaded to mount my mare, while I remained in the carriage. Thereupon the other carriage
company were fired with a desire *also* to mount. So a
proper number of troopers were ordered to get down, and
the Russians were boosted into their saddles, and the
procession moved off; but suddenly —

> A horseman darted from the crowd
> Like lightning from a summer cloud.

It was a Muscovite, who had discovered that the pommel
was a great thing to hold on to, and who had grasped the

same, to the neglect of the rein; whereupon the steed, missing his usual dragoon, started at a wild gallop! Off flew the flat cap and away went the horse and rider, with a Staff officer in full chase! Example is contagious, and, in two minutes, the country was dotted with Russians, on the wings of the wind, and vainly pursuing officers and orderlies. Some tumbled off, some were caught and brought back; and one chief engineer was discovered, after dark, in the woods, and in the unpleasant vicinity of the enemy's picket line. However, the most of them were at last got up and viewed the troops from their uncertain positions. After which they were filled up with large quantities of meat and drink and so sent in a happy frame of mind to Washington. The Captain was a very intelligent man; but most of the rest had no character or manliness in their faces, and two or three of them seemed to me almost full-blooded Jews. . . .

To-morrow[1] I lose my tent-mate, the phlegmatic countryman of Gustav Adolf and Charles XII. He could not get permission to remain on General Hunt's Staff and so will have the satisfaction of joining his cavalry regiment, which is hutted somewhere in the mud, near Culpeper! In his place I shall probably have Rosencrantz, another Swede, and for some time at Headquarters as A.D.C. He is a courteous man, an old campaigner, and very amusing with his broken English.

[1] This final paragraph is from a letter dated December 15.

II

IN WINTER QUARTERS

[TOWARD the end of December, the army being then well settled in winter quarters, Lyman obtained leave of absence, passed Christmas at home, and returned to the army about the middle of January. He found Headquarters almost deserted, General Meade sick in Philadelphia with an attack of inflammation of the lungs, General Humphreys, and his tent-mate Rosencrantz, away on leave of absence, and Barstow sick and weak, with a cold on the lungs.]

HEADQUARTERS, ARMY OF POTOMAC
January 23, 1864

Yesterday came General Humphreys, to my great content. His son, with Worth and myself, rode down to bid him welcome. Such a sea of mud round Brandy Station was enough to engulf the most hardy. There is no platform to get on; nothing but the driest spot in the mud. You should have seen the countenances of the unfortunate officers' wives, as they surveyed, from the height of the platform, this broad expanse of pap! Then the husband would appear, in great excitement, and encourage them to descend, which they presently would do, and dab across to an ambulance, seeming mutely to say, that this wasn't quite what they expected. The neat General (who left in hard weather) was entirely aghast, and said, in painful accents, "What! must I get down *there?* Oh, the deuce!" I do believe that officers will next be trying to bring down grand pianos. You needn't talk of coming here with

"small hoops." I have too much respect for you to allow
the shadow of such an idea. As Frank Palfrey sensibly
observed: "I think I should consider some time before I
brought my wife to a mud-hill." . . . The whole country,
besides the mud, is now ornamented with stumps, dead
horses and mules, deserted camps, and thousands upon
thousands of crows. The deserted camps (than which
nothing more desolate) come from the fact that several
divisions have lately changed position. General Meade
has been seriously ill at home; but we have a telegraph
that he is much better, and I have forwarded him, for his
edification, a variety of letters, opened by me at General
Williams's request.

HEADQUARTERS ARMY OF POTOMAC
January 29, 1864

If you saw the style of officers' wives that come here, I
am sure you would wish to stay away. *Quelle expérience*
had I yesterday! I was nearly bored to death, and was two
hours and a half late for my dinner. Oh, list to my har-
rowing tale. I was in my tent, with my coat off, neatly
mending my maps with a little paste, when Captain
Cavada poked in his head (he was gorgeous in a new frock-
coat). "Colonel," said he, "General Humphreys desires
that you will come and help entertain some ladies!" I held
up my pasty hands in horror, and said, "What!" "Ladies!"
quoth Cavada with a grin; "a surprise party on horseback,
thirteen ladies and about thirty officers." There was no
moyen; I washed my hands, put on the double-breaster,
added a cravat, and proceeded, with a sweet smile, to the
tent, whence came a sound of revelry and champagne
corks. Such a set of feminine humans I have not seen
often; it was Lowell factories broken loose and gone mad.
They were all gotten up in some sort of long thing, to ride

6

in. One had got a lot of orange tape and trimmed her jacket in the dragoon style; another had the badge of the Third Corps pinned all askew in her hat; a third had a major's knot worked in tarnished lace on her sleeve; while a fourth had garnitured her chest by a cape of grey squirrel-skin. And there was General Humphreys, very red in the face, smiling like a basket of chips, and hopping round with a champagne bottle, with all the spring of a boy of sixteen. He spied me at once, and introduced me to a Mrs. M——, who once married somebody who treated her very badly and afterwards fortunately went up; so Mrs. M—— seemed determined to make up lost time and be jolly in her liberty. She was quite bright; also quite warm and red in the face, with hard riding and, probably, champagne. Then they said they would go over to General Sedgwick's, and General Humphreys asked if I would not go, too, which invitation it was not the thing to refuse; so I climbed on my horse, with the malicious consolation that it would be fun to see poor, modest Uncle John with such a load! But Uncle John, though blushing and overcome, evidently did not choose to be put upon; so, with great politeness, he offered them sherry, with naught to eat and no champagne. Then nothing would do but go to Headquarters of the 3d Corps, whither, to my horror, the gallant Humphreys would gang likewise. Talk about cavalry raids to break down horses! If you want to do that, put a parcel of women on them and set them going across the country. Such a Lützow's wild hunt hath not been seen since the day of the respected L. himself! Finally one lady's horse ran away, and off went the brick, Humphreys, like a shot, to stop her. Seeing her going into a pine tree, he drove his horse between the tree and her; but, in so doing, encountered a hidden branch, which slapped the brisk old gent out of his saddle, like a shuttle-cock! The Chief-of-Staff was up in a second, laughing at his mishap; while I galloped up, in serious alarm at his accident. To make short a long story, the persistent H. tagged after those womenfolk (and I tagged after *him*) first to Corps Headquarters, then to General Carr's Headquarters, and finally to General Morris's Headquarters, by which time it was dark! I was the only one that knew the nearest way home (we were four miles away) and didn't I lead the eminent soldier through runs and mud-holes, the which he do hate!

To-day we have had a tremendous excitement: a detail of 250 men to "police" the camp, under charge of Biddle, just appointed Camp Commandant. They have been sweeping, cutting down stumps, burning brush, and, in general, making the worst-looking camp in the army neat and respectable.

HEADQUARTERS ARMY OF POTOMAC
January 31, 1864

As I was riding the other day, I came on a rare bird, a real old family nigger; none of your lying, stealing, camp contrabands, but a real, grey-headed, old-fashioned Virginian nigger. He seemed to be living in a little log hut. His battered, white broad-brim, and coat of faded snuff-color, did speak of days before the war, when Master lived in the big house, now burned flat. "Good morning, Uncle!" said I, after the manner of our Southern brethren. The ancient darky looked up in surprise, at this once familiar greeting, and then, taking his hat off in a way that knocked Louis XIV entirely, he replied, "Good mornin', saar! a beautiful mornin', saar!" I asked where Beverly Ford was, and thanked him for his information. Whereupon I was favored with more of the Great Monarch, and retired much impressed with him. His day is gone. More houses and better houses will be built in Culpeper country, and a few years will leave no trace of the war, but the decaying head-board, here and there, of some poor chap, and the bits of shell that the farmers will sometimes pick up. But Master, who lived in the big house, is shot, long ago — he and his régime both.

February 5, 1864

General Humphreys sent for me and showed me a cipher correspondence between Butler and Halleck, and Halleck and Sedgwick. B. telegraphed that large reinforcements had been sent from the Rapid Ann to North Carolina, and that he wished a demonstration to "draw their forces from Richmond." S. replied that, with the exception of some two or three brigades, nobody had been sent to that place from the army in our front. B. then said he was going to move on Richmond, or something of the sort, and would like a demonstration not later than Saturday (to-morrow). S. said it was too short a time to make any great show and that it would spoil our chances for a surprise on their works, in future. H. then telegraphed to do, at any rate, what we could. So Kilpatrick has been sent to their right *via* Mine Ford, and Merritt is to threaten Barnett's Ford; and to threaten Raccoon Ford, while the 2d will make a stronger demonstration at Morton's Ford. Old Sedgwick and General Humphreys are cross at the whole thing, looking on it as childish.

February 7, 1864

It is one in the morning and I have, so to speak, just taken a midnight dinner, having come in from the front between 11 and 12 oclock. Well, who would have thought of marching out of comfortable winter quarters, to go poking round the Rapidan! . . . Only last night orders were suddenly issued to the 1st and 2d Corps to march at sunrise, the one on Raccoon, the other on Morton's Ford; where they were to make a strong demonstration and perhaps cross at Morton's (Raccoon being too strong). Certain cavalry, also, were to go to other points, with special orders. The whole thing was very sudden, all round, and none of *our* fish. This morning we took an early breakfast, which, with the ready horses, quite reminded one of campaigning times. General Sedgwick was over, being in command, as viceroy. At 10.30 we began to hear the cannon, but General Humphreys would not stir, as he said he must stay to attend to the despatches and telegraph. However, at 3 P.M., he suddenly *did* start, with his own aides and Biddle, Mason, Cadwalader and myself, *de la part de* General Meade; also Rosencrantz. To Morton's Ford is some ten miles, but you might as well call it fifty, such is the state of the roads. Mud, varying from fetlocks to knees, then holes, runs, ditches and rocks — such was the road. With utmost diligence it took fully two hours. . . . Here we had thrown across a division, and General Warren was with them. The enemy had offered a good deal of opposition, with a skirmish fire and with artillery; despite which the whole division had waded the stream, up to their waists (cold work for the 6th of February!), and were now in line, behind some ridges; while a heavy skirmish line covered their front. Enclosing them, almost in a semi-circle, were the Rebel earthworks. It looked a shaky position for us! All was quiet; the men were making coffee, and nothing broke the stillness but an occasional shot from the sharpshooters. "Well," said General Humphreys, "I must go across and look about, while there is light left. I don't want many to go. McClellan, you will come; and Major Biddle and Colonel Lyman, if you would like, I shall be glad of your company." So off we four rode, and met Warren coming back, before we got to the river. But he at once turned horse and kept on with us. The ford was very bad, deep and with steep sides, but we floundered over, and I was once again south of the Rapid Ann. . . . As we got to the main line, "Now," said General Warren, "get off here and I will take you as far as you can go, very soon." We dismounted and remained, while the two Generals went some 150 yards to Morton's house on the crest of the ridge, where they no sooner got than a sharpshooter fired at them and the ball flew harmless over our heads, though it came close to General Warren. But hang it all! We had not been there five minutes when that infernal old sound came, *whing-z-z-z-z*, and over went a spherical case! "Fall in, fall in!" shouted the colonels, and the men took their arms. *Whing-z-z!* *Bang!* came another, right into the infantry, killing a poor man. "Steady! steady!" roared the colonels. *Whing-z-z-z-z!* *Bang!* and one of the pieces struck close to me, while one of the bullets struck the scabbard of the orderly next me, who coolly picked up the missile. We were a little sheltered by the road, but, I don't care who knows it, I did duck when that spherical case came over. By this time the Generals got back and mounted, the enemy continuing the fire but throwing their shot too high. We had not got far towards the river, when they began with musketry, a very heavy skirmish fire, and seemed about to make a general attack; but it turned out to be a strong attempt to drive back our skirmish line from a favorable fence they had secured; and the artillery was a cover for their advance. When we got back to the high ground by Robinson's, we could look across and see the fight, though it was growing dark and the air was very foggy. Our artillery opened on them also, and, in course of an hour or so, night set in, and the firing ceased, our line holding its own everywhere. And now the poor wounded fellows began to come in, some alone, some supported, and some in ambulances. The surgeons were numerous and all that could be wished for. Except one or two mortally hurt, there was nothing sad in it, so manly were the men and so cheerful. Not a groan, not a complaint. I asked one man who was staggering along, if he were much hurt. "Very slightly," he remarked, in a lively tone. I found what he called "very slightly" was a musket-ball directly through the thigh. These men are wonderful, much more so, I think (proportionately), than the officers. There was a whole division wet to the waist, on a rainy February day, exposed each instant to attack, and yet making little pots of coffee; in the open air, as calmly as if at Revere House.

Oh! what a ride had we home! It took us over three hours, with the help of a lantern. . . .

HEADQUARTERS ARMY OF POTOMAC
February 12, 1864

In this epistle I shall describe to you the whirl of fashion, the galaxy of female beauty, the grouping of manly grace. Behold, I have plunged into the wild dissipation of a military dinner-party. The day before yesterday, there appeared a mysterious orderly, with a missive from Colonel Hayes (my classmate) saying that he should next day entertain a select circle at dinner at five of the clock, and wouldn't I come and stay over night. To which I returned answer that I should give myself that pleasure. The gallant Colonel, who commands the 3d Brigade, 1st Division, 5th

Corps, has his Headquarters on the north side of the river, about half a mile from Rappahannock station. At 4 P.M. I was ready, very lovely to look on, with full tog and sash, neatly finished by white cotton gloves and my thick laced shoes. With great slowness did I wend on my sable mare, for fear of splashing myself in a run or a puddle. On the other side of the pontoon bridge I fell in with Lieutenant Appleton wending the same way — he splashed his trousers in Tin Pot Run, poor boy! The quarters were not far, and were elegantly surrounded by a hedge of evergreen, and with a triumphal arch from which did float the Brigade flag. Friend Hayes has an elegant log hut, papered with real wall-paper, and having the roof ornamented with a large garrison flag. The fireplace presented a beautiful arch, which puzzled me a good deal, till I found it was made by taking an old iron cog-wheel, found at the mill on the river, and cutting the same in two. Already the punctual General Sykes, Commander of the Corps, was there, with Mrs. S., a very nice lady, in quite a blue silk dress. . . . Also several other officers' wives, of sundry ages, and in various dresses. Then we marched in and took our seats, I near the head and between Mrs. Lieutenant Snyder and Mrs. Dr. Holbrook. Next on the left was General Bartlett, in high boots and brass spurs. There must have been some twenty-four persons, in all. The table ran the length of two hospital tents, ingeniously floored with spare boards from the pontoon-train and ornamented with flags and greens. The chandeliers were ingeniously composed of bayonets, and all was very military. Oyster soup had we; fish, biled mutting, roast beef, roast turkey, pies, and nuts and raisins; while the band did play outside. General Sykes, usually exceeding stern, became very gracious and deigned to laugh, when one of his captains said: "He was the mildest-mannered man that ever cut a throat or scuttled ship."

After dinner, songs were encouraged, and General Sykes told two of his Staff, if they didn't sing immediately, he would send them home at once! I sang two comic songs, with immense success, and all was festive. I passed the night there, and took breakfast this morning, when Albert came down with the horses. Joe Hayes is a singular instance of a man falling into his right notch. In college he was not good at his studies at all; but, as an officer, he is remarkable, and has a reputation all through the Corps. Though only a colonel, he was entrusted, at Mine Run, with bringing off the picket line, consisting of 4000 men, which he did admirably. . . .

HEADQUARTERS ARMY OF POTOMAC
February 22, '64

General Meade is in excellent spirits and cracks a great many jokes and tells stories. You can't tell how different he is when he has no movement on his mind, for then he is like a firework, always going bang at someone, and nobody ever knows who is going to catch it next, but all stand in a semi-terrified state. There is something sardonic in his natural disposition, which is an excellent thing in a commander; it makes people skip round so. General Humphreys is quite the contrary. He is most easy to get on with, for everybody; but, practically, he is just as hard as the Commander, for he has a tremendous temper, a great idea of military duty, and is very particular. When he does get wrathy, he sets his teeth and lets go a torrent of adjectives that must rather astonish those not used to little outbursts. There came down with the General (who returned yesterday from Washington) a Mr. Kennedy, Chief of the

Census Bureau, a very intelligent man, full of figures. He can tell you how many people have pug noses in Newton Centre, and any other little thing you want. There was a bill passed in the House of Reps to raise 100,000 negro troops, from the *free* colored men of the North. When the bill came before the Senate, Mr. Kennedy sent in word that there were less than 50,000 colored men who were free and capable of bearing arms in the whole North, which rather squelched the bill! He says that the free negroes South increase hardly at all; while those in the North even decrease; but the *slaves* increase more than any other class. So I think it will be best to free the whole lot of them and then they will sort of fade out.

There are perfect shoals of womenkind now in the army — a good many, of course, in Culpeper, where they can live in houses. The rest of them must live a sort of Bedouin life. The only one I have seen of late is Mrs. Captain Commissary Coxe, for behold we had a service *al fresco*, near General Patrick's tent. There was Mr. Rockwell as clergyman, quite a good preacher, and very ready to speak, nevertheless not too long in his remarks. I marched over with a camp-stool very solemnly. There were quite a collection of officers from the Headquarters, also a company of cavalry, which was marched down dismounted and stood meekly near by; for this cavalry belongs to General Patrick, and the General is pious, and so his men have to be meek and lowly. Likewise came some of the red-legs, or Zouaves, or 114th Pennsylvania, who finally had an air of men who had gone to a theatre and did not take an interest in the play. There too were some ladies, who were accommodated with a tent open in front, so as to allow them to see and hear. The band of the Zouaves sang the hymns and were quite musical. . . . To-night is a great ball of the 2d Corps. The General has gone to it; also General Humphreys. None of the Staff were invited, save George Meade, to the huge indignation of the said Staff and my great amusement.

. . . I went yesterday to a review of the 2d Corps gotten up in honor of Governor Sprague. It was some seven or eight miles away, near Stevensburg, so that it was quite a ride even to get there. General Meade, though he had been out till three in the morning at the ball, started at eleven, with the whole Staff, including General Pleasonton and *his* aides, the which made a dusty cavalcade. First we went to the Corps Headquarters, where we were confronted by the apparition of two young ladies in extemporaneous riding habits, mounted on frowsy cavalry horses and prepared to accompany. General Meade greeted them with politeness, for they were some relations of somebody, and we set forth. The review was on a large flat (usually very wet, but now quite dry, yet rather rough for the purpose) and consisted of the Corps and Kilpatrick's division of cavalry. When they were all ready, we rode down the lines, to my great terror, for I thought the womenkind, of whom there were half a dozen, would break their necks; for there were two or three ditches, and we went at a canter higglety-pigglety. However, by the best of luck they all got along safe and we took our place to see the troops march past. We made a funny crowd: there were the aforesaid ladies, sundry of whom kept chattering like magpies; then the Hon. Senator Wilkinson of Minnesota, in a suit of faded black and a second-hand felt that some officer had lent him. The Honorable rode bravely about, with a seat not laid down in any of the textbooks, and kept up a lively and appropriate conversation at the most serious parts of the ceremony. "Wall, Miss Blunt, how do you git along? Do you think you will stan' it out?" To which Miss Blunt would reply in shrill tones: "Wall, I feel kinder tired, but I guess I'll hold on, and ride clear round, if I can." And, to do her justice, she did hold on, and I thought, as aforesaid, she would break her neck. Then there was his Excellency, the Vice-President, certainly one of the most ordinary-looking men that ever obtained the suffrages of his fellow citizens. Also little Governor Sprague, a cleanly party, who looked very well except that there is something rather too sharp about his face. Likewise were there many womenkind in ambulances discreetly looking on. The cavalry came first, headed by the valiant Kilpatrick, whom it is hard to look at without laughing. The gay cavaliers themselves presented their usual combination of Gypsy and Don Cossack. Then followed the artillery and the infantry. Among the latter there was a good deal of difference; some of the regiments being all one could wish, such as the Massachusetts 20th, with Abbot at its head; while others were inferior and marched badly. Thereafter Kill-cavalry (as scoffers call him) gave us a charge of the 500, which was entertaining enough, but rather mobby in style. And so home, where we did arrive quite late; the tough old General none the worse.

HEADQUARTERS ARMY OF POTOMAC
March 1, 1864

. . . For some days General Humphreys has been a mass of mystery, with his mouth pursed up, and doing much writing by himself, all to the great amusement of the bystanders, who had heard, even in Washington, that some expedition or raid was on the tapis, and even pointed out various details thereof. However, their ideas, after all, were vague; but they should not have known *anything*. *Que voulez-vous?* A secret expedition with us is got up like a picnic, with everybody blabbing and yelping. One is driven to think that not even the prospect of immediate execution will stop Americans from streaming on in their loose, talking, devil-may-care ways. Kilpatrick is sent for by the President; oh, ah! everybody knows it at once: he is a cavalry officer; it must be a raid. All Willard's chatters of it. Everybody devotes his entire energies to pumping the President and Kill-cavalry! Some confidential friend finds out a part, tells another confidential friend, swearing him to secrecy, etc., etc. So there was Eleusinian Humphreys writing mysteriously, and speaking to nobody, while the whole camp was sending expeditions to the four corners of the compass! On Saturday, at early morn, Uncle John Sedgwick suddenly picked up his little traps and marched with his Corps through Culpeper and out towards Madison Court House, away on our right flank. The next, the quiet Sabbath, was broken by the whole of Birney's division, of the 3d Corps, marching also through Culpeper, with the bands playing and much parade. We could only phancy the feeling of J. Reb contemplating this threatening of his left flank from his signal station on Clark's Mountain. Then the flaxen Custer, at the head of cavalry, passed through, and wended his way in the same direction. All this, you see, was on our right. That night Kilpatrick, at the head of a large body of cavalry, crossed at Ely's Ford, on our *extreme left*, and drew a straight bead on Richmond! At two oclock that night he was at Spotsylvania C. H., and this is our last news of him. He sent back word that he would attack Richmond at seven this morning. The idea is to liberate the prisoners, catch all the rebel M. C.'s that are lying round loose, and make tracks to our nearest lines. I conceive the chances are pretty hazardous, although the plan was matured with much detail and the start was all that could be asked. . . .

HEADQUARTERS ARMY OF POTOMAC
March 5, 1864

I found myself late and galloped four miles in about twenty minutes, only to find I had heated the mare for nothing, insomuch that the venerable Humphreys had put off dinner to six P.M. That young man of fifty has gone in his ambulance to see, I presume, some ladies, and I will here and now wager that we don't dine till eight P.M. Sich is his nature. Really he should be dismissed the service for conduct to the prejudice of good order and military discipline. *Au reste*, there never was a nicer old gentleman, and so boyish and peppery that I continually want to laugh in his face. I am in fear he won't be confirmed as major-general. There are some persons, the very dregs of politicians, whom he tried by court-martial, when under him, that now do all they can against his promotion. I find that politicians, like Sumner and company, have a way of saying of officers who have had their very clothes shot off their back and have everywhere displayed the utmost skill and courage, that "their hearts are not in the cause," or "they are not fully with us"; meaning that these officers do not happen to fully agree with every political dogma the party may choose to enunciate. I am of the opinion that the question is: Does such and such an officer fight bravely and with skill? Anyone who has been under fire will be ready to acknowledge that it is a pretty good place to test principles; and

Andrew Atkinson Humphreys

if a man goes into the thick of it time and again, I do not ask any better proof of his earnestness. However, it would appear that Washington people often think the best test of faithfulness is to stay away from the fighting and make a good many speeches to people who entirely agree with your sentiments. To my certain knowledge, great exertions are now making to put a man at the head of this army who has made one of the most bloody failures of the War, and who is utterly incompetent to the post. Why is he pushed? Because he professes to be an ultra-Republican, ah, *voila!* . . .

Pa Meade is at Washington but I hope to have him back to-morrow. Behold my prophecy in regard to Kill-cavalry's raid fulfilled. I have heard many persons very indignant with him. They said he went to the President and pressed his plan; told Pleasonton he would not come back alive if he didn't succeed; that he is a frothy braggart, without brains and not over-stocked with desire to fall on the field; and that he gets all his reputation by newspapers and political influence. These charges are not new and I fancy Kill has rather dished himself. It is painful to think of those poor prisoners hearing the sound of his guns and hoping a rescue was at hand! Now all that cavalry must be carried back in steamers, like a parcel of old women going to market! Bah! *Pour moi,* I say nothing, as I never criticize superior officers; but I have mine own opinions, quite strong. However, these raids and the like do not much affect the War one way or the other. Nor does such a thing as the Florida reverse. Things have narrowed down now to two or three great centres, and upon large operations there depends the result. It is a favorite remark of General Meade, that "there is but one way to put down this rebellion, namely, to destroy the military power of the Rebels." Their great armies must be overwhelmed, and there will end their hopes. . . .

[A few days later Lyman left for the North on a three weeks' leave. While he was dining in Washington, at Willard's, "General Grant[1] came in, with his little boy; and was immediately bored by being cheered, and then shaken by the hand by οἱ πολλοί! He is rather under middle height, of a spare, strong build; light-brown hair, and short, light-brown beard. His eyes of a clear blue; forehead high; nose aquiline; jaw squarely set, but not sensual. His face has three expressions: deep thought; extreme determination; and great simplicity and calmness."]

HEADQUARTERS ARMY OF POTOMAC
March 30, 1864

I am pretty well, I thank you, and not so blue as when I came back the other time, perhaps because the generals are here and it is not so utterly *triste*. However, I am fain to say I draw invidious comparisons between it and home, *mais* that helps nothing. There have been marvellous changes within these three weeks. Generals Sykes, Newton, French, and Pleasonton are ordered off. I do feel sorry for Sykes, an excellent soldier, always sure to do his duty, and with this army for a long time. I fear they displaced him at Washington because they disliked his rough manners. General Pleasonton was always very civil to me

---

[1] On February 29 Congress revived the grade of Lieutenant-General, and Lincoln had appointed Grant, much in the public eye since his successful campaign in the West, to that rank, and to command the Armies of the United States. Motley writes at the time: "In a military point of view, thank Heaven! the coming man, for whom we have so long been waiting, seems really to have come."

and I am sorry therefore to see him go. I have not yet got it clearly in my head how the corps have been shifted about, but I suppose I shall in a few days. . . .

The latest joke is the heavy sell that has been practised on some regiments of "Heavy Artillery," which had re-enlisted and had been sent home to recruit. Now these gentry, having always been in fortifications, took it for granted they should there continue; consequently the patriotic rush of recruits (getting a big bounty) was most gratifying; one regiment swelled to 1900; another to 2200, etc., etc. *Bon!* Then they returned to the forts round Washington, with the slight difference that the cars kept on, till they got to Brandy Station; and now these mammoth legions are enjoying the best of air under shelter-tents! A favorite salutation now is, "How are you, Heavy Artillery?" For Chief of Cavalry we are to have a General Sheridan, from the West. He is, I believe, on his way. If he is an able officer, he will find no difficulty in pushing along this arm, several degrees. . . .

HEADQUARTERS ARMY OF POTOMAC
April 12, '64

Yesterday we all rode to Culpeper, and saw General Grant, who went last night to Washington, and did go thence to Annapolis. I was well pleased with all the officers down there; among others was a Lieutenant-Colonel Comstock, a Massachusetts man. He had somewhat the air of a Yankee schoolmaster, buttoned in a military coat. Grant is a man of a good deal of rough dignity; rather taciturn; quick and decided in speech. He habitually wears an expression as if he had determined to drive his head through a brick wall, and was about to do it. I have much confidence in him.

7

April 13, 1864

We went to a review of Birney's Division near J. M. Bott's house. The two brigades are under H. Ward and Alex. Hays. About 5000 men were actually on the ground. Here saw General Hancock for the first time. He is a tall, soldierly man, with light-brown hair and a military heavy jaw; and has the massive features and the heavy folds round the eye that often mark a man of ability. Then the officers were asked to take a little whiskey *chez* Botts. Talked there with his niece, a dwarfish little woman of middle age, who seems a great invalid. She was all of a tremor, poor woman, by the mere display of troops, being but nervous and associating them with the fighting she had seen round the very house. Then there was a refreshment at Birney's Headquarters, where met Captain Briscoe (said to be the son of an Irish nobleman, etc., etc.); also Major Mitchell on General Hancock's Staff. The Russ was delighted with the politeness and pleased with the troops. Introduced to General Sheridan, the new Chief of Cavalry — a small, broad-shouldered, squat man, with black hair and a square head. He is of Irish parents, but looks very like a Piedmontese. General Wilson, who is probably to have a division, is a slight person of a light complexion and with rather a pinched face. Sheridan makes everywhere a favorable impression.

HEADQUARTERS ARMY OF POTOMAC
April 18, 1864

I have seen some high-bush blackberries that already had wee leaves, just beginning to open; and the buds of the trees are swelling; and hundreds of little toads sing and whistle all night, to please other hundreds of Misses toads. The sap is rising so in the oak trees that the wood won't

burn without some trouble. It really looks like a beginning of spring; and everything is so quiet that it is quite
amazing; whether it is that old soldiers get lazy and sleep
a good deal during the day, I don't know, but really just a
short way from camp, it is as still as if not a human being
were near; and here at Headquarters, the only sounds are
the distant car-whistles and the drums and trumpets
sounding the calls; except, indeed, the music of the band,
which is hardly a noise and is very acceptable. I suppose
we may call this the lull before the hurricane, which little short of a miracle can avert. There is Grant, with his
utterly immovable face, going about from Culpeper to
Washington and back, and sending no end of cipher messages, all big with strategy. He evidently means to do
something pretty serious before he gives up. To-day was
a great day for him; he reviewed the entire 6th Corps,
which, as you know, has been strengthened by a division
of the late 3d Corps. The day has been fine, very. At
eleven o'clock we started and rode towards Culpeper, to
meet General Grant, who encountered us beyond Brandy
Station. He is very fond, you must know, of horses, and
was mounted on one of the handsomest I have seen in the
army. He was neatly dressed in the regulation uniform,
with a handsome sash and sword, and the three stars of a
lieutenant-general on his shoulder. He is a man of a natural, severe simplicity, in all things — the very way he
wears his high-crowned felt hat shows this: he neither puts
it on behind his ears, nor draws it over his eyes; much less
does he cock it on one side, but sets it straight and very
hard on his head. His riding is the same: without the
slightest "air," and, *per contra*, without affectation of
homeliness; he sits firmly in the saddle and looks straight
ahead, as if only intent on getting to some particular point.

General Meade says he is a very amiable man, though his eye is stern and almost fierce-looking.

Well, we encountered him, as aforesaid, followed by three or four aides; one of whom, Lieutenant-Colonel Rowley, was oblivious of straps, and presented an expanse of rather ill-blacked, calfskin boots, that took away from his military ensemble a good deal. When a man *can* ride without straps, he may do so, if he chooses; but, when he possesseth not the happy faculty of keeping down his trousers, he should make straps a part of his religion! We took our station on a swell of ground, when we could see a large part of the Corps in line; but there was so much of it, that, though drawn up by battalions (that is, ten men deep), there could be found, in the neighborhood, no ground sufficiently extensive, without hollows. At once they began to march past — there seemed no end of them. In each direction there was nothing but a wide, moving hedge of bright muskets; a very fine sight. . . . General Grant is much pleased and says there is nothing of the sort out West, in the way of discipline and organization. . . .

May 3

At last the order of march, for to-morrow at 5 A.M.! Of it more when it is over — if I am here to write. Only spring waggons go for our little mess kits and baggage; other things go with the main train. May God bless the undertaking at last and give an end to this war! I have made all preparations for the campaign.

III

THE WILDERNESS AND SPOTSYLVANIA

[On the night of May 3, the Army of the Potomac started across the Rapidan into the Wilderness. Lee did not molest them, for, knowing every inch of that difficult country, he expected to trap them when the Union Army got into the woods.

Lyman's letters for the first ten days are short, hasty notes from the front. By the middle of the month he finds time to write a detailed account of events in the lulls between the battles about Spotsylvania Court House, where Grant, finding he could not force his way through the Wilderness, had manœuvred the army by a flank movement to the left.]

Headquarters Army of Potomac
10 p.m. *Sunday, May 15, 1864*

Well, to be more or less under fire, for six days out of seven, is not very good for the nerves, or very pleasant. But now that there is a quiet day, I thought I would make a beginning of describing to you the sad, bloody work we have been at. I will write enough to make a letter and so go on in future letters, only writing what can now be of no importance to the enemy. The morning of Wednesday the 4th of May (or rather the night, for we were up by starlight) was clear and warm. By daylight we had our breakfast, and all was in a hurry with breaking up our winter camp. To think of it to-night makes it seem a half-year ago; but it is only eleven days. About 5.30 a.m. we turned our backs on what had been our little village for six months.

85

Already the whole army had been some hours in motion. The 5th Corps, followed by the 6th, was to cross at Germanna Ford, and march towards the Orange pike. The 2d Corps to march on Chancellorsville, crossing at Ely's Ford; each corps was preceded by a division of cavalry, to picket the roads and scour the country. The main waggon-train rested on the north side at Richardsville. So you see the first steps were much like the Mine Run campaign.

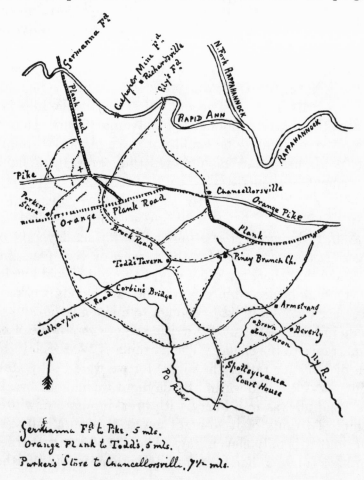

Germanna Fd to Pike, 5 mls.
Orange Plank to Todd's, 5 mls.
Parker's Store to Chancellorsville, 7½ mls.

I have drawn a little map to help you in understanding; not very exact in proportions, but still enough so.

The roads were hard and excellenᵗ, full of waggons and black with troops; as we got past Stevensburg and went through a more wooded country, there were the little green leaves just opening, and purple violets, in great plenty, by the wayside. As the sun got fairly up, it grew much warmer, as one could see by the extra blankets and overcoats that our men threw away, whenever they halted. By 8 A.M. we drew near the Ford, and halted at a familiar spot, where we had our camp on the Mine Run campaign. How bitterly cold it was then! And now there was green grass all about, and wild flowers. Griffin's division was already over, and the others were following steadily on. At 9.30 we went over ourselves, and, for a long time, I sat on the high bank, some seventy feet above the river, watching the steady stream of men and cannon and trains pouring over the pontoons. It was towards six in the evening before the last were across; and then one bridge was left for Burnside to cross by; for he was marching in all haste, from Rappahannock station. Meantime the head of the 5th Corps had reached the Orange pike, and that of the 2d, Chancellorsville. The Headquarters pitched their now reduced tents on the bank of the river that night, and I went down and took a slight bath in the stream, by way of celebrating our advance. General Grant came up betimes in the morning and had his tents near ours. He has several very sensible officers on his Staff, and several very foolish ones, who talked and laughed flippantly about Lee and his army. But they have changed their note *now*, and you hear no more of their facetiousness. The more experienced officers were sober, like men who knew what work was ahead. Our first grief was a ludicrous one. Our cook, a small Gaul, had mysteriously disappeared, and all we had left to cook for us was a waiter lad, who however rose with the occasion and was very conspicuous for activity. It turned out after, that the cook was arrested as a suspicious person, despite his violent protestations. . . .

We were off betimes the next morning (Thursday, May 5th), and about 7 o'clock got to the junction of the plank and pike, the troops meantime marching past us, as we stood waiting news from the front. Presently Griffin (5th Corps), who was two miles out on the pike (going west), reported the enemy in his front; while the cavalry, thrown out on the plank road, towards Parker's Store, sent to say that the Rebel infantry were marching down in force, driving them in. General Wright's division of the 6th Corps was turned off the Germanna plank to the right and ordered to march down the cross-road you see on the map, leading to the pike; and he and Griffin were directed to press the enemy and try to make a junction by their wings. At 10.40 A.M. General Getty's division (6th Corps) was sent to hold the Orange plank road. It marched down the Germanna plank and took the little cross-road where the dotted line is, and got to the Orange plank just in time to stop the advance of A. P. Hill's Corps. Meantime the rest of the 5th Corps was ordered into position on the left of, or in support of, General Griffin, about parallel to the most westerly dotted line, crossing the pike. Word was sent to 2d Corps, near Chancellorsville, that the Rebels were moving on us, and ordering Hancock to at once bring his men across to the Brock road and so take position on the left in support of General Getty. At noon, I was sent to General Getty, to tell him the disposition of the various troops and to direct him to feel along to his right, and find roads to communicate with the left of the 5th Corps, where, you will see, there was a considerable gap. Our Headquarters were on a piney knoll near the join of the Germanna plank and the pike. I rode down the dotted cross-road and came immediately on General Eustis, just putting his brigade into the woods, on Getty's right. I stopped and directed him to throw out well to the right and to try to find Crawford, or a road to him.

Here it is proper to say something of the nature of this country, whereof I have already spoken somewhat during Mine Run times. A very large part of this region, extending east and west along the plank and pike, and the south, nearly to Spotsylvania, is called "The Wilderness," a most appropriate term — a land of an exhausted, sandy soil, supporting a more or less dense growth of pine or of oak. There are some cleared spaces, especially near Germanna plank, where our Headquarters are marked. The very worst of it is parallel with Orange plank and upper part of the Brock road. Here it is mostly a low, continuous, thick growth of small saplings, fifteen to thirty feet high and seldom larger than one's arm. The half-grown leaves added to the natural obscurity, and there were many places where a line of troops could with difficulty be seen at fifty yards. This was the *terrain* on which we were called to manœuvre a great army. I found General Getty at the plank road (a spot I shall remember for some years) and gave him instructions. He told me the whole of Hill's Corps was in his front and the skirmishers only 300 yards from us. For all I could see they might have been in Florida, but the occasional wounded men who limped by, and the sorry spectacle of two or three dead, wrapped in their blankets, showed that some fighting had already taken place. I got back and reported a little before one o'clock, and had scarcely got there when

B-r-r-r-r wrang went the musketry, in front of Griffin and of Wright, which for the next hour and a half was continuous — not by volley, for that is impossible in such woods; but a continuous crackle, now swelling and now abating, and interspersed with occasional cannon. Very soon the ambulances began to go forward for their mournful freight. A little before two, I was sent with an order to a cavalry regiment, close by. The pike was a sad spectacle indeed; it was really obstructed with trains of ambulances and with the wounded on foot; all had the same question, over and over again; "How far to the 5th Corps' hospital?" As I returned, I saw, coming towards me, a mounted officer — his face was covered with blood and he was kept in the saddle only by an officer who rode beside him and his servant who walked on the other side. "Hullo, Lyman!" he cried, in a wild way that showed he was wandering; "here I am; hurt a little; not much; I am going to lie down a few minutes, and then I am going back again! Oh, you ought to have seen how we drove 'em — I had the first line!" It was my classmate, Colonel Hayes, of the 18th Massachusetts; as fearless a soldier as ever went into action. There we were, three of us together, for the officer who supported him was Dr. Dalton. Three classmates together, down in the Virginia Wilderness, and a great fight going on in front. I was afraid Hayes was mortally hurt, but I am told since, he will recover. I trust so.

Gradually the musketry died away; and, at a quarter before three, General Griffin rode up — his face was stern and flushed, as it well might be. He said he had attacked and driven Ewell's troops three quarters of a mile, but that Wright had made no join on his right and Wadsworth had been forced back on his left, so that with both flanks exposed he had been obliged to fall back to his former position.[1] Meantime we got word that the head of Hancock's column had moved up the Brock road and made a junction with Getty. At 3.15 I was sent with an order to General Getty to attack at once, and to explain to him that Hancock would join also. He is a cool man, is Getty, quite a wonder; as I saw then and after. "Go to General Eustis and General Wheaton," he said to his aides, "and tell them to prepare to advance at once." And so we were getting into it! And everybody had been ordered up, including Burnside, who had crossed that very morning at Germanna Ford. General Grant had his station with us (or we with him); there he took his seat on the grass, and smoked his briarwood pipe, looking sleepy and stern and indifferent. His face, however, may wear a most pleasing smile, and I believe he is a thoroughly amiable man. That he believes in his star and takes a bright view of things is evident. At 4.15 P.M. General Meade ordered me to take some orderlies, go to General Hancock (whose musketry we could now hear on the left) and send him back reports, staying there till dark. Delightful! At the crossing of the dotted cross-road with the plank sat Hancock, on his fine horse — the *preux chevalier* of this campaign — a glorious soldier, indeed! The musketry was crashing in the woods in our front, and stray balls — too many to be pleasant — were coming about. It's all very well for novels, but *I*

[1] Of this incident Lyman writes in his journal: "2.45. Griffin comes in, followed by his mustering officer, Geo. Barnard. He is stern and angry. Says in a loud voice that he drove back the enemy, Ewell, ¾ of a mile, but got no support on the flanks, and had to retreat — the regulars much cut up. Implies censure on Wright, and apparently also on his corps commander, Warren. Wadsworth also driven back. Rawlins got very angry, considered the language mutinous, and wished him put in arrest. Grant seemed of the same mind and asked Meade: 'Who is this General *Gregg?* You ought to arrest him!' Meade said: 'It's Griffin, not Gregg; and it's only his way of talking.'"

don't like such places and go there only when ordered. "Report to General Meade," said Hancock, "that it is very hard to bring up troops in this wood, and that only a part of my Corps is up, but I will do as well as I can." Up rides an officer: "Sir! General Getty is hard pressed and nearly out of ammunition!" "Tell him to hold on and General Gibbon will be up to help him." Another officer: "General Mott's division has broken, sir, and is coming back." "Tell him to stop them, sir!!" roared Hancock in a voice of a trumpet. As he spoke, a crowd of troops came from the woods and fell back into the Brock road. Hancock dashed among them. "Halt here! halt here! Form behind this rifle-pit. Major Mitchell, go to Gibbon and tell him to come up on the double-quick!" It was a welcome sight to see Carroll's brigade coming along that Brock road, he riding at their head as calm as a May morning. "Left face — prime — forward," and the line disappeared in the woods to waken the musketry with double violence. Carroll was brought back wounded. Up came Hays's brigade, disappeared in the woods, and, in a few minutes, General Hays was carried past me, covered with blood, shot through the head.

HEADQUARTERS ARMY OF POTOMAC
Monday, May 16, 1864

I will continue the letter of this morning, describing our first day's fight. I had got as far as the death of General Hays and the wounding of Carroll. This was between five and six o'clock. Hays commanded one brigade of Birney's division. He was a strong-built, rough sort of man, with red hair, and a tawny, full beard; a braver man never went into action, and the wonder only is that he was not killed before, as he always rode at the very head of his men, shouting to them and waving his sword. Mott's division behaved badly (as you observed, it broke and came back). This is a curious instance of a change of morale. It is Hooker's old fighting division, but has since been under two commanders of little merit or force of character; then there was some discontent about re-enlistments and about the breaking up of the old 3d Corps, to which it had belonged; and the result has been that most of this once crack division has conducted itself most discreditably, this campaign. However, the fresh troops saved the day, and, at dark, we occupied our old line (the dotted one along the Brock road). . . .

It was long after dark when I rode back, and, with some difficulty, found our camp, now pitched in a dusty, ploughed field. The fight of this day had been an attack by parts of our three corps against the Corps of Ewell on our right, and of Hill on our left. The fight had swayed back and forth and ended in a drawn battle, both sides holding their lines. General Grant ordered the attack all along the line, the next morning at 4.30; but put it off to 5 o'clock on the representation that Burnside could not get up in time. He was ordered to get in position by daylight and to go in on Hill's left flank, where you see a dotted line nearly parallel to the Parker's Store road. We were all up right early on that Friday the 6th of May, you may depend. "Lyman," said the General, "I want you to take some orderlies and go to General Hancock and report how things go there during the day." It was after five when I mounted, and already the spattering fire showed that the skirmishers were pushing out; as I rode down the cross-road, two or three crashing volleys rang through the woods, and then the whole front was alive with musketry. I found General Hancock at the crossing of the plank: he

was wreathed with smiles. "We are driving them, sir; tell
General Meade we are driving them most beautifully.
Birney has gone in and he is just cleaning them out be-au-
ti-fully!" This was quite apparent from the distance of
the receding firing and the absence of those infernal minié
balls. "I am ordered to tell you, sir, that only one division
of General Burnside is up, but that he will go in as soon as
he can be put in position." Hancock's face changed. "I
knew it!" he said vehemently. "Just what I expected. If
he could attack *now*, we would smash A. P. Hill all to
pieces!" And very true were his words. Meantime, some
hundreds of prisoners were brought in; all from Hill's
troops. Presently, however, the firing seemed to wake
again with renewed fury; and in a little while a soldier
came up to me and said: "I was ordered to report that
this prisoner here belongs to Longstreet's Corps." "Do
you belong to Longstreet?" I hastened to ask. "Ya-as,
sir," said grey-back, and was marched to the rear. It was
too true! Longstreet, coming in all haste from Orange
Court House, had fallen desperately on our advance; but
he had uphill work. Birney's and Getty's men held fast
and fought with fury, a couple of guns were put in the
plank road and began to fire solid shot over the heads of
our men, adding their roar to the other din. The streams
of wounded came faster and faster back; here a field
officer, reeling in the saddle; and there another, hastily
carried past on a stretcher. I stood at the crossing and
assisted in turning back stragglers or those who sought to
go back, under pretext of helping the wounded. To some
who were in great pain I gave some opium, as they were
carried past me.

It was about seven o'clock, I think, that Webb's brigade
marched along the Brock road, and, wheeling into the pike,

advanced to the support of Birney. Among them was the 20th Massachusetts. Abbot smiled and waved his sword towards me, as he rode by, and I called out to him wishing him good luck; and so he went on to his death, as gallant a fellow as fell that day; a man who could ride into the fight with a smile on his face. Just before eight o'clock came one brigade of Stevenson's division (Burnside's Corps) which had been sent to strengthen Hancock; the other brigade came later and was put on our left, where we were continually paralyzed by reports that the enemy was coming up the Brock road to take us in the flank. This prevented proper mobility of our left, and, after all, they turned out to be a division of Rebel cavalry, who were defeated later in the day by our men. Stevenson's brigade was now put in to relieve the advanced lines that had long been under fire, and all other fresh troops were marched to the front. But Longstreet knew full well (they know everything, those Rebels) that Burnside was coming up with two divisions, on his flank; and knew too that he was late, very late. If Hancock could first be paralyzed, the day was safe from defeat, which now impended. Gathering all his forces, of both corps, he charged furiously. At a little after eleven Mott's left gave way. On the right the brigade of Stevenson, consisting of three raw Massachusetts regiments miscalled "Veterans," broke, on being brought under a tremendous fire. . . . The musketry now drew nearer to us, stragglers began to come back, and, in a little while, a crowd of men emerged from the thicket in full retreat. They were not running, nor pale, nor scared, nor had they thrown away their guns; but were just in the condition described by the Prince de Joinville, after Gaines's Mill. They had fought all they meant to fight for the present, and there was an end of it! If there is anything that will make your heart sink and take all the back-bone out of you, it is to see men in this condition! I drew my sword and rode in among them, trying to stop them at a little rifle-pit that ran along the road. I would get one squad to stop, but, as I turned to another, the first would quietly walk off. There was a German color-bearer, a stupid, scared man (who gave him the colors, the Lord only knows!), who said, "Jeneral Stavenzon, he telled me for to carry ze colors up ze road." To which I replied I would run him through the body if he didn't plant them on the rifle-pit. And so he did, but I guess he didn't stick. Meanwhile there was no danger at all; the enemy did not follow up — not he. He was busy swinging round to op-pose Burnside, and was getting his men once more in order. At half-past one I rode to General Meade and reported the state of affairs. The Provost-General went out at once and stopped and organized the stragglers. At two o'clock Burnside, who had been marching and countermarching, *did* attack. He made some impression, but it was too late, and he had not enough force to follow on. About this time I returned to General Hancock.[1] His men were rallied

[1] Lyman says in his journal: "*1.15* (about). Back to Hancock. He alone, in rear of Brock road; and there he asked me to sit down under the trees, as he was very tired indeed. All his Staff were away to set in order the troops. They had now constructed a tolerable rifle-pit ex-tending along the Brock and to the head of the cross-road. He said that his troops were rallied but very tired and mixed up, and not in a condition to advance. He had given orders to have the utmost exer-tions put forth in putting regiments in order, but many of the field officers were killed and wounded, and it was hard. At 2 P.M. Burnside, after going almost to Parker's Store and again back, made a short attack with loud musketry. Ventured to urge Hancock (who was very pleasant and talkative) to try and attack too; but he said with much regret that it would be to hazard too much, though there was nothing in his immediate front, which had been swept by Stevenson's other brigade, which marched from left to right."

along the road; but regiments and brigades were all mixed up; and we were obliged to listen to Burnside's fighting without any advance on our part. In our front all was quiet; and I got permission to go back to the 2d Corps hospital and look up the body of Major Abbot. Two miles back, in an open farm surrounded by woods, they had pitched the hospital tents. I will not trouble you with what I saw there, as I passed among the dead and dying. Abbot lay on a stretcher, quietly breathing his last — his eyes were fixed and the ashen color of death was on his face. Near by lay his Colonel, Macy, shot in the foot. I raised Macy and helped him to the side of Abbot, and we stood there till he died. It was a pitiful spectacle, but a common one on that day. I left in haste, after arranging for sending the remains home, for the sudden sound of heavy firing told of some new attack. The Rebels (unquenchable fellows they are!), seeing that Burnside had halted, once more swung round and charged furiously on Hancock in his very rifle-pits. I rode at once to General Meade, to ask that Burnside might attack also. This he did, without further orders and with excellent effect. When I got back to the cross-road, I was told the enemy had broken through on the plank and cut us in two; this turned out an exaggeration. They did get into a small part of a rifle-pit but were immediately driven out leaving near sixty dead in the trench at the point.

HEADQUARTERS ARMY OF POTOMAC
Tuesday, May 17, 1864

. . . Just at dark there occurred a most disgraceful stampede in the 6th Corps — a thing that has been much exaggerated in the papers, by scared correspondents. You will remember I told you that we had two dubious divisions in the army: one, the Pennsylvania Reserves, has done finely and proved excellent; but the other, General Ricketts's division of the 6th Corps, composed of troops from Winchester, known as "Milroy's weary boys," never has done well. They ran on the Mine Run campaign, and they have run ever since. Now, just at dark, the Rebels made a sort of sortie, with a rush and a yell, and as ill-luck would have it, they just hit these bad troops, who ran for it, helter-skelter. General Seymour rode in among them, had his horse shot, and was taken. General Shaler's brigade had its flank turned and Shaler also was taken. Well, suddenly up dashed two Staff officers, one after the other, all excited, and said the *whole 6th Corps* was routed; it was *they* that were routed, for Wright's division stood firm, and never budged; but for a time there were all sorts of rumors, including one that Generals Sedgwick and Wright were captured. In a great hurry the Pennsylvania Reserves were sent to the rescue, and just found all the enemy again retired. A good force of them did get round, by a circuit, to the Germanna plank, where they captured several correspondents who were retreating to Washington! Gradually the truth came out, and then we shortened the right by drawing back the 5th and 6th Corps, so as to run along the interior dotted line, one end of which ends on the Germanna plank.

General Meade was in favor of swinging back both wings still more, which should have been done, for then our next move would have been more rapid and easy.

The result of this great Battle of the Wilderness was a drawn fight, but strategically it was a success, because Lee marched out *to stop our advance on Richmond*, which, at this point, he did not succeed in doing. We lost a couple of guns and took some colors. On the right we made no impression; but, on the left, Hancock punished the enemy so fearfully that they, that night, fell back entirely from his front and shortened their own line, as we shortened ours, leaving their dead unburied and many of their wounded on the ground. The Rebels had a very superior knowledge of the country and had marched shorter distances. Also I consider them more daring and sudden in their movements; and I fancy their discipline on *essential* points is more severe than our own — that is, I fancy they shoot a man when he ought to be shot, and we do not. As to *fighting*, when two people fight without cessation for the best part of two days, and then come out about even, it is hard to determine.

HEADQUARTERS ARMY OF POTOMAC
Wednesday, May 18, 1864

I have no right to complain: I have less hardship, more ease, and less exposure than most officers, and, if I must be with the army in the field, I have as good a place as one can well expect. I did hope (though there was no proper ground for it) that we might have the great blessing of an overwhelming victory. Such things you read of in books, but they do not happen often, particularly with such armies to oppose as those of the Rebels. . . .

The great feature of this campaign is the extraordinary use made of earthworks. When we arrive on the ground, it takes of course a considerable time to put troops in position for attack, in a wooded country; then skirmishers must be thrown forward and an examination made for the point of attack, and to see if there be any impassable obstacles, such as streams or swamps. Meantime what does the enemy? Hastily forming a line of battle, they then collect rails from fences, stones, logs and all other materials, and pile them along the line; bayonets with a few picks and shovels, in the hands of men who work for their lives, soon suffice to cover this frame with earth and sods; and within one hour, there is a shelter against bullets, high enough to cover a man kneeling, and extending often for a mile or two. When our line advances, there is the line of the enemy, nothing showing but the bayonets, and the battle-flags stuck on the top of the work. It is a rule that, when the Rebels halt, the first day gives them a good rifle-pit; the second, a regular infantry parapet with artillery in position; and the third a parapet with an abattis in front and entrenched batteries behind. Sometimes they put this three days' work into the first twenty-four hours. Our men can, and do, do the same; but remember, our object is offense — to advance. You would be amazed to see how this country is intersected with field-works, extending for miles and miles in different directions and marking the different strategic lines taken up by the two armies, as they warily move about each other.

The newspapers would be comic in their comments, were not the whole thing so tragic. More absurd statements could not be. Lee is *not* retreating: he is a brave and skilful soldier and he will fight while he has a division or a day's rations left. These Rebels are not half-starved and ready to give up — a more sinewy, tawny, formidable-looking set of men could not be. In education they are certainly inferior to our native-born people; but they are usually very quick-witted within their own sphere of comprehension; and they know enough to handle weapons with terrible effect. Their great characteristic is their stoical manliness; they never beg, or whimper, or complain; but look you straight in the face, with as little animosity as if they had never heard a gun.

Now I will continue the history a little. But first I will

remark that I had taken part in two great battles, and heard the bullets whistle both days, and yet I had *scarcely seen a Rebel* save killed, wounded, or prisoners! I remember how even line officers, who were at the battle of Chancellorsville, said: "Why, we never saw any Rebels where we were; only smoke and bushes, and lots of our men tumbling about"; and now I appreciate this most fully. The great art is to *conceal* men; for the moment they show, *bang, bang,* go a dozen cannon, the artillerists only too pleased to get a fair mark. Your typical "great white plain," with long lines advancing and manœuvring, led on by generals in cocked hats and by bands of music, exist not for us. Here it is, as I said: "Left face — prime — forward!" — and then *wrang, wr-r-rang,* for three or four hours, or for all day, and the poor, bleeding wounded streaming to the rear. That is a great battle in America.

Well! to our next day — Saturday, May 7th. At daylight it would be hard to say what opinion was most held in regard to the enemy, whether they would attack, or stand still; whether they were on our flanks, or trying to get in our rear, or simply in our front. However, it was not long before they were reported as fallen back — a good deal back from the left and right and somewhat from our centre on the pike. Reconnaissances were at once thrown out; and the General sent me to the front, on the pike, to learn how matters stood; where I found, on the most undoubted evidence, that we were throwing solid shot and shell at the rebels, and they were throwing solid shot and shells at us. . . .

There was heavy skirmishing, with some artillery, all that morning, until we determined that the enemy had swung back both wings; and shortened and straightened his line. There lay both armies, each behind its breastworks, panting and exhausted, and scowling at each other. At five this morning a novel sight was presented to the Potomac Army. A division of black troops, under General Ferrero, and belonging to the 9th Corps, marched up and massed in a hollow near by. As I looked at them, my soul was troubled and I would gladly have seen them marched back to Washington. Can we not fight our own battles, without calling on these humble hewers of wood and drawers of water, to be bayonetted by the unsparing Southerners? We do not dare trust them in the line of battle. Ah, you may make speeches at home, but here, where it is life or death, we dare not risk it. They have been put to guard the trains and have repulsed one or two little cavalry attacks in a creditable manner; but God help them if the grey-backed infantry attack them! . . .

As General Grant sat under a pine tree, stoically smoking his briarwood pipe, I heard him say: "To-night Lee will be retreating south."[1] Ah! General, Robert Lee is not Pemberton; he will retreat south, but only far enough to get across your path, and then he will retreat no more, if he can help it. In fact, orders were out for the whole army to move at dark on Spotsylvania Court House. But Lee knew it all: he could see the waggons moving, and had scouts besides. As night fell, his troops left their works and were crowding down the Parker's Store road, towards Spotsylvania — each moment worth untold gold to them! Grant had no longer a Pemberton! "His best friend," as he calls him. And we marched also. . . .

We [Headquarters] did not start till nearly nine o'clock. . . . It was a sultry night — no rain for many days; the

[1] The day before, "Grant told Meade that Joe Johnston would have retreated after two such days' punishment. He recognized the difference of the Western Rebel fighting." — Lyman's *Journal*, May 6.

horses' hoofs raised intolerable clouds of dust, which, in this sandy region, is fine almost like flour. I never saw — nobody could well see — a more striking spectacle than that road as we passed slowly along. All the way was a continuous low breastwork behind which lay crowded the sleeping infantry. They were so close as almost to be on top of each other; every man with his loaded musket in his hand, or lying at his side. A few yards outside stood a line of sentries, their muskets cocked, and others sat on top of the breastwork. Few of the officers allowed themselves any rest, but paced up and down, in their great coats and slouched hats, looking sharply after the sentries. That looked like war, I do assure you. By the roadside was Gibbon, and a tower of strength he is, cool as a steel knife, always, and unmoved by anything and everything. There we lay down, literally in the dust, after a drink of iced water (for all the farms have ice-houses in this region, which our men are not slow to hunt out), and then we waited for General Meade, who had waited behind to speak with Hancock. By and by he came, with more clouds of dust, and then on again, past more sleeping men, and batteries in position, losing the road, finding it again, tearing our clothes among trees and bushes, then coming to cavalry pickets and finally to Todd's Tavern, where General Gregg had his Headquarters, with his division of cavalry camped about there. . . . There was a porch in front with a dirt floor, and there I lay down, with my head on a timber, and got some sleep. On Sunday morning, May 8th, — it was not much like a Sabbath, — we were all staring sleepily about us, forlorn with dust and dirt. The road was full of the infantry, passing at a rapid rate; in light order they were, many without knapsacks, or coats: most had thrown away all baggage but a blanket and haversack. Then came batteries, then more infantry, all of the 5th Corps; the Second had not yet begun to pass. An old nigger made us some coffee and hoe-cake — very acceptable. . . .

HEADQUARTERS ARMY OF POTOMAC
Thursday, May 19

To continue my history a little — I had struggled with much paper to the morning of the 8th. It proved a really hot day, dusty in the extreme and with a severe sun. We staid till the morning was well along, and then started for Piney Branch Church. On the way passed a cavalry hospital, I stopped and saw Major Starr, who had been shot directly through both cheeks in a cavalry fight the day before. He was in college with me, and when I first came to the army commanded the Headquarter escort, the same place Adams[1] now has. . . .

Near Piney Branch Church we halted, pitched tents and had something cooked. Meanwhile there was firing towards Spotsylvania, an ill omen for us. The Rebels were there first and stood across the way. Warren attacked them, but his were troops that had marched and fought almost night and day for four days and they had not the full nerve for a vigorous attack. General Robinson's division behaved badly. Robinson rode in among them, calling them to attack with the bayonet, when he was badly shot in the knee and carried from the field. They failed to carry the position and lost a golden opportunity, for Wilson's cavalry had occupied Spotsylvania, but of course could not keep there unless the enemy were driven from our front. . . .

A little before two we moved Headquarters down the Piney Branch Church road, south, to near its junction

[1] Charles F. Adams, Jr.

with the Todd's Tavern road. Meantime the 6th Corps had come up and formed on the left of Warren, the lines running in a general easterly and westerly direction, a mile and a half north of Spotsylvania. There was a high and curving ridge on which was placed our second line and batteries, then was a steep hollow, and, again, a very irregular ridge, or broken series of ridges, much of them heavily wooded, with cleared spaces here and there; along these latter crests ran the Rebel lines in irregular curves. Preparations were pushed to get the corps in position to attack, but it was plain that many of the men were jaded and I thought some of the generals were in a like case. About half-past four what should Generals Grant and Meade take it into their heads to do but, with their whole Staffs, ride into a piece of woods close to the front while heavy skirmishing was going on. We could not see a thing except our own men lying down; but there we sat on horseback while the bullets here and there came clicking among trunks and branches and an occasional shell added its discordant tone. I almost fancy Grant felt mad that things did not move faster, and so thought he would go and sit in an uncomfortable place. General Meade, not to be bluffed, stayed longer than Grant, but he told me to show the General the way to the new Headquarters. Oh! with what intense politeness did I show the shortest road! for I had picked out the camp and knew the way.

Well, they could not get their attack ready; but there was heavy skirmishing.[1] . . . I think there was more nervous prostration to-day among officers and men than on any day before or since, the result of extreme fatigue

---

[1] "Sheridan now came to Headquarters — we were at dinner. Meade told him sharply that his cavalry was in the way, though he had sent him orders to leave the road clear. S. replied that he never

and excitement. General Ward was relieved from his command, for misbehavior and intoxication in presence of the enemy during the Battle of the Wilderness. I had always supposed him to be a brave but rough man. . . .

HEADQUARTERS ARMY OF POTOMAC
Friday, May 20, 1864

To-day has been entirely quiet, our pickets deliberately exchanging papers, despite orders to the contrary. These men are incomprehensible — now standing from daylight to dark killing and wounding each other by thousands, and now making jokes and exchanging newspapers! You see them lying side by side in the hospitals, talking together in that serious prosaic way that characterizes Americans. The great staples of conversation are the size and quality of rations, the marches they have made, and the regiments they have fought against. All sense of personal spite is sunk in the immensity of the contest.

In my letter of yesterday I got you as far as the evening of Sunday the 8th. On Monday, the 9th, early, Burnside was to come down the Spotsylvania and Fredericksburg road to the "Gate," thus approaching on the extreme left; Sedgwick and Warren respectively occupied the left and right centre, while Hancock, in the neighborhood of Todd's Tavern, covered the right flank; for you will remember that the Rebel columns were still moving down the Parker's Store road to Spotsylvania, and we could not be sure they would not come in on our right flank and rear. Be-

---

got the order. Meade then apologized, but Sheridan was plainly full of suppressed anger, and Meade too was in ill temper. S. went on to say that he could see nothing to oppose the advance of the 5th Corps; that the behavior of the infantry was disgraceful, etc., etc. Maybe this was the beginning of his dislike of Warren and ill-feeling against Meade." — Lyman's *Journal*.

JOHN SEDGWICK

times in the morning General Meade, with three aides, rode back to General Hancock, and had a consultation with him. The day was again hot and the dust thicker and thicker. As we stood there under a big cherry tree, a strange figure approached; he looked like a highly independent mounted newsboy; he was attired in a flannel checked shirt; a threadbare pair of trousers, and an old blue *képi;* from his waist hung a big cavalry sabre; his features wore a familiar sarcastic smile. It was General Barlow, commanding the 1st division of the 2d Corps, a division that for fine fighting cannot be exceeded in the army. There, too, was General Birney, also in checked flannel, but much more tippy than Barlow, and stout General Hancock, who always wears a clean *white* shirt (where he gets them nobody knows); and thither came steel-cold General Gibbon, the most American of Americans, with his sharp nose and up-and-down manner of telling the truth, no matter whom it hurts. . . .

It was about ten o'clock, and I was trotting down the Piney Branch road, when I met Colonel McMahon, Adjutant-General of the 6th Corps; I was seriously alarmed at the expression of his face, as he hurriedly asked where General Meade was. I said, "What is the matter?" He seemed entirely unnerved as he replied: "They have hit General Sedgwick just here under the eye, and, my God, I am afraid he is killed!" It was even so: General Sedgwick, with a carelessness of consequences for which he was well known, had put his Headquarters close on the line of battle and in range of the sharpshooters. As he sat there, he noticed a soldier dodging the bullets as they came over. Rising from the grass, he went up to the man, and, laying his hand on his shoulder, said, "Why, what are you dodging for? They could not hit an elephant at that distance." As he spoke the last word, he fell, shot through the brain by a ball from a telescopic rifle. . . . The dismay of General Sedgwick's Staff was a personal feeling; he was like a kind father to them, and they loved him really like sons. So fell "good Uncle John," a pure and great-hearted man, a brave and skilful soldier. From the commander to the lowest private he had no enemy in this army. . . .

I found General Meade with Generals Wright, Warren, and Humphreys consulting together in the same spot where Grant sat yesterday among the bullets, for no apparent reason. You never saw such an old bird as General Humphreys! I do like to see a brave man; but when a man goes out for the express purpose of getting shot at, he seems to me in the way of a maniac. . . . In the afternoon there was some fighting on the right centre, without result; Burnside pushed down on the left, driving the enemy before him; and so the day closed, our army crowding in on Lee and he standing at bay and throwing up breastworks.

[At this period Lyman was in the habit of writing a few lines about the events of the day, and then taking up his narrative several days back. A bit of foresight of which he characteristically remarks: "I make a rule to speak chiefly of what has passed, not deeming it prudent to properly describe the present." To avoid confusion, the letters have been chronologically separated.]

May 10, 1864

[Tuesday] there was sharp fighting all along the line. General Mott's division of the 2d Corps was put on the left of the 6th Corps, with the idea of making a connection with Burnside and then swinging our left to take the enemy in flank. I was ordered early to go to General Wright and explain to him, then to General Mott and direct him to

demonstrate along his front and feel on the left for Burnside. General Wright had moved his Headquarters and
had put them a little back and on one side, being moved
thereto by the fact that the first selection was a focus for
shells. Then I rode along the lines to General Mott and
got his position as well as I could, and gave him the order.
Coming back to General Wright, I had a sharp corner to
go through. A battery was firing at one of ours and the
shells coming over struck right among our infantry. They
cut the pine trees about me in a manner I didn't like, and
one burst close by, throwing the pieces round just as you
see them in French battle pictures. All day there was firing. About eleven came General Meade and told me to go
out at once to Mott and to get a written report from him,
which I did; and a sharpshooter shot at me, which I hate
— it is so personal. More by token, poor General Rice, a
Massachusetts man and very daring, was to-day killed by
a sharpshooter. The ball broke his thigh, and, when they
amputated his leg, he never rallied. As he lay on the
stretcher, he called out to General Meade: "Don't you
give up this fight! I am willing to lose my life, if it is to be;
but don't you give up this fight!" All day we were trying
to select places for an assault. Barlow crossed the Po on
the right, but was afterwards ordered back, and had a
brilliant rear-guard fight in which he punished the enemy.
From five to six P.M. there was heavy cannonading, the
battalions firing by volley. At 6.30· Upton, with a heavy
column of picked men, made a most brilliant assault with
the bayonet, at the left of the Sixth Corps. The men
rushed on, without firing a shot, carried the breastworks in
the face of cannon and musketry, and took 900 prisoners.
Some of the men, who faltered, were run through the body
by their comrades! But Mott's men on the left behaved

shamefully, and so Upton was obliged again to fall back, bringing his prisoners with him.[1] . . .

May 12, 1864

This was the date of one of the most fearful combats, which lasted along one limited line, and in one spot, more than fourteen hours, without cessation. I fancy this war has furnished no parallel to the desperation shown here by both parties. It must be called, I suppose, the taking of the Salient.

Hancock was ordered to attack with his corps as soon after four in the morning as possible and Burnside was to follow the example. A little after daylight we were all gathered round General Grant's tent, all waiting for news of importance. The field telegraph was laid to all corps Headquarters and there we could hear from all parts. At a little after five o'clock, General Williams approached from the telegraph tent; a smile was on his face: Hancock had carried the first line! Thirty minutes after, another despatch: he had taken the main line with guns, prisoners and two generals! Great rejoicings now burst forth. Some of Grant's Staff were absurdly confident and were sure Lee was entirely beaten. My own experiences taught me a little more scepticism. Hancock presently sent to ask for a vigorous attack on his right, to cover and support his right flank. General Wright was accordingly ordered to attack with a part of the 6th Corps. As I stood there wait-

[1] "11 p.m. Grant in consultation with Meade. Wright came up also; he uttered no complaints, but said quietly and firmly to Meade: 'General, I don't *want* Mott's men on my left; they are not a support; I would rather have no troops there!' Warren is not up to a corps command. As in the Mine Run move, so here, he cannot spread himself over three divisions. He cannot do it, and the result is partial and ill-concerted and dilatory movements." — Lyman's *Journal*.

ing, I heard someone say, "Sir, this is General Johnson."
I turned round and there was the captured Major-General,
walking slowly up. He was a strongly built man of a stern
and rather bad face, and was dressed in a double-breasted
blue-grey coat, high riding boots and a very bad felt hat.
He was most horribly mortified at being taken, and kept
coughing to hide his emotion. Generals Meade and Grant
shook hands with him, and good General Williams bore
him off to breakfast. His demeanor was dignified and
proper. Not so a little creature, General Steuart, who insulted everybody who came near him, and was rewarded
by being sent on foot to Fredericksburg, where there was
plenty of mud and one stream up to his waist. Our attack
was a surprise: the assaulting columns rushed over the
breastworks without firing a shot, and General Johnson,
running out to see the reason of the noise, found himself
surrounded by blue blouses. I was now sent by General
Meade to see how far General Wright's column of attack
was prepared. I found the columns going into the woods
south of the Brown house; the enemy had seen them and
the shells were crashing through the thick pines. When I
came back and reported, the General said: "Well, now
you can take some orderlies and go to General Wright and
send me back intelligence from time to time." There are
some duties that are more honorable than pleasant! As I
turned into the pines, the musketry began, a good way in
front of me. I pressed past the column that was advancing.
Presently the bullets began to come through the pine trees.
Then came back a Staff officer, yelling: "Bring up that
brigade! Bring it up at the double-quick!" "Double-
quick," shouted the officers, and the column started on a
run.

HEADQUARTERS ARMY OF POTOMAC
Monday, May 23, 1864

. . . I asked on all sides for General Wright. One said
he had gone this way; another that he had gone that; so
finally I just stood still, getting on the edge of the woods,
on a ridge, where I dismounted and wrote a short despatch
to General Meade, midst a heavy rain that now began to
come down. Just before me was a very large field with
several undulations, close to me was a battery firing, and
in the wood beyond the field was the fighting. I stood there
a short time, while the second line was deployed and advanced in support of the first. The Rebels were firing a
great many explosive bullets, which I never saw before.
When they strike they explode, like a fire-cracker, and
make a bad wound; but I do not suppose, after all, that
they are worse than the others. Presently there came
along Captain Arthur McClellan (brother of the General
and a very nice fellow). He said he would show me where
General Wright was, which proved to be not far off, in a
little hollow place. There was the stout-hearted General,
seated with his aides, on the ground. He had just been hit
on the leg by a great piece of shell, but was smiling away,
despite his bruises. A sterling soldier he is! I soon found
that the hollow did not exclude missiles, which fly in
curves, confound them! There came a great selection of
bullets about our ears, in the first of it. By-and-by a Rebel
battery began to suspect that, from the number of horses,
there must be a general about that place, and so, *whing!
smash, bang!* came a shell, striking in the woods just beyond. "My friend," said calm Colonel Tompkins, addressing the invisible gunner, "if you want to hit us you must
cut your fuses shorter" — which indeed he *did* do, and
sent all sorts of explosives everywhere except in our little

group, which was only reached by a fragment or two. None of us got hurt, but one horse was wounded and another killed. There I staid for five hours (very long ones), and pelted all the time, but most of the balls flew too high, and, as is well known, shells make a horrid noise, but hurt comparatively few.

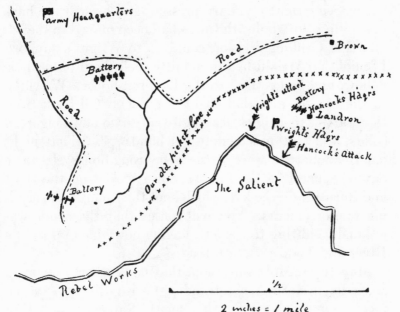

THE ATTACK ON THE SALIENT

All this time the enemy was rolling up his fresh troops and frantically endeavoring to regain that salient. He made as many as five desperate charges with the bayonet, but in vain. At one place called the "Corner" the lines stood within fifty feet of each other, for hours![1] The breast-

[1] "The great historical fight of this day extended over a front of only 1000 to 1500 yards, along the faces of the salient, or the 'Death-angle,' as it was afterwards called. Within that narrow field two corps were piled up to assault and in support. Indeed we had *too many*

9

work made a ridge between, and any living thing that showed above that line fell dead. The next day the bodies of friend and foe covered the ground. Some wounded men were then taken out from under three or four dead ones. One body, that lay exposed to the fire, had eighty bullets in it. At 12.30 I rode back to General Meade, to tell him our extreme right was hard pressed; and he sent me back to say that the whole 5th Corps had been moved to the left and that Griffin's division could go to Wright's support. I found that Wright had been fairly shelled out of his little hollow, and had retired to the Landron house. We clung to the salient, and that night the Rebels fell back from that part of their lines, leaving twenty-two guns, eighteen colors, and 3500 prisoners in our hands. . . . That night our Headquarters were at the Armstrong house. It was a day of general battle, for Warren attacked on the right and Burnside on the left, which kept the enemy from sending reinforcements. You will notice that the army was gradually shifting to the left, having now given up the Po River and Todd's Tavern road.

May 16. — Mott's division, that had hitherto behaved so badly, was broken up and put with Birney — a sad record for Hooker's fighting men! Napoleon said that food, clothing, discipline, and arms were one quarter, and

---

troops, as the generals justly said. The lines got mixed and jammed together and were hard to handle. The amount of bullets fired may be known from the fact that a red oak, twenty-three inches in diameter, was reduced, about six feet from the ground, to a fibrous structure and blew down that night! Bodies that lay between the lines were shot to pieces and could only be raised in a blanket! The result was damaging to the enemy — very — but the army of Lee was not cut in two — an issue clearly looked for by Rawlins and some others of Grant's Staff, but not so confidently assumed by those who knew a little more." — Lyman's *Journal*.

morale the other three quarters. You cannot be long midst hard fighting without having this brought home to you. This day was a marked one, for being fine, nearly the whole of it; we have been having a quantity of rain and a fine bit was quite a wonder. There did appear a singular specimen to behold, at my tent, a J. Bull — a Fusileer — a doctor Think of an English fusileer surgeon — what a combination! He walked on the tips of his toes, with his knees bent, was dressed in full uniform, and had a smirk on his face as much as to say: "Now I know a good deal; and I am coming to see; and I am not going to be put off." Poor Medical Director McParlin was horribly bored with him; but finally got him to the 6th Corps hospital, where I afterwards saw him, running round with some large instrument. I hope they didn't let him do much to the wounded. We were honored at dinner by the company of Governor Sprague and Sherman of the Senate. The Governor is a brisk, sparrowy little man with perky black eyes, which were shaded by an enormous straw hat. He is very courageous, and went riding about in various exposed spots. Sherman is the tallest and flattest of mortals — I mean physically. He is so flat you wonder where his lungs and other vitals may be placed. He seems a very moderate and sensible man.

Tuesday, May 17. — Our Headquarters were moved to the left, and back of the Anderson house. We rode, in the morning, over, and staid some time at the house, one of the best I have seen in Virginia. It was a quite large place, built with a nest of out-houses in the southern style. They have a queer way of building on one thing after another, the great point being to have a separate shed or out-house for every purpose, and then a lot more sheds and out-houses for the negroes. You will find a carpenter's shop,

tool-room, coach-shed, pig-house, stable, out-kitchen, two
or three barns, and half-a-dozen negro huts, besides the
main house, where the family lives. Of the larger houses,
perhaps a quarter are of brick, the rest of wood. They are
plain, rarely with any ornament; in fact, these "mansions"
are only farmhouses of a better class. Anderson was re-
puted a rich man, but he had carpets on very few rooms;
most were floored with hard pine. Round these houses are
usually handsome trees, often locusts, with oaks and, perhaps, some flowering shrubs. Often there is a small corner
with a glass front, to serve as a greenhouse in winter. It is
hard to judge what this country once was; but I can see
that each house of the better class had some sort of a
flower-garden; also, there are a great number of orchards
in this part of the country and plenty of peach trees.
Nothing gives such an air of desolation as a neglected
flower-patch! There are the perennial plants that start
each spring, all in disorder and struggling with weeds; and
you are brought to think how some woman once took an
interest in the flowers, and saw that they were properly
kept. These little things appeal more pointedly to you
than great ones, because they are so easily understood. In
the few days' fighting I have seen, I have come to be entirely unmoved by the appearance of the horrible forms of
wounds or death; but to-day I had quite a romantic twinge
at finding in a garden a queer leaf, with scallops on it,
just like one I found in Bologna and put in your scrap-
book. . . .

At Anderson's I saw quite a galaxy of generals, among
others the successor of General Stevenson, Major-General
Crittenden. He is the queerest-looking party you ever
saw, with a thin, staring face, and hair hanging to his coat
collar — a very wild-appearing major-general, but quite

FROM POLOPOTAMOY CREEK TO CHICKAHOMINY RIVER.

a kindly man in conversation, despite his terrible looks.
. . . The waggoners and train rabble and stragglers have
committed great outrages in the rear of this army. Some
of the generals, particularly Birney and Barlow, have punished pillagers in a way they will not forget; and they will
be shot if they do not stop outrages on the inhabitants.
The proper way to stop the grosser acts is to hang the per-
petrators by the road where the troops pass, and put a
placard on their breasts. I think I would do it myself, if I
caught any of them. All this proceeds from one thing —
the uncertainty of the death penalty through the false
merciful policy of the President. It came to be a notorious
thing that no one could be executed but poor friendless
wretches, who had none to intercede for them; so that the
blood of deserters that was shed was all in vain — there
was no certainty in punishment, and certainty is the es-
sence of all punishment. Now we reap the disadvantage in
a new form. People must learn that war is a thing of life
or death: if a man won't go to the front he must be shot;
but our people can't make up their minds to it; it is repul-
sive to the forms of thought, even of most of the officers,
who willingly expose their own lives, but will shrink from
shooting down a skulker.

IV

COLD HARBOR

[After Spotsylvania the Confederate Army was gradually forced back on Richmond. At Cool Arbor, or Cold Harbor as it is usually called, almost in sight of the southern capital, Grant ordered a frontal attack of the strongly entrenched enemy. The engagement was unsuccessful and the Union losses heavy. This battle has been much criticized, and is considered the most severe blemish on Grant's military reputation. He now determined to make for the James River. Leaving Richmond to the west, the army marched south, and the advanced guard reached the river on June 13. The Army of the Potomac was moved across the James, and took up its position in the neighborhood of City Point — a district already in the possession of Federal forces, which had advanced up the river under Butler.

The loss of the Union Army, from the time it crossed the Rapidan 122,000 strong until it reached the James, was within a few men of 55,000, which was almost equal to Lee's whole force in the Wilderness. The Confederate loss is unknown, but it was certainly very much smaller.[1]]

HEADQUARTERS ARMY OF POTOMAC
Sunday evening, May 22, 1864 [2]

I don't know when I have felt so peaceful — everything goes by contrast. We are camped, this lovely evening, in

[1] J. F. Rhodes, *History of the United States*, IV, 440, 447.
[2] "Gen. Meade said to me at breakfast: 'I am afraid the rebellion cannot be crushed this summer!'" — Lyman's *Journal*.

a great clover field, close to a large, old-fashioned house, built of bricks brought from England in ante-revolutionary times. The band is playing "Ever of Thee I'm Fondly Dreaming" — so true and appropriate — and I have just returned from a long talk with two ultra-Secessionist ladies who live in the house. Don't be horrified! You would pity them to see them. One, an old lady, lost her only son at Antietam; the other, a comparatively young person, is plainly soon to augment the race of Rebels. Poor creature! Our cavalry raced through here yesterday and scared her almost to death. Her eyes were red with crying, and it was long before she fully appreciated the fact that General Meade would *not* order her to instant death. To-night she has two sentries over her property and is lost in surprise. Have I not thence obtained the following supplies: five eggs, a pitcher of milk, two loaves of corn bread, and a basket of lettuce — all of which I duly paid for. I feel well to-night on other accounts. If reports from the front speak true, we have made Lee let go his hold and fall back some miles. If true, it is a point gained and a respite from fighting. Hancock had got away down by Milford. Warren had crossed at Guinea Bridge and was marching to strike the telegraph road, on which the 6th Corps was already moving in his rear. The 9th Corps would cross at Guinea Bridge, last, and follow nearly after the 2d Corps.

We started ourselves not before noon, and crossed the shaky little bridge over the Po-Ny (as I suppose it should be called), and so we kept on towards Madison's Ordinary, crossing, a little before, the Ta, a nice, large, clear brook. An "Ordinary" in Virginia seems to be what we should call a fancy variety store, back in the country. Madison's is a wooden building, just at cross-roads, and was all shut, barred, and deserted; and, strange to say, had not been broken open. On the grass were strewn a quantity of old orders, which people had sent by their negroes, to get — well, to get every conceivable thing. I saved one or two, as curiosities, wherein people ask for quarts of molasses, hymn-books, blue cotton, and Jaynes's pills! The 5th Corps was passing along, as we stood there. After a while we went across the country, by a wood road, to the church you will see south of Mrs. Tyler's. Close to Madison's Ordinary was one of those breastworks by which this country is now intersected. A revival of the Roman *castrum*, with which the troops of both sides protect their exposed points every night. This particular one was made by the heavy artillery, whose greenness I have already spoken of. When they put it up the enemy threw some shells. Whereupon an officer rode back in all haste to General Hancock, and said: "General, our breastwork is only bullet-proof and the Rebels are shelling us!" "Killed anybody?" asked the calm commander. "Not yet, sir," quoth the officer. "Well, you can tell them to take it comfortably. The Rebels often throw shells, and I am sure I cannot prevent them." We passed, on the wood road, some of the finest oak woods I have seen; nothing could be finer than the foliage, for the size, fairness, and rich, polished green of the leaves. The soil, notwithstanding, is extremely sandy and peculiarly unfavorable to a good sod. At the church (do I call it Salem? I am too lazy to hunt after my map; no, it is New Bethel), the 9th Corps was marching past, and Burnside was sitting, like a comfortable abbot, in one of the pews, surrounded by his buckish Staff whose appearance is the reverse of clerical. Nothing can be queerer (rather touching, somehow or other) than to see half a dozen men, of unmistakable New York *bon ton*, arrayed in soldier clothes, midst this desolated coun-

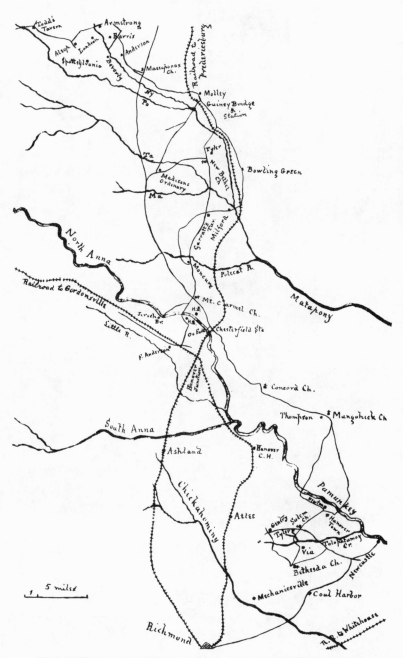

THE NORTH AND SOUTH ANNAS AND PAMUNKEY RIVER

try. I am glad to see that such men have the energy to be here. They are brave and willing, though, like your hub, their military education has been rather neglected.

And this leads me to remark that it is a crying mistake to think, as many do, that an aide is a sort of mounted messenger — an orderly in shoulder-straps. An aide *should* be a first-rate military man; and, at least, a man of more than average intelligence and education. It is very difficult, particularly in this kind of country, to deliver an order verbally, in a proper and intelligent way; then you must be able to report positions and relative directions, also roads, etc.; and in these matters you at once see how deficient some men are, and how others have a natural turn for them. To be a good officer requires a good man. Not one man in ten thousand is fit to command a brigade; he should be one who would be marked anywhere as a person (in that respect) of superior talent. Of good corps commanders I do not suppose there are ten in this country, after our three-years' war. Of army commanders, two or three. When we had seen enough of the 9th Corps and had found out that Hancock had mistaken Birney's line of battle (down by Milford) for that of the enemy, — whereat there was a laugh on the chivalric H., — we departed for the Tyler house. In one of Burnside's regiments are a lot of Indian sharpshooters, some full, some half-breeds. They looked as if they would like to be out of the scrape, and I don't blame them. . . .

May 23, 1864

It was with regret that early this morning we left the fine clover field of Dame Tyler, and wended our way towards the North Anna. We crossed the Mat (or what is called South River, I am not sure which, at any rate a mere brook), and kept straight on for Garrett's Tavern. Grant,

mounted on the purloined black pony, ambled along at a
great pace, but General Meade, who got his pride up at
Grant's rapidity, set off at a rate that soon raised a cloud
of dust and left the Lieutenant-General far behind; whereat George G. was much pleased, and his aides much the
contrary, as they had to scramble after. About ten we got
to a side road, leading to the right, and here we turned off
the 9th Corps, so as to keep the telegraph road open for
the passage of the 5th. Then we took a bend to the left
again and came out by the Moncure house, crossing the
Polecat Creek by the way — a pleasant stream running
over stones, and with the trees quite growing into it.
There, I knew, Biddle and Mason "straggled" and took a
bath. We passed also a house where dwelt four women,
all alone; we left them a guard, to stay till next morning.
A hazardous position for these people, with all the stragglers and camp scoundrels about! Old Ma'am Moncure
was a perfect old railer, and said: "They should soon see us
coming back on the double-quick." However, they (the
family) were amazing sharp and eager in selling us sheep,
and took our greenbacks with avidity. A gold dollar now
is worth about $30 in Confederate money! This afternoon
Warren crossed the North Anna at Jericho Bridge, and
was fiercely attacked on the other side by Longstreet; but
he repulsed him with heavy loss, after a sharp fight. Hancock coming along more to the left, stormed the rifle-pits
near Chesterfield station and seized the bridge, ready to
cross. I have been lately up at three and four in the morning and I am *so* sleepy I must stop.

May 24, 1864

We started quite early — a little before six — to go towards the North Anna; and halted at Mt. Carmel Church,
where this road from Moncure's strikes the "telegraph

road" (so called, because the telegraph from Fredericksburg ran along it). If you want a horrible hole for a halt, just pick out a Virginia church, at a Virginia cross-roads, after the bulk of an army has passed, on a hot, dusty Virginia day! There was something rather funny, too. For in the broad aisle they had laid across some boards and made a table, round which sat Meade, Grant, General Williams, etc., writing on little slips of paper. It looked precisely like a town-hall, where people are coming to vote, only the people had unaccountably put on very dusty uniforms. General Meade is of a perverse nature; when he gets in a disagreeable place, he is apt to stay there. I think he likes to have officers who are prone to comfort feel decidedly *un*comfortable. That reminds me of an anecdote. The day before yesterday, when we had our bloody attack along the whole line, General Meade had ordered his whole Staff ready at four in the morning. Now, such people as the Judge-Advocate-General are Staff officers and at Headquarters, but not aides. Ours is an old army officer, with many characteristics of a part of his class, that is, rather lazy and quite self-sufficient. He came to the front with us and staid some time; but, as dinner-time approached, late in the afternoon, he thought it would be bright to go to the camp and arrange a snug dinner. Pretty soon the suspicious and not very kindly gray eyes of the chief began to roll about curiously. "General Williams! did you give orders that *all* my Staff should accompany me?" "Yes, sir; certainly, sir." (Seth is rather scared at his superior, as are many more.) "Where is Major Platt?" "I think he must have gone to camp for a moment, sir." "Send at once for him!" In no great time the Major arrived at a gallop. "Major Platt," said the General slowly and solemnly, "I wish you to ride along our whole lines (possibly about eight miles) and ascertain as accurately as possible the amount of our casualties during the day!" Somewhere about nine o'clock that night Platt returned with his statement, having missed a nice, six o'clock dinner, and happily *been* missed by stray balls and shells. . . .

I am glad to hear that you take once more an interest in the furniture coverings; an excellent sign! Keep a-going; that's the way! That is the way I do: heart in my mouth for half a day; then come home and eat a good supper; there is no use in "borrowing trouble" — you do learn that here. You know I am not sanguine in my military hopes; but I have the strongest hopes of ultimate success, taking into consideration the uncertainty of war. You must go by the general features; and these are: 1st: Watchfulness, caution, and military conduct of our generals. 2d: The defensive attitude of the enemy; an attitude which Lee never assumes unless driven to it. 3d: The obstinacy and general reliability of our troops. 4th: The fact, that we have worked them, from one position to another, to within nine miles of Richmond across a highly defensible country. 5th: That their counter-attacks on us have been few and comparatively weak, and of no great moment, showing that they have no large force with a "free foot."; but have to put all their men on their lines. Nevertheless, I look on the future as still long and full of the common hazards of war. If the Rebels are forced to abandon Richmond, I believe the effect would be very heavy on them. This I judge not only on general grounds but also from the stupendous efforts, the general concentration, they are using to defend it. Do not, for a moment, look for the "annihilation," the "hiving," or the "total rout" of Lee. Such things exist only in the New York *Herald*.

To return to our Mt. Carmel. About seven came a negro who reported the whole Rebel army retreating on Richmond — a vague expression which left them room to halt anywhere this side of it. Soon after "Tick" Wadsworth — son of the late General — came in from General Sheridan and reported the cavalry corps at Dunkirk. This was welcome news to us. Sheridan had been sent on a raid towards Richmond and had destroyed railroads and depots of stores to a considerable extent. Also recaptured some hundreds of our prisoners on their way to the capital. He was delayed on his return by the rise of the Pamunkey, but got pontoons from Fortress Monroe and crossed it. On his way down, Stuart's cavalry tried to stop him, but he pitched into them, took two guns and a number of prisoners, and killed Stuart, driving off his command completely. It is curious that the southern cavalry cannot now cope with ours. We have beaten them every time this campaign; whereas their infantry are a full match for us. Sheridan was a great help on his return, to watch our flanks and threaten the enemy's rear. . . . About ten there came in a very entertaining nigger, who had been servant of Colonel Baldwin, Rebel Chief of Ordnance. He gave a funny description of Lee's Headquarters. From him and from other sources I judge that the reports of Lee's humble mode of living are true. He has only corn bread and bacon for the "chief of his diet," and this sets an example to all his men. There can be no doubt that Lee is a man of very high character (which you may reconcile as you may with his treacherous abandonment of the flag). He carries on war in a merciful and civilized way, his correspondence is dignified and courteous, and his despatches are commonly (not always) frank and not exaggerated.

General Meade got awfully mad, while waiting at the

church. There came a cipher despatch from Sherman, in
the West. Mr. Dana, Assistant Secretary of War, hastened — with considerable want of tact — to read it to
the General. Sherman therein told Grant that the Army
of the West, having fought, could now afford to manœuvre,
and that, if his (Grant's) inspiration could make the Army
of the Potomac do its share, success would crown our
efforts. The eyes of Major-General George Gordon Meade
stood out about one inch as he said, in a voice like cutting
an iron bar with a handsaw: "Sir! I consider that despatch
an insult to the army I command and to me personally.
The Army of the Potomac does not require General Grant's
inspiration or anybody's else inspiration to make it fight!"
He did not get over it all day, and, at dinner, spoke of the
western army as "an armed rabble." General Grant, who
is one of the most candid men I ever saw, has repeatedly
said that this fighting throws in the shade everything he
ever saw, and that he looked for no such resistance. Colonel Comstock and others, who have fought with both
armies, say distinctly that our troops are fifty per cent
better than the western, and that the good Rebel soldiers
have always been kept near Richmond except when Longstreet went temporarily to the West. At dusk we rode
down to cross the North Anna, midst a fearful thunder-
storm; some of the lightning fell so near that it really
hissed, which was disagreeable, as there was an ammunition train close by. The North Anna is a pretty stream,
running between high banks, so steep that they form
almost a ravine, and, for the most part, heavily wooded
with oak and tulip trees, very luxuriant. It is perhaps 125
feet wide and runs with a tolerably swift and deep stream,
in most places over one's head. The approaches are by
steep roads cut down the banks, and how our waggons and

artillery got across, I don't know! Indeed I never *do* know
how the trains get up, seeing that you are not over well
off, sometimes, on a horse. . . .

May 25, 1864

Burnside's Corps, hitherto a sort of fifth wheel, was to-
day incorporated in the A. of P., and so put under Meade.
. . . The enemy, with consummate skill, had run their
line like a V,[1] with the point on the river, so that our army
would be *cut in two*, if we attacked, and either wing subject
to defeat; while the enemy, all the time, covered Hanover
Junction. At 7.30, I was sent to General Warren, to stay
during the day, as long as anything of interest was going
on, and send orderlies back to report. I found the General
among the pines, about halfway up his line. In front a
heavy skirmish was going on, we trying to push on our
skirmish line and they resisting obstinately. Presently we
rode down to where Griffin was, near the spot where the
common road crosses the Gordonsville rail. Griffin always
goes sitting in unpleasant places. There was a sharpshooter or two who, though we were hid by the small
trees, would occasionally send a bullet through, as much
as to say: "I know you are there — I'll hit you presently." Appleton was shot through the arm near here,
while placing a battery in position. Then we rode to
the extreme right, near to the picket reserve of the
22d Massachusetts. Warren, who is always very kind to
me, told all the others to stay behind, but let me come.
We rode under the crests, and along woods a little, and

---

[1] "Lee, concentrating his troops, interposed them between the two
wings of the Union Army, which were widely separated, and could
reinforce neither the other without passing over the river twice.
'Grant,' wrote Nicolay and Hay, 'was completely checkmated'" —
Rhodes, IV, 444.

were not shot at; and went as far as a log barn, where we stopped carefully on the *off* side, and talked to the picket officer.   When we left, we cantered gracefully and came off all right.   Then to General Wright at E. Anderson's house; a nice safe place, and the family still there; likewise iced water, very pleasant this hot weather.   After which, once more for a few minutes to Griffin, passing on the road one of his aides, on a stretcher, exceeding pale, for he had just been hit in the artery of the arm and lost a deal of blood before it could be stopped.   Also there came a cheery soldier, shot through the leg, who said: "Never mind, I hit five or six of *them* first."   Finally we rode the whole length of Warren's and Crittenden's lines, seeing Weld on the way. . . .

May 27, 1864

Last night Russell's trusty division of the 6th Corps set out on a very long march, as our advanced guard in a flank movement to the Chickahominy. . . . This necessitated our early "getting out of that," for we were on the bank of the river, and the Rebel skirmishers would be sure to follow right down with the first daylight to the opposite side. Indeed, a little while after we were gone they did come down and fired into the telegraph waggon, wounding the side of the same.   By four we had taken our breakfast and were in the saddle.   Wonderful how promptly all the servants pack the things and strike the tents when they expect to be shot at! We rode first to Burnside, into whom the General pitched for cutting the march of General Warren and not sending up the brigades to hold the fords; and B. rather proved that he was right and Warren wrong.   I can tell you aquafortis is mild to the Major-General commanding when he gets put out; which is quite not at all unfrequently; but I have seen him in no such fits as in the falling back from

Culpeper to Centreville. *Here* he can lean upon Grant
more or less, though he does all the work; so much so that
Grant's Staff really do nothing, with the exception of two
or three engineer officers. Then we passed by the gushing
Hancock, who explained what he was going to do, in his
usual flowing style. At Chesterfield Station we found two
divisions of the 6th Corps massed, and just then beginning
to march out. They were issuing rations, to each man his
bit of beef and his "hard tack." We got ahead of the infantry and kept on the way, sending some cavalry ahead
in case of wandering Rebels. The road was strown with
dead horses, worn out and shot by the cavalry, when they
came this way from their raid. Really whenever I may
see civilized parts again, it will seem strange to see no
deceased chargers by the roadside. We made a halt to let
the column get up, at a poor house by the way. There
were a lot of little children who were crying, and the
mother too, for that matter — a thin ill-dressed common-
looking woman. They said they had been stripped of
nearly everything by the cavalry and expected to starve.
So the soft-hearted General, who thought of his own small
children, gave them his lunch, and five dollars also; for he
is a tender-hearted man. We kept on, through a very poor
and sandy country, scantily watered; for this was the
ridge and there was no water except springs. At 9.30 we
dismounted again at an exceptionally good farm, where
dwelt one Jeter, . . . who was of a mild and weak-minded
turn. He said he was pleased to see such well-dressed
gentlemen, and so well-mannered; for that some others,
who had been there two days since, had been quite rude
and were very *dusty;* whereby he referred to the cavalry,
who, I fear, had helped themselves. . . . About one
o'clock, having ridden some twenty-two miles in all, we

stopped at the house of one Thompson and, that afternoon, camped near by, just close to Mangohick Church.
. . . Mr. Thompson was an odd specimen. He talked
just like a nigger, and with a squeaky voice. He was sharp
withal, and pretended to have been entirely stripped; but
I presently discovered he had a good deal, or, as he would
have said, right smart, of corn. I discovered to-day that
the Lieutenant-General has sick-headaches periodically —
one now, for example, for which he put some chloroform
on his head.

May 28, 1864

A little before eight we left the neighborhood of the
squeaky Mr. Thompson and, turning presently to the
right, pushed along towards the Pamunkey. We now had
struck a classic ground where the old McClellan men began to have "reminiscences," worse than you and Anna
Curtis, when you get together. "Ah," says Cadwalader,
"that is the house, the very house, where I came up with
my regiment — Rush's Lancers. We drove the Rebs
across that field, and then we burned the bridge, and
picketed the river," etc. The bridge destroyed by the
valiant Cadwalader had never been replaced, and now our
engineers had thrown a pontoon, over which the artillery
of the 6th Corps was rapidly passing, while the flat was
full of batteries, and of waggons waiting their turn. These
canvas pontoons are funny looking; they consist of a boat-
shaped frame, which is wrapped in a great sheet of canvas
and put in the water, this making a boat, on which part of
the bridge-floor may rest. It looks as if the Commander-
in-Chief had undertaken the washing business on a large
scale, and was "soaking" his soiled clothing. At about
half-past ten I crossed (having been told to go back and
inform General Grant of General Meade's whereabouts)

and tried to find my General on the south side; but I got among a lot of German artillery men, who could not tell whether they were on their heads or heels, much less whether they had seen the Staff go that way. Really it is surprising how poorly the Germans show, out of their own country, where they are an honest and clever, though rather slow people. But *here* they seem almost idiotic, and, what is worse, they will plunder and they won't fight. Really, as soldiers, they are miserable. Actually, a Yankee regiment would drive a brigade of them. They have no grit as a rule. The Paddies, on the contrary, will go in finely, and if well officered, stand to it through everything. . . .

Having ascertained the Headquarters, I rode over to Mrs. Newton's, where I found a romantic lot of officers reposing, very flat on the grass. . . . Poor Mrs. Newton! — she was the one whose husband fell in my Raccoon Ford fight. . . . Presently arrived an aunt, a Mrs. Brockenbrough, a conceited, curious, sallow, middle-aged woman, itching to "tackle" a Northerner. She said the Cavalry Provost-Marshal had been very kind to her. She then began to catechize Grant, with an eager relish, who replied with entire calmness and candor, whereat she was plainly taken aback, as she looked for a volley of gasconade! Their negro houses were full of wounded cavalry men, some of them Rebels. As we sat there the cavalry cannon began again, in the direction of Haw's store, and there followed, in the afternoon, a very desperate engagement in which we lost from 400 to 500 men, including the extraordinary proportion of nearly fifty officers killed and wounded. We drove them at all points, after a desperate resistance. Our cavalry is full of confidence and does wonders. The whole army had crossed by evening. . . .

May 30, 1864

It has been a tolerably quiet day, though there was a quite sharp fight at evening on our left — the Rebels badly used up. The people in Richmond must hear plainly the booming of our cannon: they scarcely can feel easy, for we are closing in on the old ground of McClellan. Fair Oaks was two years ago this very day. What armies have since been destroyed and rebuilt! What marchings and counter-marchings, from the James to the Susquehanna! Still we cling to them — that is the best feature. There is, and can be, no doubt of the straits to which these people are now reduced; particularly, of course, in this distracted region; there is nothing in modern history to compare with the conscription they have. They have swept this part of the country of all persons under 50, who could not steal away. I have just seen a man of 48, very much crippled with rheumatism, who said he was enrolled two days ago. He told them he had thirteen persons dependent on him, including three grandchildren (his son-in-law had been taken some time since); but they said that made no differ-ence; he was on his way to the rendezvous, when our cav-alry crossed the river, and he hid in the bushes, till they came up. I offered him money for some of his small vege-tables; but he said: "If you have any bread, I would rather have it. Your cavalry have taken all the corn I had left, and, as for meat, I have not tasted a mouthful for six weeks." If you had seen his eyes glisten when I gave him a piece of salt pork, you would have believed his story. He looked like a man who had come into a fortune. "Why," said he, "that must weigh four pounds — that would cost me forty dollars in Richmond! They told us they would feed the families of those that were taken; and so they did for two months, and then they said they had no more meal." What is even more extraordinary than their extreme suffering, is the incomprehensible philosophy and endurance of these people. Here was a man, of poor health, with a family that it would be hard to support in peacetimes, stripped to the bone by Rebel and Union, with no hope from any side, and yet he almost laughed when he described his position, and presently came back with a smile to tell me that the only two cows he had, had strayed off, got into a Government herd, and "gone up the road" — that's the last of *them.* In Europe, a man so situated would be on his knees, tearing out handfuls of hair, and calling on the Virgin and on several saints. There were neighbors at his house; and one asked me if I supposed our people would burn his tenement? "What did you leave it for?" I asked. To which he replied, in a concise way that told the whole: "Because there was right smart of bullets over thaar!" The poorest people seem usually more or less indifferent or adverse to the war, but their bitterness increases in direct ratio to their social position. Find a well-dressed lady, and you find one whose hatred will end only with death — it is unmistakable, though they treat you with more or less courtesy. Nor is it extraordinary: there is black everywhere; here is one that has lost an only son; and here another that has had her husband killed. People of this class are very proud and spirited; you can easily see it; and it is the officers that they supply who give the strong framework to their army. They have that military and irascible nature so often seen among an aristocracy that was once rich and is now poor; for you must remember that, before the war, most of these landowners had ceased to hold the position they had at the beginning of this century.

There, that is enough of philosophizing; the plain fact

being that General Robert Lee is entrenched within can-non range, in a sort of way that says, "I will fight you to my last gun and my last battalion!" We had not well got our tents pitched before the restless General, taking two or three of us, posted off to General Hancock. That is his custom, to take two or three aides and as many orderlies and go ambling over the country, confabbing with the generals and spying round the country roads. There, of course, was Hancock, in a white shirt (his man Shaw must have a hard time of it washing those shirts and sheets) and with a cheery smile. His much persecuted aides-de-camp were enjoying a noon-tide sleep, after their fatigues. The indefatigable Mitchell remarked that there were many wood-ticks eating him, but that he had not strength to fight them! The firing was so heavy that, despite the late hour, General Meade ordered Hancock and Burnside to advance, so as to relieve Warren. Only Gibbon had time to form for an attack, and he drove back their front line and had a brief engagement, while the other commands opened more or less with artillery; and so the affair ended with the advantage on our side. — The swamp magnolias are in flower and the azaleas, looking very pretty and mak-ing a strong fragrance.

May 31, 1864

Last night, what with writing to you and working over some maps of my own, I got to bed very late, and was up tolerably early this morning, so to-day I have passed a good deal of time on my back fast asleep; for the General has not ridden out and has sent out very few officers. As I im-plied, to-day has been an occasion of Sybarite luxury. What do you think we mustered for dinner? Why, green peas, salad, potatoes, and fresh milk for the coffee! Am I not a good forager? Yes, and iced water! The woman (a

fearful Secesh) asked two dollars for half a bushel of ice;
upon which I, in a rage, sent a sergeant and told him to
pay only a reasonable price and to take what we needed.
But, in future, I will not pay for ice; it costs these Rebels
nothing, and they can't eat it. For food I will always pay
the scoundrels. They have usually plenty of ice for the
hospitals, and the bands are kept there to play for the
wounded, which pleases them. The Sanitary are doing, I
believe, a great deal of good at the rear, between this and
Washington. There is room for any such people to do good,
when there are such multitudes of wounded. I was amused
to read a letter from one of the Sanitaries at Fredericksburg, who, after describing his good works, said that, for
eight days, his ears were "bruised by the sound of cannon." To me, Fredericksburg and Montreal seem about
equally far away!

The armies lay still, but there was unusually heavy
fighting on the skirmish line the whole time; indeed there
was quite an action, when Birney, Barlow, and Wright advanced and took the front line of the enemy. We used, too,
a good deal of artillery, so that there was the noise of battle from morning to night. We took in some cohorn mortars, as they are called. These are light, small mortars,
that may be carried by two or three men, and are fired
with a light charge of powder. They throw a 24-lb. shell
a maximum distance of about 1000 yards. As these shells
go up in the air and then come down almost straight, they
are very good against rifle-pits. General Gibbon says there
has been a great mistake about the armies of Israel marching seven times round Jericho blowing on horns, thereby
causing the walls to fall down. He says the marching
round was a "flank movement," and that the walls were
then blown down with cohorns. Some of the heavy artil-

lerists of the German regiment were first sent to fire these mortars; but it was found that they could give no definite account of where the projectiles went, the reason of which was that, every time they fired, the officer and his gunners tumbled down flat in great fear of Rebel sharpshooters!

"Baldy" Smith arrived, by steamer, at Whitehouse, from Bermuda Hundreds, with heavy reinforcements for this army. The Rebels, on their side, have been also bringing up everything — Breckinridge from the valley of the Shenandoah, Hoke from North Carolina, and everything from the South generally. . . . General Wilson's division of cavalry was sent out towards our rear and right, to cover that quarter and to continue the destruction of the railroads below Hanover Junction. General Sheridan, with the remaining cavalry, swung round our left flank and pressed down towards Shady Grove and Cool Arbor (this name is called Coal Harbor, Cold Harbor, and Cool Arbor, I can't find which is correct, but choose "Arbor" because it is prettiest, and because it is so hideously inappropriate). In vain I try to correct myself by the engineer maps; they all disagree. The topographical work of the engineers is rather uphill in this country. Before we opened the campaign the engineers prepared a series of large maps, carefully got up from every source that they could come upon, such as state, county, and town maps, also the information given by residents and refugees, etc., etc. In spite of all this the result has been almost ludicrous! Some places (e.g. Spotsylvania) are from one to two miles out of position, and the roads run everywhere *except* where laid down. I suppose the fact is that there was no material whatever wherewith to make a map on a scale so large as one inch to a mile. It is interesting to see now how the engineers work up the country, as they go along. Topographers are sent out as far as possible in the front and round the flanks. By taking the directions of different points, and by calculating distances by the pacing of their horses, and in other ways, they make little local maps, and these they bring in in the evening, and during the night they are compiled and thus a map of the neighborhood is made. If the next day is sunny, photographic copies are taken of this sketch and sent to the principal commanders, whose engineers add to, or correct it, if need be, and these corrections are put on a new sketch. Much information is gotten also by the engineers sent with the cavalry. . . .

June 1, 1864

At 1.30 last night, General Wright with the 6th Corps passed round our left flank and marched on Cool Arbor, which already was occupied by our cavalry last night. They would have fallen back, in view of the advance of the enemy's infantry, but General Meade sent an order to hold it, which they did; and had a very heavy fight early this morning, remarkable from the fact that our cavalry threw up breastworks and fought behind them, repulsing the enemy till Wright could arrive. Baldy Smith too was marching from Whitehouse and came up during the day, forming on the right of the 6th Corps. Meantime, of course, the enemy was marching to his own right, in all haste, and formed so as to cover the roads leading to Mechanicsville and also to continue his line on his right. . . . There was a desperate charge on Smith and Wright at Cool Arbor and the sound of musketry was extremely heavy long after dark, but the Rebels could not do it and had to go back again. Nor did the right of the line escape where they attacked Birney, and were driven back just the same way. . . . Smith had orders to report to General

Meade and so became part of the Army of the Potomac. General Meade was in one of his irascible fits to-night, which are always founded in good reason though they spread themselves over a good deal of ground that is not always in the limits of the question. First he blamed Warren for pushing out without orders; then he said each corps ought to act for itself and not always be leaning on him. Then he called Wright slow (a very true proposition as a general one). In the midst of these night-thoughts, comes here from General Smith bright, active, self-sufficient Engineer-Lieutenant Farquhar, who reports that his superior had arrived, fought, etc., etc., but that he had brought little ammunition, no transportation and that "he considered his position precarious." "Then, why in Hell did he come at all for?" roared the exasperated Meade, with an oath that was rare with him.

June 2, 1864

To-day has been occupied with strategy; but our strategy is of a bloody kind, and even the mere movements have not passed without the sounds of cannon and musketry for two or three hours. Sharp as steel traps those Rebs! We cannot shift a hundred yards, but presto! skirmishers forward! and they come piling in, *pop, pop, pop;* with reserves close behind and a brigade or two hard on the reserves, all poking and probing as much as to say: "Hey! What! Going are you! Well, where? How far? Which way? How many of you are there?" — And then they seem to send back word: "There they go — down there; head 'em off! head 'em off quick!" And very soon General So-and-so, who thinks he has entirely got round the Rebel line, begs to report that he finds them strongly entrenched in his front! Yesterday the 6th Corps drove the enemy

from their lines, in their front, and took a good many
prisoners. The division of Ricketts, which Hancock called
a "weakly child," suddenly blazed out, and charged with
the bayonet; an example I hope it will follow up! The
"weary boys" at first broke and ran as usual, but Ricketts,
their new commander, a man of great personal courage,
pitched into them and kept at them, till finally, on the 1st
of June, he got them to storm breastworks, and now I hope
and believe they will continue good troops. Such are the
effects of good pluck in generals. You hear people say:
"Oh, everyone is brave enough; it is the head that is
needed." Doubtless the head is the first necessity, but I
can tell you that there are *not* many officers who of their
own choice and impulse will dash in on formidable positions. They will go anywhere they are *ordered* and anywhere they believe it is their *duty* to go; but fighting for
fun is rare; and unless there is a little of this in a man's
disposition he lacks an element. Such men as Sprigg Carroll, Hays (killed), Custer and some others, attacked
wherever they got a chance, and of their own accord. Very
few officers would hold back when they get an order; but
the ordeal is so awful, that it requires a peculiar disposition
to "go in gaily," as old Kearny used to say.

Last night the 2d Corps marched, to form on the left
of the 6th at Cool Arbor; it was badly managed, or rather
it was difficult to manage, like all those infernal night
marches, and so part of the troops went fifteen miles instead of nine and there was any amount of straggling and
exhaustion. I consider fifteen miles by night equal to
twenty-five by day, and you will remember our men have
no longer the bodily strength they had a month before;
indeed, why they are alive, I don't see; but, after a day's

rest, they look almost as fresh as ever. . . . We set out in
the morning by half-past seven and, partly by roads,
partly by cross-cuts, arrived at Kelly's via Woody's house.
Of all the wastes I have seen, this first sight of Cool Arbor
was the most dreary! Fancy a baking sun to begin with;
then a foreground of breastworks; on the left, Kelly's
wretched house; in the front, an open plain, trampled fet-
lock deep into fine, white dust and dotted with caissons,
regiments of many soldiers, and dead horses killed in the
previous cavalry fight. On the sides and in the distance
were pine woods, some red with fires which had passed
through them, some grey with the clouds of dust that rose
high in the air. It was a Sahara intensified, and was called
Cool Arbor! Wright's Headquarters were here, and here,
too, I first beheld "Baldy" Smith, a short, quite portly
man, with a light-brown imperial and shaggy moustache,
a round, military head, and the look of a German officer,
altogether. After getting all information, General Meade
ordered a general assault at four P.M. but afterwards coun-
termanded it, by reason of the exhausted state of the 2d
Corps. We pitched camp in the place shown on my map
by a flag, where we since have remained — ten whole
days. Towards evening Warren was to close in to his left
and join with the rest of the line, his right resting near
Bethesda Church, while Burnside was to mass and cover
his movement; but they made a bad fist of it between them.
The enemy, the moment the march began, rushed in on
the skirmishers. A division, 5th Corps, got so placed that
it bore the whole brunt (and a fine division too). Between
the two corps — both very willing — the proper support
was not put in. The enemy in force swung round by Via's
house and gobbled up several miles of our telegraph wire,

besides several hundred prisoners.[1] We *ought* to have just
eaten them up; but as it was, we only drove them back into
some rifle-pits we had formerly abandoned, and then the
line was formed as originally ordered, with Burnside swung
round to cover our right flank from Bethesda Church
towards Linney's house, while the enemy held Via's
house and a line parallel to our own. . . .

You know I was never an enthusiast or fanatic for any
of our generals. I liked McClellan, but was not "daft"
about him; and was indeed somewhat shaken by the great
cry and stories against him. But now, after seeing this
country and this campaign, I wish to say, in all coolness,
that I believe he was, both as a military man and as a
manager of a country under military occupation, the greatest general this war has produced. You hear how slow he
was; how he hesitated at small natural obstacles. Not so.
He hesitated at an obstacle that our ultra people steadily
ignore, the Rebel Army of Northern Virginia; and anyone
that has seen that army fight and march would, were he
wise, proceed therewith with caution and wariness, well
knowing that defeat by such an enemy might mean destruction. When I consider how much better soldiers, as soldiers, our men now are than in his day; how admirably
they have been handled in this campaign; and how heroically they have worked, marched, and fought, and *yet*,
how we still see the enemy in our front, weakened and
maimed, but undaunted as ever, I am forced to the con-

---

[1] "When Grant heard of it, he said to Meade: 'We ought to be able
to eat them up; they have placed themselves in such a position. Generally I am not in favor of night attacks; but I think one might be justi-
fied in such a case as the present.' Indeed it was a wretched affair." —
Lyman's *Journal*.

clusion that McClellan (who did not have his own way as
we have) managed with admirable skill. Mind, I don't say
he was perfect. I say he was our best. Think how well we
are off. Do we want the very garrison of Washington?
Grant beckons, and nobody is hardy enough to say him
nay. McClellan had over 20,000 men taken from him at
the very crisis of the campaign. Suppose at the culmina-
tion of our work, a telegraph from the President should
come: "Send General Wright and 25,000 men at once to
Winchester." How would that do? In all this I *praise* the
present commanders. The *handling* of this army, in
especial, has been a marvel. Through narrow roads (the
best of them not better than the "lane" opposite our back
avenue), ill known and intricate, over bogs and rivers, we
have transported cannon and army waggons in thousands,
and a vast army has been moved, without ever getting in
confusion, or losing its supporting distance. I don't believe
there is a marshal of France that could do it with his army.
I am sure there is not.

[It was known that the order had been given to attack
next morning. Rhodes says:[1] "Officers and men had a
chance to chew upon it, and both knew that the undertaking was hopeless. Horace Porter, an aide-de-camp of
Grant, relates that, when walking among the troops on
Staff duty, the evening before the battle, he noticed many
of the soldiers of one of the regiments designated for the
assault pinning on the backs of their coats slips of paper
on which were written their names and home addresses, so
that their dead bodies might be recognized on the field,
and their fate be known to their families at the North."]

[1] *History*, IV, 446.

June 3, 1864

We had very severe fighting this morning, all along the lines. If you look on the map you may follow our lines. The line of battle faced westerly, towards Gaines's Mill and Mechanicsville, with a corps covering the right flank, and the left refused (a wing is "refused" when it is swung back from the direction of the main line). In some sort this was the battle of Gaines's Mill reversed. . . . The Rebel lines were about parallel with ours and they were throwing up dirt as hard as they could. No country could be more favorable for such work. The soldiers easily throw up the dirt so dry and sandy with their tin plates, their hands, bits of board, or canteens split in two, when shovels are scarce; while a few axes, in experienced hands, soon serve to fell plenty of straight pines, that are all ready to be set up, as the inner face of the breastwork. I can't say I heard with any great hope the order; given last night, for a general assault at 4.30 the next morning! You see Wright and Smith took their front line and drove them back Wednesday afternoon. Thursday afternoon was twenty-four, and Friday morning would be thirty-six hours, for them to bring up and entrench their whole army. If we *could* smash them up, the Chickahominy lay behind them; but I had no more hope of it, after Spotsylvania, than I had of taking Richmond in two days. Half-past four found us at Kelly's, the Headquarters of General Wright; the brave General himself, however, had gone to the front. At that moment the cannon opened, in various directions, and the Rebels replied vigorously. There has been no fight of which I have seen so little as this. The woods were so placed that the sound, even, of the musketry was much kept away, and the fighting, though near us, was completely shut from view. All the warfare for us was an occasional roundshot, or shell, that would come about us from the Rebel batteries. In the direction of the 18th Corps the crash of the musketry was very loud, but elsewhere, scarcely to be noticed. . . . About five we had a gleam of hope for our success. News came that Barlow had carried their works and taken seventeen guns; and so he did; but it is one thing to get in, another to stay in. His men advanced heroically and went over the breastworks with a rush; but the enemy had reserves massed behind, well knowing that his extreme right was seriously threatened. Before our supports could get up, their forces were down on our men, while a heavy enfilade of canister was kept up from flanking batteries. Barlow was driven out with heavy loss, and succeeded in getting off only about 300 of the prisoners he took. Like good soldiers, however, his men stopped and turned about, close to the works, and there entrenched themselves. At six we got notice that Russell's division could not carry the line in their front. Ricketts, however, on the right of the 6th Corps, got their first line, and so did the 18th Corps on his right; but the 18th people were forced back, and this left Ricketts a good deal exposed to enfilade; but he held on. A singular thing about the whole attack, and one that demonstrated the staunchness of the troops, was, that our men, when the fire was too hot for them to advance and the works too strong, did not retreat as soldiers often do, but lay down where some small ridge offered a little cover, and there staid, at a distance from the enemy varying from forty to perhaps 250 yards. When it was found that the lines could not be carried, General Meade issued orders to hold the advanced position, all along, and to trench. The main fight lasted, I suppose, some three

hours, but there was sharp skirmishing and artillery firing
the whole day. The Rebels threw canister in large quantities, doing much damage. . . .

In the afternoon came Wright and Hancock, with their
Staff officers, to consult with General Meade. They looked
as pleasant as if they had been out to dine, instead of standing all day with shells, bullets and canister coming about
them; for we now have a set of corps commanders who, in
action, go, as they say, where they "can see"; which means
sitting calmly in places where many people would be so
scared they wouldn't know the left wing from the right.
Which reminds me of a ludicrous circumstance — there
always *is* something of the ludicrous mixed in every
tragedy. Three or four vulgar and very able-bodied civilians had got down to the army, in some way or other, and
were at our standpoint for a little while. Having come
from the White House and hearing little musketry, they
concluded it would be quite safe to go further to the front.
"Come," said one, in a flippant way, "let's go forward
and see the fun." So off they trotted down the Gaines's
Mill road. One of Wright's aides said they came pretty
soon, as far as where they were standing. All was quiet,
but these braves had hardly dismounted when the Rebel
guns again opened and the shells came with fearful precision over the spot! One gentleman, a fat man, rushed
wildly to his horse, convulsively clutched the mane and
tumbled on the saddle, galloping hotly off. But it so happened that two successive shells, passing with their hideous
scream, burst just behind his horse, giving him the wings
of panic! The other cit, quite paralyzed, lay down flat behind a ridge; in a few minutes he looked up at a Staff officer
and, with the cold sweat rolling off him, exclaimed: "Oh!

11

I wish they would stop! Don't you think, sir, they will stop pretty soon?" What became of the third I know not; but they all "saw the fun." Not a thing did I have to do till six in the evening, when General Meade told me to go to General Birney, ascertain his position and what he thought of the force in his front; then keep on to Warren and ask him if he could so close in his Corps to the left as to set Birney free to return to the Second Corps. I found General Birney, with his usual thin, Puritanic face, very calmly eating tapioca pudding as a finish to his frugal dinner. He remarked drily that his man had selected that hollow as particularly safe; but, as half a dozen shells had already plumped in there, he did not exactly believe the theory a good one. I had a great mess finding General Warren.[1] First I went, by the road leading through the woods, to Bethesda Church. There were his aides and his flag: but the General had "ridden out along the lines" — confound that expression! That is the luck of a Headquarters aide. You say: "Is the General here?" "No, sir, he has gone, I believe, along the line." "Do you know where?" "Well, Colonel, he did not say exactly; but, if you will follow down the breastworks, I think you will find him." (Delightful vision of a line of two miles or so of breastworks with the infantry safely crouched behind, and you perched on a horse, riding down, taking the chance of stray shot, canister, and minié balls, looking for a general who probably is not there.) The greatest piece of coolness is when you are advised to make a short cut by the picket line! . . .

---

[1] "This was Warren's great way, to go about, looking thus after details and making ingenious plans; but it kept him from generalities, and made it hard to find him, so that he finally came to trouble as much by this as by anything else." — Lyman's *Journal*.

GOUVERNEUR KEMBLE WARREN

Warren looks care-worn. Some people say he is a selfish man, but he is certainly the most tender-hearted of our commanders. Almost all officers grow soon callous in the service; not unfeeling, only accustomed, and unaffected by the suffering they see. But Warren feels it a great deal, and that and the responsibility, and many things of course not going to suit him, all tend to make him haggard. He said: "For thirty days now, it has been one funeral procession, past me; and it is too much! To-day I saw a man burying a comrade, and, within half an hour, he himself was brought in and buried beside him. The men need some rest." . . .

At nine at night the enemy made a fierce attack on a part of Gibbon's division, and, for a time, the volleys of musketry and the booming of the cannon were louder, in the still night, than the battle had been by day. But that sort of thing has not done with the Rebels, since the brilliant attack of Johnson, the second night of the Wilderness. This time they were repulsed completely. It was then that our men called out: "Come on! Come on! Bring up some more Johnnies! You haven't got enough!" . . .

To-night all the trenching tools were ordered up and the lines were strengthened, and saps run out, so as to bring them still closer to the opposing ones. And there the two armies slept, almost within an easy stone-throw of each other; and the separating space ploughed by cannon-shot and clotted with the dead bodies that neither side dared to bury! I think nothing can give a greater idea of death-less tenacity of purpose, than the picture of these two hosts, after a bloody and nearly continuous struggle of thirty days, thus lying down to sleep, with their heads almost on each other's throats! Possibly it has no parallel in history. So ended the great attack at Cool Arbor. The losses were far greater for us than for the Rebels. From what I can gather I doubt not we lost four or five to one. We gained nothing save a knowledge of their position and the proof of the unflinching bravery of our soldiers.[1] . . .

June 4, 1864

Although there was no battle to-day, both sides were as sensitive as Hotspur when he was "all smarting from my wounds being cold." The slightest movement would provoke a volley, and any unusual stir would open a battery. This is characteristic of troops in a *new* position. When they have remained awhile, they begin to be more quiet, the skirmishers fire less and less, and finally cease entirely. The General took three or four of us and went on a sort of tour to his Generals; after a brief visit to General Hancock (who had a battery roaring away close to his Headquarters) and a few words with General Wright, we paid a long visit to "Baldy" Smith, whose tents were pitched between the Woody house and the line of battle. His tent was much better than General Meade's and he displayed, for his benefit, a lunch with champagne, etc., that quite astonished us. Whether it was the lunch, or Baldy, or "Bully" Brooks (a General of that name), I do not know, but the Commander staid there several hours, talking and smoking.

[1] "I do think there has been too much assaulting, this campaign! After our lessons of failure and of success at Spotsylvania, we assault here, after the enemy had had thirty-six hours to entrench, and that time will cover them over their heads and give them slashings and traverses besides! The best officers and men are liable, by their greater gallantry, to be first disabled; and, of those that are left, the best become demoralized by the failures, and the loss of good leaders; so that, very soon, the men will no longer charge entrenchments and will only go forward when driven by their officers." — Lyman's *Journal*.

June 4 (continued)

Let me see, I left the party sitting, as it appeared to me, an unnecessarily long time at Baldy Smith's. I say "unnecessarily," first, because it was several hours, and General Meade had nothing to discuss of any moment; and, secondly, because a round-shot would, every now and then, crash through the neighboring trees, or go hoppity-hop along the open field on the edge of which the tents were. You ought to see them skip! It would be odd, if it were not so dangerous. When they have gone some distance and are going slower, you can see them very plainly, provided you are in front of, or behind them. They pass with a great *whish*, hit the ground, make a great hop, and so go skip, skip, skip, till they get exhausted, and then tumble — *flouf* — raising a puff of sand. That is the reason round-shot are more dangerous than conical, which strike perhaps once, vault into the air with a noise like a catherine's wheel, topple over and over, and drop without further trouble. . . . At last the General's confab was broken up by the arrival of Burnside,[1] who, in Fredericksburg days, had a furious quarrel with Baldy and Brooks — or they with him. So they don't speak now; and we enjoyed the military icicle in great perfection! All the day there was sharpshooting and cannonading along our front.

June 5, 1864

This afternoon I carried a flag of truce — quite an episode in my military experiences. At three in the afternoon General Meade sent for me and said, as if asking for a piece of bread and butter: "Lyman, I want you to take

---

[1] "Burnside has a short, military jacket, and, with his bell-crowned felt hat, the brim turned down, presents an odd figure, the fat man!" — Lyman's *Journal*.

this letter from General Grant and take it by a flag of truce, to the enemy's lines. General Hancock will tell you where you can carry it out." I recollect he was lying on his cot at the time, with his riding boots cocked up on the footboard. My ideas on flags of truce were chiefly medi- aeval and were associated with a herald wearing a tabard. However, I received the order as if my employment had been that from early youth, and proceeded at once to array myself in "store" clothes, sash, white gloves and all other possible finery. After searching in vain for a bugler who could blow a "parley," I set forth with only a person- able and well-dressed cavalry sergeant, and found the gal- lant Hancock reposing on *his* cot. "Well, Colonel," says H., "now you can't carry it out on my front, it's too hot there. Your best way is to go to the left, where there are only pickets, and the officers there will get it out." So the ever-laborious Major Mitchell was summoned and told to provide some whiskey for the Rebs and a flag. The last was a great point: there seemed nothing white about, except the General's shirt, but at last he found a pillow- case which was ripped up and put on a staff, and you would have admired it when it was completed! Then we made our way towards the left and found General Birney's men moving that way, who furnished us information about the road, and a guide, Colonel Hapgood of the 5th New Hamp- shire, corps officer of the day. He was a live Yankee, a thorough New Hampshire man — tall, sinewy, with a keen black eye, and a driving way about him. He was ornamented with a bullet-hole through his hat, another through the trousers, and a third on his sword scabbard. We rode forward till we struck the breastwork at Miles's Headquarters. It was a curious sight! Something like an Indian family camped half underground. Here was the breastwork, behind which were dug a number of little cellars, about two feet deep, and, over these, were pitched some small tents. And there you could see the officers sitting, with only their heads above ground, writing or perhaps reading; for it was a quiet time and there were no bullets or shells. We followed the line to its end, near by, and then rode through the pine woods a little way. Here Colonel Hamyl remarked in a ghostly voice: "Do you know where you are going? There have been two field officers killed just here." To whom Colonel Hapgood (with injured pride): "Yes *sir!* I *do* know where I am going. There's some bullets comes through here; but *none to hurt.*" Without definitely settling what precise minimum of balls was "none to hurt," we continued on. Presently the cautious Hapgood pulled up and peered round; and I could see an open field through the trees and another taller wood behind. "Now," said the New Hampshire patriot, "those tallest trees are full of their sharpshooters; if we strike into the field fifty yards above here, they will fire; but, just below, they can't see." So we followed on, and, as soon as we were in the open ground, started at a gallop and got into another wood, close to where I have put my flag on the map. There was here a road, leading past a mill-pond, which however was some quarter of a mile away. Our pickets held this road for some hundred or two yards from us, and then came the enemy's pickets. The Colonel said he knew a good place to approach, and went forward to call to some of them. After a great deal of delay, the lieutenant on our side got one of them to send for an officer, and then word was sent down each line to cease firing in that command, as a flag of truce was going in. Then we left our horses and went forward, the sergeant carrying the flag. As we turned a corner, close by, we came almost upon their party, standing some paces off. It looked exactly like a scene in an opera; there was never anything that so resembled something got up for stage effect. The sun was near setting, and, in the heavy oak woods, the light already began to fade. On the road stood a couple of Rebel officers, each in his grey overcoat, and, just behind, were grouped some twenty soldiers — the most gipsy-looking fellows imaginable; in their blue-grey jackets and slouched hats; each with his rusty musket and well-filled cartridge-box. I walked up in all stateliness (fully aware, however, that white cotton gloves injured the ensemble), and was introduced to Major Wooten of the 14th North Carolina sharpshooters, belonging to A. P. Hill's Corps. He was a well-looking man, with quiet and pleasing manners; and, to see us all together, you would suppose we had met to go out shooting, or something of that kind. I am free to confess that the bearing of the few Rebel officers I have met is superior to the average of our own. They have a slight reserve and an absence of all flippancy, on the whole an earnestness of manner, which is very becoming to them. They get this I think partly from the great hardships they suffer, or, still more, the hardships of those at home, and from a sense of their ruin if their cause fails. We attack, and our people live in plenty, with no one to make them afraid; it makes a great difference. . . .

Major Wooten said he would enquire if the despatch could be received, and soon got notice that it could, if in a proper form. So it was sent in, an answer promised in a couple of hours, and we all sat down on the grass to wait — or rather on the leaves, for this sandy soil produces no grass to speak of. As I had time to look about and, still more to sniff about, I became aware that the spot was not

so charming as it looked.   There had been a heavy cavalry
skirmish in the woods and they were full of dead horses,
which, as the evening closed, became, as Agassiz would say,
"highly offensive." It was positively frightful! and there I
waited till eleven at night! Not even the novelty of the
position was enough to distract one's attention. As to the
pickets, *they* were determined to have also a truce, for,
when a Reb officer went down the line to give some order,
he returned quite aghast, and said the two lines were *together*, amiably conversing. He ordered both to their posts,
but I doubt if they staid. At half-past eight we had quite
a disagreeable experience. There suddenly was heard a
shot or two towards our left centre, then quite a volley,
and then, *whir-r-r-r*, the musketry came running down
right towards us, as one regiment after another took it up!
The next thing I expected was that both sides just near us
would take a panic and begin blazing away. The officers
sprung to their feet and ran down the lines, to again caution the men; so nobody fired; and there we sat and listened to the volleys and the cannonading, that opened
very heavily. . . .

As it got to be after ten, Major Wooten said he would go
back and see what was the delay. There came back a lieutenant soon, that is about eleven, with a note from a
superior officer, saying that "General Grant's aide-de-
camp need not be delayed further," but that an answer
would be sent in at the same point, which could be received
by the picket officer. So we shook hands with the Rebs
and retreated from the unsavory position. . . . We
stopped at Barlow's Headquarters, and then I kept on to
camp, where the General greeted me with: "Hullo, Lyman,
I thought perhaps the Rebs had gobbled you during that
attack." . . .

June 7, 1864

After extraordinary delays an armistice was concluded between six and eight P.M. this evening. It was very acceptable for burying the dead; but the wounded were mostly dead too, by this time, having been there since the 3d. I fancy there were not many, for our men make extraordinary exertions in the night to get in their comrades, and those who were not thus reached usually had their sufferings shortened by some stray ball, among the showers that continually passed between the works. We here found the body of Colonel McMahon, brother of Sedgwick's Adjutant-General. He was wounded and sat down by a tree, where he was soon hit by two or three other bullets. . . . Some extraordinary scenes occurred during the armistice. Round one grave, where ten men were laid, there was a great crowd of both sides. The Rebels were anxious to know who would be next President. "Wall," said one of our men, "I am in favor of Old Abe." "He's a damned Abolitionist!" promptly exclaimed a grey-back. Upon which our man hit his adversary between the eyes, and a general fisticuff ensued, only stopped by the officers rushing in. Our entrenchments were most extraordinary in their extent, with heavy traverses, where exposed to enfilade, and all done by the men, as it were, spontaneously. An officer told a man it was not worth while to go on with a little private bomb-proof he was constructing, as he would only be there two or three days. "I don't care," replied he, "if we only stay two or three hours; I ain't going to have my head knocked off by one of them shells!" . . .

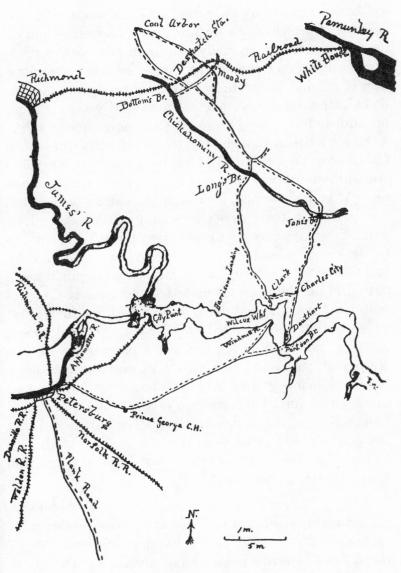

RICHMOND–PETERSBURG

June 12, 1864[1]

General Grant has appeared with his moustache and beard trimmed close, giving him a very mild air — and indeed he is a mild man really. He is an odd combination; there is one good thing, at any rate — he is the concentration of all that is American. He talks bad grammar, but he talks it naturally, as much as to say, "I was so brought up and, if I try fine phrases, I shall only appear silly." Then his writing, though very terse and well expressed, is full of horrible spelling. In fact, he has such an easy and straightforward way that you almost think that he must be right and you wrong, in these little matters of elegance. . . . At 3 P.M. tents were struck and we all rode to Despatch Station, where we turned up to the left and went as far as Moody's house. . . . We halted in a field hard by and waited for the train, an operation that required much patience: for the waggons undertook to go over a sort of mill-dam, and tumbled down a bank and had many mishaps, so that they arrived only at ten. General Grant, however, had made a big fire, got a piece of board, lain down on it, with a bag under his head, and was fast asleep. At eleven, before getting to bed, we had news that Wilson's cavalry had forced the passage of the Chickahominy at Long's Bridge (the bridge was long since burnt) and that the pontoon was going down for the passage of the 5th Corps. Fain would I write more, but I am so stupid and sleepy that I am not equal to it.

June 13, 1864

Last night, at dark, the whole army was in motion for "Charles City" on the James River (there is no "city" there, but I believe a house and a barn). . . . This morn-

---

[1] On this date the army began its march to the James River.

ing we were on our way by 5.30 and, making a cut across
the woods, we soon came on Barlow's division of the 2d
Corps going rapidly toward the river, close to which we
found Hancock, sitting on the grass and waiting for his
Corps. At this point the Chickahominy is nothing of a
stream, but, as it is bordered by considerable flats, it suddenly widens, during heavy floods, to perhaps half a mile,
the water being just deep enough to stop waggons. This
was a great trouble McClellan had: we have met with no
such obstacle. This river is characteristic; a good drawing
of this very scene at Long's Bridge might pass as the incar-
nation of malaria and swamp fever. Fancy a wide ditch,
partly choked with rotten logs, and full of brown, tepid,
sickly-looking water, whose slow current would scarcely
carry a straw along. From the banks of dark mould rises
a black and luxuriant vegetation: cypresses of immense
size, willow oaks, and swamp magnolias, remind you that
you are within the limits of a sub-tropical climate, and so
does the unhealthy and peculiar smell of decaying leaves
and stagnant water. A great contrast to this landscape,
so suggestive of silence and loneliness, was the rumbling
and clatter of Barlow's batteries, as they passed over the
resounding pontoon bridge. We clattered over too, as soon
as the last of the regiments had passed (which was about
10.30), designing to follow in rear of this division. . . .
We kept on, on the flank of the column, admiring its excellent marching, a result partly due to the good spirits of the
men, partly to the terror in which stragglers stand of Barlow. His provost guard is a study. They follow the column, with their bayonets fixed, and drive up the loiterers,
with small ceremony. Of course their tempers do not improve with heat and hard marching. There was one thin,
hard-featured fellow who was a perfect scourge. "Blank

you! — you —" (here insert any profane and extremely abusive expression, varied to suit the peculiar case) "get up, will you? By blank, I'll kill you if you don't go on, double-quick!" And he looked so much like carrying out his threat that the hitherto utterly prostrate party would skip like the young lamb. Occasionally you would see a fellow awaiting the charge with an air of calm superiority, and, when the guard approached, pull out the ægis of a "surgeon's pass." The column marched so fast that I was sent forward to tell General Barlow to go more gently. I found that eccentric officer divested of his coat and seated in a cherry tree. "By Jove!" said a voice from the branches, "I knew I should not be here long before Meade's Staff would be up. How do you do, Theodore, won't you come up and take a few cherries?" However, I could not stay, and so kept on till we came, somewhat suddenly, on well-cultivated fields with good crops of wheat, oats, and clover. I was speculating on the reason of this when somebody said we were within a mile of James River! and just after, General Meade ordered me to ride down and see what sort of a position there was and how the land lay.

It was about four o'clock in the afternoon that I caught the first sight of the water, as I cantered round the corner of a little grove. To appreciate such a sight you must pass five weeks in an almost unbroken wilderness, with no sights but weary, dusty troops, endless waggon-trains, convoys of poor wounded men, and hot, uncomfortable camps. Here was a noble river, a mile wide, with high green banks, studded with large plantation houses. In the distance, opposite, was Fort Powhatan, below which lay two steamers; and, what seemed strangest of all, not a Rebel soldier to be seen anywhere! . . . There was a signal-man

waving away with his flag to attract the attention of the
steamers, to notify all concerned that the head of the Army
of the Potomac had struck the James. We went to a field
by the Tyler house for our camp — the birthplace of John
Tyler, he of the big nose and small political principles —
once Vice President, with Tippy-canoe and Tyler too.
Nobody was there, save a lot of nigs, that were too funny;
for there suddenly appeared among them one of our black
servants, who had left that very place in McClellan's time.
Such a."Lord a-a massy! is dat a-ar you? Wha-ar d'ge
come from?" as never was heard, and great rejoicings
over the distinguished traveller! What was more to the
purpose, I got some green peas, a great *coup;* likewise
milk, though "them a-ar infants" (meaning infantry) got
the most of it. . . . A pontoon bridge, 2000 feet long, was
made in ten hours, and over this passed a train of waggons
and artillery thirty-five miles long; more than half the
infantry in the army and 3500 beef cattle; besides 4000
cavalry; all of which was chiefly accomplished within the
space of forty-eight hours![1] In civil life, if a bridge of this
length were to be built over a river with a swift current and
having a maximum depth of eighty-five feet, they would
allow two or three months for the making of plans and col-
lecting of materials. Then not less than a year to build it.
This was a busy night on the river, messages going to City
Point and Fort Monroe, and ferryboats and gunboats
coming up as fast as possible to the neighborhood of
Charles City. . . .

[1] As before stated, these letters were written after the events described.

V

MANŒUVRES ABOUT PETERSBURG

["IF we only *could* have been a little quicker and more driving, we might have had Petersburg at a mouthful," wrote Lyman some days after the Army of the Potomac had crossed the James. "The strategy of Grant had deceived Lee, who failed to divine the movement, and did nothing therefore to impede it."[1]

Butler, in command of the Army of the James, was encamped at Bermuda Hundred. Grant ordered him to advance and capture Petersburg. But Butler did not rise to the occasion; he sent only part of his forces, under Baldy Smith, who had reinforced Butler, which captured some strong outer fortifications but which did not advance on the city, although it was feebly garrisoned. When Grant and Meade arrived, the town had been reinforced. The attacks of June 16, 17, and 18 were repulsed with great loss to the Union forces. No new assaults were ordered, and the investment of Petersburg began.]

HEADQUARTERS ARMY OF POTOMAC
June 15, 1864

Of course, the first thing was to visit the great bridge. The approach to it lay along the river border, under the bank, and had been prepared with much labor, for, a day or two previous, it had been covered with great cypresses, some of them at least three and a half feet in diameter, and these had to be cut close to the ground, and the debris care-

[1] Rhodes, IV, 488.

160

fully cleared away; in a portion of the road too there was a muddy swamp, which had to be laboriously spanned by a causeway; but there was the whole thing, finished, and of course a photographer making a "picture" of it. It was very simple: you have only to fancy a bridge of boats, thirteen feet wide and 2000 long, the while looking so light as scarcely to be capable of bearing a man on horseback. In the middle of the river were anchored two schooners, which gave greater stability to the bridge, by being attached to it with ropes. What added to the strangeness of the scene was the *ci-devant* Rebel iron-clad Atlanta, lying there, like a big mud-turtle, with only its back exposed. The group was completed by two or three gunboats and several steamers anchored near by. It was funny to run against the marine in this inland region, and to see the naval officers, all so smug and well brushed in their clean uniforms. Admiral L—— came to visit the General — a pleasant old lady apparently. While we were at dinner came Colonel Babcock, from Grant at City Point, with news that Baldy Smith had marched thence before daylight, engaged the enemy at five A.M., and was driving them towards Petersburg. Orders were immediately given to halt the waggon-train, now passing the bridge, and allow the 9th Corps to pass over and push on towards Petersburg (by the same route that Hancock had been following, during the day), and there form on his left. Smith, meantime, had hit the enemy, some three or four miles from City Point, in a wood, near where the main road crossed the rail. . . . How many there were I do not know, but they made a considerable fight with help of field batteries. Harry,[1] with 300 of his men, had the extreme left, and was wounded in this wood, early in the engagement.

[1] Mrs. Lyman's brother.

12

A soldier told me he held on for an hour after he was hit; and I was further told his men did remarkably well. Within about two and a half miles of the town, Smith ran on the strong works long since constructed for its defence. These consist of a series of redoubts, with regular ditches and barbettes for guns, and connected in a chain by a heavy infantry parapet. The line was defended by Wise's men[1] (who look to me just like other Confederate soldiers) and by the local militia. What a difference that makes!! Their batteries opened a well-directed fire as our people advanced; but no sooner did the lines of battle debouch from the woods and push over the open ground, than the militia got shaky behind their works and, when our troops charged, they broke and ran, leaving sixteen guns and 300 or 400 prisoners in our hands. Everyone gives great credit to the negroes for the spirit they showed. I believe there is no question their conduct was entirely to their credit. . . .

I shall never forget meeting, on the City Point road, five Confederate soldiers, under guard of nigs! . . . Three of the prisoners looked as if they could have taken off a tenpenny nail, at a snap. The other two seemed to take a ludicrous view of the matter and were smiling sheepishly. As to the negroes, they were all teeth, so to speak, teeth with a black frame. Hancock got up that evening and joined the 18th Corps. Their troops were all exhausted, but, oh! that they had attacked at once. Petersburg would have gone like a rotten branch. In war there is a critical instant — a night — perhaps only a half hour, when everything culminates. He is the military genius who recognizes this instant and acts upon it, neither precipitating nor postponing the critical moment. There is thus good reason why great soldiers should be so rare that genera-

[1] "Wise's Legion."

tions pass without producing a single one. A great soldier must have, in addition to all usual traits of intellect, a courage unmoved by the greatest danger, and cool under every emergency, and the quickness of lightning, not only in conceiving, but in enforcing an order. . . .

June 16, 1864

At four in the morning they began to ferry over the 5th Corps; of this, two divisions were loaded from Wilcox's wharf and two from a wharf near the bridge; the bridge itself being in constant use for the passage of the main train. The 5th Corps would then march on Petersburg and take position on the left of the 9th. . . . Our information was that part of Lee's army, quitting Malvern Hill, had crossed at Drury's Bluff and was moving on Petersburg. About nine o'clock the General, with Sanders and myself, went on board the ironclad Atlanta. The Captain sent a boat ashore and took us out in state. How sailor-like the Americans look, with their blue shirts and flat caps! And these poor infantry, artillery, and cavalry of ours, why, the more they serve, the less they look like soldiers and the more they resemble day-laborers who have bought second-hand military clothes. I have so come to associate good troops with dusty, faded suits, that I look with suspicion on anyone who has a stray bit of lace or other martial finery. . . .

At 10.30 General Humphreys and General Meade, taking only Sanders and myself, embarked on a boat with General Ingalls, for City Point. The boat started up the river with us, and we found it an hour's trip to City Point. The river is very pretty, or rather fine, with banks that remind one of Narragansett Bay, going to Newport, only they are, I think, higher. . . . City Point is a jut of land at the junction of the Appomattox and the James. It must once have been a quite pretty place, and consisted of a large number of scattered private houses, several of them very good ones; especially that near which General Grant had his camp, which is just on the river. . . . Grant had gone to the front, some seven miles away, and we presently rode out on the Petersburg road, and met Grant returning,[1] a couple of miles from the Point. It was on going out of the place that it occurred to me that someone had said that Hal's[2] regiment was there; so, as I passed a shipshape-looking camp, I asked, "What regiment is that?" "Fifth Massachusetts Cavalry," said the darkie. "Is Colonel Russell there?" "No, sa-ar. He's in der hospital. He was wounded yesterday!" I felt a quite cold perspiration, as I asked if he were badly hurt. The man thought not, but said he was hit in two places. It was tough to ride right past him so, but the General had but two aides; we were expecting a fight, and I had no business to stop in a road where I could not again find him. Meeting Colonel Rowley, however, I asked him to see that Hal had everything and to say that I would be in that night to see him. We rode on along an almost deserted road, till we crossed the rail, when we came on Burnside's column, moving wearily along. The men had done awful marching in a dry country, with a hot sun and midst a stifling dust. I hate to see troops so used up. Passing through some woods, we again got to an open country, then went a little way more in woods, and came full on an open space in front of the captured line of works. . . . Just here Han-

[1] "Presently we met Grant and his Staff coming back. 'Well,' he said; 'Smith has taken a line of works there, stronger than anything we have seen this campaign! If it is a possible thing, I want an assault made at 6 o'clock this evening!'" — Lyman's *Journal*.

[2] Mrs. Lyman's brother.

cock had his flag and General Meade was soon busy consulting about an assault, which finally was ordered for six
P.M. . . . From the place we then stood I could see two or
three spires of the town. Of this attack I saw more than of
most previous fights, or rather of the cannonade. The line
of our batteries was in plain sight, a little in front of where
General Meade took his stand, because the Rebels had
long since cut down a wide zone of timber in their front, to
get a good field of fire. It was a most striking sight! The
air, hazy with dust, gave a copper-red color to the declin-
ing sun, which was soon heightened by the powder-smoke
that rose from the batteries. The firing was very heavy
and there was the continual whiz of our shells or those of
the enemy. It is curious, but the scene reminded me of one
of those stiff but faithful engravings of Napoleon's battles
that one sees in European collections; especially the artillerists loading and discharging their pieces. The musketry
was pretty heavy too. Birney and part of the others carried the first line, but the assault was not a success such as
we wanted; however, General Meade ordered a column
of 5000 men to be prepared for a moonlight attack, which,
as you will learn, took place at daylight next morning.
The General had a quite narrow escape, as we stood watching; for a round shot came bounding over the country and
hopped right in front of him and General Humphreys. The
attack over, I asked leave to go in and see Harry, and the
General told me I could have stopped when we came
through had I asked then. So I got a fresh horse and two
men and started. It was an elegant night, with a fine
moon — quite perfect indeed. You could never have supposed yourself near a great army, after getting past the
railroad. There was scarcely a soul on the route. As I got
near the village there were some waggons going out to But-

ler, but these were pretty much all. Nobody halted me,
though I rode past a picket guard and through the breastworks. It was not till I drew near Hal's camp that his sentry roared out in a military voice, indicating much study
of phonetics: "Halt! Who goes there?" Then came a corporal of the guard in due style. . . . I ascended the stairs
of what had been a private house. It was about ten at
night when I got in. There were a number of cots arranged
in a large upper room, each occupied by a wounded officer.
On the mantelpiece were medicine bottles, a pitcher of
lemonade and a candle; and this was a ward. Master Hal
lay fast asleep on one of the cots, quite unconscious of
dusty brothers-in-law. . . . He was mightily glad to see
me, and we talked some time, in a low voice, not to disturb
others. I remember there was a wounded lieutenant next
us, a good deal under morphine, who had a great fancy
that Lee had captured our whole supply train. Finally I
departed with a humble gift of two oranges and some tea,
which I had brought in my holsters. . . .

Then to Headquarters and found General Grant just
going to bed. He sat on the edge of his cot, in shirt and
drawers, and listened to my report. I told him the General
would put in a column of 5000 men of the 9th Corps, by
moonlight. He smiled, like one who had done a clever
thing, and said, "I think it is pretty well to get across a
great river, and come up here and attack Lee in his rear
before he is ready for us!" He prepared a despatch to
General Meade, which I took back.

June 17, 1864

At daylight Potter, of the 9th Corps, assaulted the
enemy's works at a point near what was then our left. He
took the works very handsomely, with four guns and 350
prisoners, and had his horse shot under him. Potter (a son

of the Bishop of Pennsylvania) is a grave, pleasant-looking man, known for his coolness and courage. He is always very neatly dressed in the full uniform of a brigadier-general. His Headquarters are now at the house where he took two of the cannon. You ought to see it! It is riddled with bullets like the cover of a pepper-box. In a great oak by his tent a cannon-ball has just buried itself, so that you can see the surface under the bark. In a few years the wood will grow over it, and there it will perhaps remain to astonish some wood-cutter of the future, when the Great Rebellion shall have passed into history. This was a brave day for Burnside. He fought in the middle of the day, with some gain, and just before evening Ledlie's division attacked and took a third line, beyond the one taken by Potter. This could have been held, I think, but for the idea that we were to advance still more, so that preparations were made to push on instead of getting reserves in position to support the advanced force. The enemy, however, after dark, concentrated and again drove out our troops, who fell back to the work taken by Potter in the morning; and so ended the anniversary of Bunker Hill. In the attack of that evening, Major Morton, Chief Engineer of the 9th Corps, was killed — a man of an eccentric disposition, but of much ability. He was son of the celebrated ethnologist, whose unrivaled collection of crania is now in the Philadelphia Academy.

June 18, 1864

A general attack was planned for an early hour, so Headquarters, which had lain down late, had scarce a chance to turn over once before it was routed out again, just at daylight. The General was in a tearing humor. (I don't think anybody felt any too pleasant.) "Lyman, you are behind time!" I had the satisfaction of stepping out, all dressed, and saying shortly: "No, sir, I am ready." Presently: "Colonel Lyman, take two or three orderlies and go to General Warren and report to me by telegraph promptly and frequently." I did not admire this duty, as there was to be an assault; but everybody must do his share, and I started immediately. The General started with me. "Do you know the way to General Hancock's?" "Yes, sir!" In a few moments: "This is not the *short cut* to Hancock's." "I did not say I knew the short cut, General." "Well, but I wanted the short cut! What's the use of the road; of course I knew the road!" Whereupon I suggested I would gallop ahead, not to lose time; which I did and left my chief to attack Biddle, who was late and was coming up very red in the face!

It was half-past four when I got to Headquarters of the 5th Corps, which consisted of a couple of tents, pitched by a solitary tree. Warren, with all his clothes on, was catching a little sleep on a camp bed. Burnside[1] was there also, sitting under the tree, and there was a telegraph operator with his little portable instrument. Our lines were advancing, and there was an inexplicable silence along the skirmish line. . . . At 6.50 came an order for all the line to advance and to attack the enemy if found. . . . A little later, after seven, Major Roebling came in and reported he

[1] "Everyone was near the breaking-point. He, Burnside, complained of the heavy artillery detailed to his corps. 'They are worthless,' said he; 'they didn't enlist to fight and it is unreasonable to expect it from them. In the attack last night I couldn't find thirty of them!' He afterwards said of Meade (to one of his Staff): 'He is irascible; but he is a magnanimous man.' Presently up comes Griffin, in one of his peculiar blusters! and all about a commissary who, he maintains, didn't follow orders. Griffin stormed and swore. 'Now! now!' said Warren (who can be very judicious when he chooses), 'let us all try to keep our tempers more, and not swear so much. I know I give way myself; but it is unworthy.'" — Lyman's *Journal*.

had discovered the enemy's new line of works, that ran along a high ground beyond the railroad, and that they were all there, with batteries in position. Soon after General Warren mounted, and we all rode to the front, over a wide oat-field past the works captured last evening, from which we were afterwards driven. In these there was one part where we seemed to have had an enfilade fire, for the Rebel dead lay there, one on top of the other. . . . We stopped under a hollow oak, just at a point of woods and at the juncture of two country roads. Some movement of our troops attracted the enemy, who immediately sent two or three round shot to enfilade the road, and which of course came about our ears in a most uncomfortable way. Ill luck would have it that the fire of two or three batteries just crossed at that point. So not a gun could open but that we got a reminder. To which may be added that stray bullets from Crawford's front came *zip! tziz!* to add their small voices. We had it intermittently all day long from eight o'clock till dark. New batteries soon came up, under charge of Captain Phillips (Appleton's commander). "I want you to go in there with your guns," said General Griffin, "but you will be under fire there." "Well," said Phillips, "I have been in those places before"; and rode on, followed by his pieces. Later, his First Lieutenant, Blake, was carried by me, dead, shot with a minié ball through the forehead. . . .

After much difficulty in advancing the different divisions, we at last drove the enemy from the railroad cut and a gully beyond, and got in, to about 200 yards of their works. At 3.30 in the afternoon the first assault took place. We rode out on an open field to watch it. In front was a broad expanse, quite flat; then the railroad cut with a fringe of bushes, and then a gradual rise crowned by the

Rebel rifle-pits and batteries, which were distant perhaps half a mile. Close to us, on each side, were our batteries, firing as fast as they could, and the rebels were sending back shot, shell, and shrapnel as hard as possible. Half a mile is no good with minié rifles; and, as soon as we attacked, the balls came tolerably numerous, cutting up little puffs of sand on the dry field. I sat up straight on my horse, *comme les autres*, but I can't say it was pleasant, though it is a help to have others cool and brave. It was as I expected — forty-five days of constant marching, assaulting and trenching are a poor preparation for a rush! The men went in, but not with spirit; received by a withering fire, they sullenly fell back a few paces to a slight crest and lay down, as much as to say, "We can't assault but we won't run." The slopes covered with dead and wounded bore testimony that they were willing to give proof of courage even in circumstances that they deemed desperate. Another attack at six resulted no better, save that the lines were at all points pressed close in on those of the enemy. Birney, during the day, made a grand attack with no better success, on the right. I returned after dark, feeling pretty sad. General Meade was much disappointed, but took it cheerfully as he does every matter which affects him personally. The whole thing resulted just as I expected. You cannot strike a full blow with a wounded hand.

June 19, 1864

It having been represented to General Meade that there were some wounded and a good many dead between the lines, he determined to send a flag to get a short armistice, as at Cool Arbor. I was again selected, as the man having good clothes, to undertake the mission. *This* time I determined to have a bugler, and so I did, and very spruce he was, with a German-silver key-bugle. Likewise was there a tall sergeant, in Sunday best, with General Seth Williams's new damask tablecloth, on an appropriate staff! Thus equipped, and furnished with a large letter, I rode forth. . . . We crossed the rail near Colonel Avery's, rode into the woods and immediately came on the picket reserves of cavalry, where we got a man to guide us to the extreme left of the infantry picket line. We floundered through a little swampy run, brushed through some brush, and came on a little clearing, at the other side of which was a gentleman, with a cocked musket, eyeing us suspiciously, but who withdrew on seeing our color. There we came on what is always a pretty sight, a picket line in a wood. The men are dotted along, ten or fifteen feet apart, with stronger parties on the roads; and you see them indistinctly, as they stand, half-hidden among trees and bushes. I found there Captain Thatcher in command of the picket line. There was some delay here, in sending word to the division commander, and to a battery that was firing. As soon as they were notified, Captain T. and myself, with the flag about five paces ahead, and the bugler behind, walked along the wood-road. Thatcher is a brisk, black-eyed little man, and kept peeping about, through the dense pines, and saying: "We are getting somewhere pretty near them. Wave your flag, Sergeant!" As for myself, I looked with some confidence for a salutation of two or three bullets; but made no observation, as being superfluous under the circumstances. Presently the flag-bearer, who, you may be sure, kept an extremely bright look-out, said: "There's one of 'em!" and immediately waved the emblem of peace in a truly conscientious manner. I looked and saw the main road, and, in an open field beyond, stood a single grey-back, looking dubiously at us, with his rifle ready for

any emergency. I told the bugler to blow a parley, which
he did in very good style, while I advanced to call to the
solitary sentry; but the effect of the bugle was most marvellous — quite as when "he whistled shrill and he was answered from the hill." In an instant, a line of some seventy-
five men rose, as if out of the ground. It was their pickets,
who had been concealed in little holes, dug in the slope of
the gentle hill. One of them laid down his musket and
came forward, when I asked for an officer; whereat, he
touched his hat (probably awestruck by my cotton gloves)
and returned to fetch one. Then came a red-faced captain,
who received my despatch, and a bundle of letters from
Rebel prisoners, and promised a speedy answer. So the
flag was stuck up on a fence and we waited. In a few minutes the commander of the pickets hastened out to do me
honor — Major Crow, of Alabama, a remarkably bright,
nice-looking man. We exchanged compliments and newspapers, and he entertained me with an amusing account,
how he had gone on a "leave" to north Alabama, and how
our cavalry suddenly rushed into the town, whereupon he
ascended briskly into the belfry of the court-house, through
the slats of which he beheld a large number of his friends
gobbled up and marched off, while he himself nearly froze
to death with the extreme cold! By this time we had the
variety of a visitor on horseback, Colonel Ring, a handsome
man, who was curious about the negro troops and said,
with an honesty unmistakable, that he would not be a bit
afraid to fight them, one against two. They, however, said
nothing at all unpleasant or rude. The next comer was
apparently a Staff officer, a young man of rather a sour
countenance, with a large pair of spurs. He brought a
message that we should immediately retire from the lines,
and hostilities would then recommence, till the answer

was ready, when they would put a white flag on their rifle-pit. This amused me, for I had already seen all that could be seen and knew just where their position was just at that point! I returned whence I came, and waited at a wretched, deserted house. . . . At seven in the evening I got the reply and carried it in. The sum of it was: "Have the honor to acknowledge your favor. As to your proposition — Ah, don't see it!"[1] And so there was no armistice. Our poor wounded fellows, I believe, we got off that night, all of them, or all but a very few. And thus ended my second diplomatic mission. Since then, General Williams has caused a regular white flag to be made, ready for use in future.

June 23, 1864

All were up at an early hour and ready for an advance, which had been ordered. On the right, towards the Gregory house, we were already against them, and I suppose my friend there, Major Crow, had seen us under more hostile circumstances. . . . By 4.30 General Meade started for General Wright's Headquarters at the Williams house, where he ordered me to stay, when he left at seven. . . . I rode about with General Wright, who visited his line, which was not straight or facing properly. That's a chronic trouble in lines in the woods. Indeed there are several chronic troubles. The divisions have lost connection; they cannot cover the ground designated, their wing is in the air, their skirmish line has lost its direction, etc.,

---

[1] "It was signed by Beauregard, and was a specimen of his mean Creole blood. 'He did not know there had been any fight of consequence and should therefore refuse. After any engagement of real moment, he should be glad to extend the courtesies of war!' He lied; for he knew full well that there had been heavy fighting and that we at least had lost some thousands. But he wished to show his dirty spite. Lee does not do such things." — Lyman's *Journal*.

etc. Then General Meade gets mad with the delay. The commanders say they do as well as they can, etc. Well, Ricketts ran one way and Russell another; and then the 2d Corps — how did that run? and were the skirmishers so placed as to face ours? and what would General Birney do about it? How long was the line? could it advance in a given direction, and, if so, how? All of which is natural with a good many thousand men in position in a dense wood, which nobody knows much about. All this while the men went to sleep or made coffee; profoundly indifferent to the perplexities of their generals; *that* was what generals were paid for. When General Wright had looked a great deal at his line, and a great deal more at his pocket compass, he rode forth on the left to look at the pickets, who were taking life easy like other privates. They had put up sun-shades with shelter-tents and branches, and were taking the heat coolly. . . .

About this time a Vermont captain (bless his soul!) went and actually did something saucy and audacious. With eighty sharpshooters he pushed out boldly, drove in a lot of cavalry, and went a mile and a quarter to the railroad, which he held, and came back in person to report, bringing a piece of the telegraph wire. . . . Some time in the morning, I don't exactly know when, the signal officers reported a large force, say two divisions, marching out from the town, along the railroad, whereof we heard more anon. At noon there still had been no advance, and General Wright went to General Birney to arrange one. There was General Meade, not much content with the whole affair. They all pow-wowed a while, and so we rode back again, through the dreary woods, through which fires had run. It was after two when we returned. Now then — at last — all together — skirmishers forward! And away they go;

steadily. Oh, yes! but Rebs are not people who let you sit
about all the day and do just as you like; remember that
always, if nothing else. There are shots away out by the
railroad — so faint that you can scarce hear them. In
comes a warm sharpshooter: "They are advancing rapidly
and have driven the working party from the railroad."
Here come the two divisions, therefore, or whatever they
are. "Stop the advance," orders General Wright. "General Wheaton, strengthen that skirmish line and tell them
to hold on." The remainder of Wheaton's division is
formed on the flank, and begins making a breastwork;
more troops are sent for. The fire of the skirmishers now
draws nearer and gets distinct; but, when the reinforce-
ment arrives, they make a stout stand, and hold them.
. . . All the while the telegraph is going: "Don't let 'em
dance round you, pitch into them!" suggests General
Meade (not in those exact words). "Don't know about
that — very easy to say — will see about it," replies the
cautious W.; etc., etc. Pretty soon the cavalry comes piling in across the Aiken oat-field; *they* don't hold too long,
you may be certain. This exposes the flank of the picket
line, which continues to shoot valiantly. In a little while
more, a division officer of the day gallops in and says they
have broken his skirmishers and are advancing in line of
battle. But the Rebels did not try an approach through the
open oat-field: bullets would be too thick there; so they
pushed through the woods in our rear. I could hear them
whooping and *ki-yi-ing*, in their peculiar way. I felt uncomfortable, I assure you. It was now towards sunset.
Our position was right in the end of the loop, where we
should get every bullet from two sides, in event of an
attack. General Grant, of the Vermont Brigade, walked
up and said, in his quiet way: "Do you propose to keep

your Headquarters here?" "Why not?" says Ricketts. "Because, when the volleys begin, nothing can live here." To which Ricketts replied, "Ah?" as if someone had re- marked it was a charming evening, or the like. I felt very like addressing similar arguments to General Wright, but pride stood in the way, and I would have let a good many volleys come before I would have given my valuable ad- vice. A column of attack was now formed by us, during which the enemy pushed in their skirmishers and the bul- lets began to slash among the trees most spitefully; for they were close to; whereat Wright (sensible man!) vouch- safed to move on one side some seventy yards, where we only got accidental shots. And what do you think? It was too dark now for us to attack, and the Rebs did *not* — and so, domino, after all my tremendous description! Worse than a newspaper isn't it? I was quite enraged to be so scared for no grand result.[1]

June 24, 1864

It is praise *not* to be pitched into by the Great Peppery: and he is very kind to me. To be sure, I watch him, as one would a big trout on a small hook, and those who don't, catch volleys at all hours! Poor Biddle, for instance, an excellent, bettyish sort of man, with no fragment of tact, when the General is full of anxiety for something that is not going right, is sure to come in, in his stuttering way, with "Ah, aw, hem, aw, General, they are going to pitch camp in a very sandy, bad place, sir; you will not be at all comfortable, and there is a nice grassy —" "Major Bid-

---

[1] "I look on June 22d and 23d as the two most discreditable days to this army that I ever saw! There was everywhere, high and low, feebleness, confusion, poor judgment. The only person who kept his plans and judgment clear was General Meade, himself. On this par- ticular occasion Wright showed himself totally unfit to command a corps." — Lyman's *Journal*.

JAMES CORNELL BIDDLE
Aide-de-Camp

dle!!!" — and then follows the volley. Sometimes it is very effective to contradict the General, provided you stick to it and are successful. I came in last night, feeling cross and not at all caring for commanders of armies or other great ones of this earth. "Well, Lyman, you're back, are you?" "Yes, sir: I reported that the enemy were moving along our rear, but they got no further than —" "Rear! not at all! they were moving along the front." "No, sir, they were not, they were moving along our rear." "What do you mean by that? There is Russell, and there is Ricketts, and here is Wheaton; now of course that's your front." "Russell isn't in such a position, sir, nor Wheaton either. They face so (dabs with a pencil), so that *is* our rear and can't be anything else." Whereupon the good chief graciously said no more. I do not know that he ever said anything pleasant about me except the day after the Wilderness battles, when I heard Hancock say that "Colonel Lyman had been useful to him, the day before." To which the General replied: "Yes, Lyman is a clear-headed man." I have heard him volunteer several favorable things about Captain Sanders; also he has remarked that Old Rosey (my tent-mate) was good at finding roads; and that is pretty much all of his praises, whereof no man is more sparing. By the way, old Rosey has his commission as captain. One thing I do *not* like — it is serious — and that is, that three years of bitter experience have failed to show our home people that, to an army on active campaign (or rather furious campaign), there must be supplied a constant stream of fresh men — by thousands. What do we see? Everyone trying to persuade himself that his town has furnished its "quota." But where are they? We *have* large armies, but nothing compared with the paper statements. No! The few produced by drafts in

13

good part run away; so too many of the "volunteers" — miserable fellows bought with money. None are shot — that is unmerciful — but the Powers that Be will let brave, high-toned men, who scorn to shirk their duty, be torn with canister and swept away with musketry, and *that* is inevitable.

This morning appeared General Grant with two French officers, who since have taken up their quarters with us and mess with us. They are two artillery officers, the elder a Colonel de Chanal, the other a Captain Guzman, both sent as a commission to observe the progress of the campaign. The Colonel is a perfect specimen of an old Frenchman, who has spent most of his life in provincial garrisons, in the study of all sorts of things, from antiquities down to rifled projectiles. He has those extraordinary, nervous legs, which only middle-aged Frenchmen can get, and is full of various anecdotes. Many years he has lived in Toulouse. The other is young and little and looks like a black-eyed and much astonished grasshopper. He is very bright, speaks several languages, and was on the Chinese expedition. General Grant staid some time in council, and took dinner with us. I was amused at him, for, the day being warm, he began taking off his coat before he got to the tent; and by the time he had said, "How are you, Meade?" he was in his shirt-sleeves, in which state he remained till dinner-time. He attempted no foreign conversation with the Gauls, simply observing; "If I could have turned the class the other end to, I should have graduated at West Point, very high in French"!

June 25, 1864

I can only say that I have "sweltered" to-day — that is the word; not only has it been remarkably broiling, but this region is so beclouded with dust and smoke of burning forests, and so unrelieved by any green grass, or water, that the heat is doubled. We have had no drop of rain for twenty days, and but a stray shower for over a month. It is hardly necessary to say that neither army is what it was: the loss of a large proportion of the best officers, the nervous prostration of the men, the immense destruction of life, all tend to injure the morale and discipline and skill of both parties. As to the next step, I do not know; Grant is as calm and as apparently sure as ever. I have got from the region of fighting now, to the realm of lying idle, and it will not be so easy to fill a daily sheet. General Meade asked me to show the Gauls somewhat about; so I clapped them on their two horses, which they had from General Grant, and took them by easy stages to General Wright near by. The good General was comfortably in the woods. I say comfortably, because everything is relative. I mean he had his tents pitched and had iced water, two important elements. He speaks no French — De Chanal no English — so they smiled sweetly at each other. Old D. C. ought to be ashamed of himself. He married an American wife, but, like a true Gaul, utterly refused to learn a word of English. It is ever a part of a Frenchman's religion to speak no language but his own. Little grasshopper Guzman chirped away and made up for two. Then Colonel Kent rode out with us, as a matter of politeness (for I knew that part of the line as well as he), and we showed them how our men made breastworks of rails, logs, and earth; how they lived and cooked; and all sorts of things. After which I took them out towards the picket line and showed them the country, and a tract of dense, young pines, through which our men advanced in double lines — a feat which I can never understand, but which is performed nevertheless. By this time, both distinguished foreigners being powdered *à la marquise*, I took them home, only showing them, before coming in, one more thing, only too characteristic of our war — the peculiar graves of our soldiers, marked each by a piece of cracker-box, with the man's name in pencil, or hastily cut with a knife. I recollect sitting on the high bank of the Rapid Ann, at Germanna Ford, and watching the 5th and 6th Corps as they marched up from the pontoon bridges; and I remember thinking how strange it would be if each man who was destined to fall in the campaign had some large badge on! There would have been Generals Sedgwick, Wadsworth, and Rice, and what crowds of subordinate officers and of privates, all marching gaily along, unconscious, happily, of their fate.

July 1, 1864

Nothing very new to-day. I took advantage of the propinquity of the nigger division (which had come to fill part of the 6th Corps' line, during its absence) to show the unbleached brethren to my Imperial commissioners. We rode first to General Ferrero's Headquarters. This officer, as his name hints, is an Italian by birth, his papa being of Milan. He is quite a well-looking man, and, like unto General Carr, was a dancing-master before he took to soldiering. He speaks Italian and some French and sputtered along very successfully with the visitors. There was turned out for them a regiment of darks. The sun was intense and the sable gents looked like millers, being indeed quite obscured except when they stood perfectly still. They did remarkably well, and the French officers, who were inclined to look favorably on them beforehand, were in ecstasies over their performances.

JOSEPH BRADFORD CARR

July 4, 1864

What shall I say of the Fourth? Our celebration could not well amount to much; the men have to stay too close in camp to do such things. The band came in the morning and serenaded, and there was saluting enough in the form of cannon and mortars from our right. This siege — if you choose to call it a siege — is a curious illustration of the customs of old soldiers. On the right — say from the Appomattox to a point opposite the Avery house — the lines are very close and more or less of siege operations are going on; so every finger, or cap, or point of a gun that shows above the works, is instantly shot at, in addition to which batteries and mortars are firing intermittently. Nothing could be more hostile! But pass to the division a little to the left of this, where our lines swing off from the enemy's, and you have a quite reversed state of things. There is not a shot! Behold the picket men, no longer crouching closely in their holes, but standing up and walking about, with the enemy's men, in like fashion, as near to them, in some places, as the length of the Brookline house. At one part, there was a brook between, and our pickets, or theirs, when they want water, hold up a canteen, and then coolly walk down to the neutral stream. All this truce is unofficial, but sacred, and is honorably observed. Also it is a matter of the rank and file. If an officer comes down, they get uneasy and often shout to him to go back, or they will shoot. The other day General Crawford calmly went down, took out an opera-glass and began staring. Very quickly a Reb was seen to write on a scrap of paper, roll it round a pebble and throw it over to our line. Thereon was writ this pithy bit of advice: "Tell the fellow with the spy-glass to clear out, or we shall have to shoot him." Near this same spot occurred a ludicrous thing, which is true, though one would not believe it if seen in a paper. A Reb, either from greenness or by accident, fired his musket, whereupon our people dropped in their holes and were on the point of opening along the whole line, when the Rebs waved their hands and cried: "Don't shoot; you'll see how we'll fix him!" Then they took the musket from the unfortunate grey-back, put a rail on his shoulder, and made him walk up and down for a great while in front of their rifle-pits! If they get orders to open, they call out, "Get into your holes, Yanks, we are ordered to fire"; and their first shots are aimed high, as a sort of warning. Their liberties go too far sometimes, as when two deliberately walked up to our breastwork to exchange papers; whereat General Crawford refused to allow them to return, saying very properly that the truce was not official, and that they had chosen to leave their own works and come over to ours, and that now they could carry back information of our position. They expected an attack on the 4th of July — I suppose as a grand melodramatic stroke on Grant's part; but, instead thereof, the Maryland brigade brought up their band to the trenches and played "Hail Columbia"; upon which, to the surprise of everyone, a North Carolina regiment, lying opposite, rose as a man and gave three cheers! The news is not precisely cheery from Maryland.[1] With the preparations on foot, we ought to bag a large part of the Rebels; but I have a sublime confidence that the movements of our troops will, as usual, be a day too late. . . .

July 5, 1864

I forgot to tell you that yesterday there appeared a waggon of the Sanitary Commission bearing a gift for the com-

[1] Early's invasion of Maryland, and advance on Washington.

fort of Headquarters. With it came the agent, Mr. Johnson, a dried-up Philadelphian, of a serious countenance.
He brought some ice, mutton, canned fruit, etc., for the
behoof of the suffering hossifers, and was received with
sweet smiles. This morning we made up a quartette, the
two Frenchies, Rosencrantz and myself, and made a
journey to City Point, distant some twelve or thirteen
miles. It was not unpleasant, though the sun was extremely hot; for we took back roads in the woods and escaped a good share of dust. Before getting to the City
Point road, near Bailey's, we stopped at one Epps's house.
Epps himself with family had been called on sudden business to Petersburg, about the time Smith moved up; but
some of his nigs remained. Among others a venerable
"Aunty," of whom I asked her age. "Dunno," replied the
Venerable, "but I know I'se mighty old: got double gran'
children." She then began to chuckle much, and said:
"Massa allers made me work, 'cause he was ugly; but since
you uns is come, I don't have to do nuphun. Oh! I'se
powerful glad you uns is come. I didn't know thar was so
many folks in the whole world as I seen round here." I told
the old lady to use up everything she could find, and left
her chuckling continuously and plainly impressed with
the idea that I was a very pleasant gentleman. Guzman,
meantime, looked on with irrepressible astonishment, having never before seen a real, live slave. At City Point I delivered some despatches at General Grant's, and after
went down and saw the Sanitary boats. They have three
of them, large ones, moored permanently side by side, and
full of all sorts of things, and especially a host of boxes, no
two alike. The upper deck, to render it attractive, was
ornamented with a pile of two or three hundred pairs of
crutches. For myself I got some iced lemonade on board,

and retired much refreshed and highly patriotic. One of the great sights down there is the huge army hospital, a whole plain, white with large tents. These are capable of receiving 7000 patients and have at present about 3000. All are under charge of my excellent classmate, Dr. Ned Dalton.

July 6, 1864

We have no rain here — never expect any; air hazy with a faint dust, finer than twice volted flour, which settles on everything — but *that* won't kill anybody. So Ewell is (or was — don't know his whereabouts at this precise moment) at Harper's Ferry. We knew he was poking up there somewhere. As to the A. of P., it is sitting here, trying to get some fresh cabbages, not very successfully, so far — the last issue, I am told, furnished one small one to every fifteen men. Old Uncle Lee is "in posish," as General Williams would say, and seems to remark: "Here I am; I have sent off Ewell; now why don't you come on?" I suppose you think I speak flippantly of what the French call the "situation"; but one gets so desperate that it is no use to be serious. Last night, after I had got to bed, I heard the officer of the day go with a despatch into the General's tent and wake him up. Presently the General said: "Very well, tell General Wright to send a good division. I suppose it will be Ricketts's." And he turned over and went asleep again. Not so Ricketts, who was speedily waked up and told to march to City Point, thence to take steamers for Washington, or rather for Baltimore. We do not appreciate now, how much time, and labor, and disappointment, and reorganization, and turning out bad officers, have to be done, before an army can be got in such condition that a division of several thousand men may be suddenly waked at midnight and, within an hour or so, be on the march, each man with his arms and ammunition ready, and his rations in his haversack. *Now*, nobody thinks of it. General Meade says, "Send Ricketts"; and turns over and goes to sleep. General Ricketts says, "Wake the Staff and saddle the horses." By the time this is done, he has written some little slips of paper, and away gallop the officers to the brigade commanders, who wake the regimental, who wake the company, who wake the non-commissioned, who wake the privates. And each particular private, uttering his particular oath, rises with a groan, rolls up his shelter-tent, if he has one, straps on his blanket, if he has not long since thrown it away, and is ready for the word "Fall in!" When General Ricketts is informed that all are ready, he says: "Very well, let the column move" — or something of that sort. There is a great shouting of "By the right flank, forward!" and off goes Ricketts, at the head of his troops, bound for City Point; and also bound, I much regret to say, for the Monocacy,[1] where I fancy his poor men stood up and did all the fighting. From what I hear, I judge we had there about 10,000, of whom a good part were next to worthless. The Rebs had, I think, some 12,000, all good troops. This General Wallace is said by officers here to be no general at all, though brave; and General Tyler is the man whom General Humphreys had tried for cowardice, or some misbehavior in the presence of the enemy; and who has, in consequence, an undying hate for the Chief-of-Staff. I remember thinking to myself, as I went to sleep — "division — why don't they send a corps and make a sure thing?" Behold my military forethought!

[1] Monocacy Bridge — the scene of Early's defeat of Lew Wallace, which terrified Washington, and caused much consternation in the North.

July 7, 1864

I paid a visit to Brigadier-General Barlow, who, as the day was hot, was lying in his tent, neatly attired in his shirt and drawers, and listening to his band, that was playing without. With a quaint hospitality he besought me to "take off my trousers and make myself at home"; which I did avail of no further than to sit down. He said his men were rested and he was ready for another assault! — which, if of real importance, he meant to lead himself; as he "wanted no more trifling." His ideas of "trifling," one may say, are peculiar. It would be ludicrous to hear a man talk so, who, as De Chanal says, "a la figure d'un gamin de Paris," did I not know that he is one of the most daring men in the army. It would be hard to find a general officer to equal him and Joe Hayes — both my classmates and both Massachusetts men. Hayes now commands the Regulars. He could not have a higher compliment.

July 10, 1864

It seems sometimes sort of lonely and hopeless, sitting here in the dust by Petersburg, and hearing nothing except now and then a cannon in the distance. Sometimes I feel like saying to the Rebels: "You're a brave set of men, as ever were; and honest — the mass of you. Take what territory you have left and your nigs, and go and live with your own delusions." But then, if I reflect, of course I see that such things won't do. Instead of being exasperated at the Southerners by fighting against them, I have a great deal more respect for them than ever I had in peace-times. They appear to much more advantage after the discipline of war than when they had no particular idea of law and order. Of course I speak only of a certain body, the army of Northern Virginia; of the rest I know nothing. Also do I not speak of their acts elsewhere; but simply of the manner of warfare of our particular opponents. It is always well, you know, to speak of what you *see*, and not of what you hear through half a dozen irresponsible persons. There is no shadow of doubt that the body of the Southerners are as honestly, as earnestly and as religiously interested in this war as the body of the Northerners. Of course such sentiments in the North are met with a storm of "Oh! How *can* they be?" — "That is morally impossible" — "No one *could* really believe in such a cause!" Nevertheless there is the fact, and I cannot see what possible good can come from throwing a thin veil of mere outcries between ourselves and the sharp truth. I am not so witless as not to be able to tell in five minutes' conversation with common men whether they are reasonably honest and sincere, or false and deceitful. I was much struck with something that Major Wooten said, when we were waiting together, by night, at Cool Arbor.[1] After listening to the tremendous noise of cannon and musketry that suddenly had burst forth, he said: "There they are, firing away; and *it is Sunday night, too.*" The great thing that troubles me is, that it is not a gain to kill off these people — now under a delusion that amounts to a national insanity. They are a valuable people, capable of a heroism that is too rare to be lost.

It is a common saying round here that the war could be settled in half an hour if they would leave it to the two armies. But I fear the two armies would settle it rather for their own convenience and in the light of old enemies (who had beaten at each other till they had beaten in mutual respect) than on the high grounds on which alone such a decision could rest. And, on second thoughts, I do

[1] On the Rebel picket line, with a flag of truce.

not think it might turn out so smoothly. Doubtless the treaty would make excellent progress the first ten minutes; but then would arise questions at which there would be hesitation, and, at the end of the half-hour, it is to be feared both parties would be back in their breastworks. General Meade is fond of saying that the whole could be settled by the exercise of common Christian charity; but (entirely *sub rosa*) I don't know any thin old gentleman, with a hooked nose and cold blue eye, who, when he is wrathy, exercises less of Christian charity than my well-beloved Chief! I do not wish to be understood as giving a panegyric on the Secesh, but merely as stating useful facts.

Little Governor Sprague appeared again. He was last with us at Spotsylvania. This time he came over with Birney, who, with his thin, pale, Puritanic face, is quite a contrast. Sprague has two rabbit teeth in front that make him look like a small boy. Birney looks rather downcast. You see he was ambitious to do well while he had temporary command of the Corps; but all went wrong. His great charge of nine brigades, on the 18th of June, was repulsed; and on the 22d the Corps had that direful affair in which the whole Corps was flanked, by nobody at all, so to speak. The more I think on that thing, the more extraordinary and disgraceful does it appear. At the same time, it is in the highest degree instructive as showing what a bold and well-informed enemy may do in thick woods, where nobody can see more than a company front. The Rebel official accounts show that Mahone, with some 6000 or 7000 men, marched in the face of two corps in line of battle, took 1600 prisoners, ten flags, and four guns, paralyzed both corps, held his position till nightfall, and retreated with a loss of not over 400 men! I was with the 6th Corps and never heard a musket from the 2d nor

FRANCIS CHANNING BARLOW

dreamed it was doing anything, till an aide came to say the line had been driven in. . . .

July 12, 1864

I sent off a detail of fifty men at daylight to prepare the ground for the new camp, and at eight o'clock, the wag-gons moved off with all our worldly effects, and the Staff remained under the shade of the abandoned *gourbis.*[1] We live very much after the way of Arabs, when you think of it — nomadic, staying sometimes a day, sometimes a month in a place, and then leaving it, with all the bowers and wells that cost so much pains. Afterwards most of the officers went to the new camp, while the General, with two or three of us, went down the road, towards the Williams house. There was an odd group at Hancock's temporary Headquarters, by a little half-torn-to-pieces house, on whose walls some fellow had inscribed "the Straggler's Rest.". Hancock lay, at full length, in a covered waggon, which had been placed under a weeping willow, one of the few green objects midst the desert of dust. He was attired in a white shirt and blue flannel pantaloons, quite enough for the intensely hot day. He lies down as much as he can, to give his wounded leg rest. General Meade mounted on the front seat, put his feet on the foot-board and lighted a cigar; and we all knew he was fixed for an hour at least. When he gets down with Hancock they talk, and talk, and talk, being great friends. Hancock is a very great and vehement talker but always says something worth hearing. Under the ruined porch was Barlow, in his costume *d'été* — checked shirt and old blue trousers, with a huge sabre, which he says he likes, because when he hits a straggler he wants to hurt him. He immediately began to pump the

[1] An Algerine word for a bower over a tent.

Captain Guzman, for he never neglects a chance to get information. After we had been well fried and dusted, General Meade rose to go, but I budged not, for I knew he would sit down again. He always rises twice or three times before he finally leaves Hancock. By the time we got to camp, it was all ready and looked quite neat.

July 13, 1864

. . . I hear this evening that General Wright has been put in command of all forces to repel the invasion.[1] But our attempt to bag the raiders may be somewhat like the domestic rural scene of surrounding an escaped pig in the vegetable garden. Don't you know how half a dozen men will get in a circle about him, and then cautiously advance, with an expression of face between confidence and timidity? The piggie stands still in the midst, with a small and a treacherous eye. Suddenly, picking out the weakest man, he makes an unexpected rush between his legs, upsets him, and canters away midst an impotent shower of sticks! I suppose you think I take a very light view of things, but in reality I do not; only, after seeing so many fine men knocked over, this business of tearing up tracks and eating all the good wife's fresh butter seems of lesser consequence. Another thing is, I *hope* it will do us good, sting us to the quick, and frighten us into a wholesome draft. You must remember that this sort of raiding has been a continual and every-day thing in the southern country, though to us it seems to be so awful.

The mail man who came down to-night says they are in a great tremble at Washington, while down here we are pleasantly building bowers against the sun, and telling stories to wile away the time. To these last our French

[1] Early's advance on Washington.

Colonel contributes many, of the Midi, which, with the peculiar accent, are very laughable. To illustrate the egotistical ideas of the Marseillais, he told of a father who was showing to his son a brigade of Zouaves who had just come from Italy and were marching through the streets. "Mon enfant! Vois-tu ces Zouaves? Eh bien, ils sont tous-e des Marseillais. Il y avait des Parisiens, *mais on les a mis dans la musique!*" You remember that long, hot street there they call the Canébière. A certain citizen, who had just been to see Paris with its present improvements, returned much gratified. "Ah," said he, "Paris est une bien jolie ville; si, ça avait une Canébière, ça serait un petit Marseille." As an offset to which we must have an anecdote of this region. Did I ever tell you of "Shaw," the valet of Hancock (formerly of General French)? This genius is a regular specimen of the ne'er-do-weel, roving, jack-of-all-trades Englishman. I fancy from his manner that he has once been a head servant or butler in some crack British regiment. He has that intense and impressive manner, only to be got, even by Bulls, in years of drill. He is a perfect character, who no more picks up anything American, than a duck's feathers soak water. He is full of low-voiced confidence. "Oh, indeed, sir! The General rides about a vast deal in the dust, sir. I do assure you, that to-day, when he got in, his undergarments and his *hose* were quite soiled, sir!"

"That fellow," said Hancock, "is the most inquisitive and cool man I ever saw. Now I don't mind so much his smoking all my cigars and drinking all my liquors — which he does — but I had a bundle of most private papers which I had hidden in the bottom of my trunk, and, the other day, I came into my tent and there was Mr. Shaw reading them! And, when I asked him what the devil he meant, he said: "Oh, General, I took the liberty of looking at them, and now I am *so* interested, I hope you will let me finish the rest!"

July 20, 1864

Our camp was this morning taken by assault by a cavalcade which turned out to be Major-General Ben F. Butler and a portion of his Staff. He *is* the strangest sight on a horse you ever saw: it is hard to keep your eyes off him. With his head set immediately on a stout shapeless body, his very squinting eyes, and a set of legs and arms that look as if made for somebody else, and hastily glued to him by mistake, he presents a combination of Victor Emmanuel, Æsop, and Richard III, which is very confusing to the mind. Add to this a horse with a kind of rapid, ambling trot that shakes about the arms, legs, etc., till you don't feel quite sure whether it is a centaur, or what it is, and you have a picture of this celebrated General. Celebrated he surely is, and a man of untiring industry and activity. Woe to those who stand up against him in the way of diplomacy! Let the history of "Baldy" Smith be a warning to all such. It is an instructive one, and according to camp rumor, runs thus. It was said that Smith, relying on his reputation with Grant, had great ideas of shelving Butler, and Fame even reported that he had ideas also of giving Meade a tilt overboard. So what do we see but an order stating that Major-General Smith was to command the "forces of the field" of the Department, while Major-General Butler would continue to command the Department, with his "*Headquarters at Fortress Monroe.*" Next day everybody says: "So, Butler has gone." Not exactly. Butler was still there, precisely as before. "As long as I command the Department, I command its troops; therefore, Headquarters where I please. I please *here.*" Off goes

Smith to Washington, mysteriously. Down pounces Butler on City Point. Long confab with General Grant. Back
comes Smith comfortably and is confronted by an order to
"proceed at once to New York and await further orders!"
Thus did Smith the Bald try the Macchiavelli against
Butler the cross-eyed, and got floored at the first round!
"Why did he do so?" asked Butler, with the easy air of a
strong man. "I had no military ambition; he might have
had all that. I have more important things in view!"
Speaking of Butler's visit, he had sent him an aide without
consulting him, and Benjamin thought it a good chance to
hit Halleck over the aide's head. "Aide-de-camp, sir!
Ordered on my Staff, sir! I'm sure I do not know what you
are to do. I have really nothing for you. All the positions
are filled. Now there is General Halleck, what has *he* to
do? At a moment when every true man is laboring to his
utmost, when the days ought to be forty hours long, General Halleck is translating French books at nine cents a
page; and, sir, if you should put those nine cents in a box
and shake them up, you would form a clear idea of General
Halleck's soul!"

July 22, 1864

I had one of the most amusing excursions that I have
had during the campaign — really quite a picnic. Colonel
de Chanal, Rosy, and myself made the party. The distance
to Butler's Headquarters, whither we were bound, is about
eight miles, and the road all the way was either through
the woods or shaded by trees, and the dust had not yet had
time to show its head after the rain. It was a new part of
the country to me and very interesting. We struck the
Appomattox at the Point of Rocks, where the river appears
double by reason of a long, swampy island in the middle.

14

The width, between the two steep, high, gravelly banks, cannot be less than 350 yards. Here is a pontoon bridge, and, near each end of it, on the top of the bank, a fort for its defence. Below it, too, lies a gunboat. Crossing this, we soon came to the Great Ben's, who received us very hospitably, and exhibited a torpedo and a variety of new projectiles, the virtues of which in the destruction of the human race I explained in pure Gallic to the Colonel. During dinner he said to me: "They spoiled a good mechanic when they made me a lawyer, and a good lawyer when they made me general." He delivered a long exposition (which I translated) on the virtues of a huge *powder-boat*, which he would explode between Moultrie and Sumter, by clockwork, and not only flatten both forts, but Charleston into the bargain! De Chanal replied (citing examples) that no such result would follow and that the effect would be limited to a very small radius. "No effect!" cried B., suddenly bursting into French, "mais pourquoi *non?*" "Ah," said De C., with his sharp French eye, "mais pourquoi *si?*" . . .

July 24, 1864

The appearance of the sky is what the sailors term "greasy," though whether that betokens rain or not I don't venture to guess. Mayhap we will have a storm, which indeed would serve to lay the dust, which already begins to return, in force. This drought has been in one respect beneficial: it has kept the soldiers from using surface water and forced them to dig wells, whence healthy water may be got. One well near this was productive of scientific results, as they got from it a quantity of shells which I shall send to Agassiz. All this country is underlain more or less by "marl beds," which are old sea-bottoms full of a good many different shells. The good Colonel de Chanal took a ride with me. He is so funny, with his sentimental French ways. He, with a true French appreciation of wood, looks with honest horror on the felling of a tree. As we rode along, there was a teamster, cutting down an oak for some trivial purpose. "Ah," cried De Chanal, "Ah! encore un chêne; encore un beau chêne!" If you tell him twenty men have been killed in the trenches, he is not interested; but actually he notices each tree that falls. "Ah," he says, "when I think what labor I have been at, on the little place I have at home, to plant, only for my grandchildren, such trees as you cut down without reason!" As he has always lived in the South of France, where greenery is scarce, he is not offended by the bareness of the soil; but when riding through a dreary pine wood, will suddenly break out: "Oh, que c'est beau, que c'est beau!"

July 30, 1864

My spirits to-night are not very high; our project of attack, which in the beginning promised well, has not been a success in the result. You must know that there has always been a point on Burnside's line that was quite near that of the enemy, say 250 feet. A mine was begun there over a month since, and has been quite finished for a week. It was at first rather an amateur affair, for the policy of the future operations had not then been fixed. However, it was steadily pushed, being in charge of Colonel Pleasants, who has a regiment of Pennsylvania coal-miners. He first ran a subterranean gallery, straight out to the enemy's bastion, where they had four guns. Then three lateral passages were made, each terminating in a chamber, to be filled with gunpowder. These chambers or magazines were

about twenty feet underground. The final springing of the
mine was delayed, in order to build heavy batteries and
get the guns and mortars in. A couple of days ago orders
were given to charge the chambers with 8000 pounds of
gunpowder (four tons).[1] The powder was laboriously carried in in kegs (the gallery was so low, the men were forced
to double themselves over in passing), and the kegs were
packed in, after removing their heads. When a chamber
was charged, loose powder was poured over the whole.
The magazines were connected by a wooden casing filled
with powder, and this was also run along the gallery for
some distance, where it was connected to a fuse which ran
to the mouth of the gallery.

To-morrow I will continue, but now it is rather late.

July 31, 1864

I will continue now my letter that broke off last night,
and confide to you in all honesty, that I went fast to sleep
on the bed and never woke till it was too late for more writing! The fact is, it was a day of extraordinary heat, and
remarkably close also. I had been up at half-past two that
morning, and I felt a great deal depressed by the day's
work. Well, I had got my fuse to the mouth of the gallery.
You must know that all the time they were putting in the
powder they could hear the enemy digging pretty near
them, over their heads; for they had suspected we were
mining, and had begun digging, to try to find it: they sunk
a "shaft" or well inside their bastion, and then ran a

[1] "Duane had sent for the mining records before Sebastopol and got
me to read them to learn the proper charge; for, what with malaria,
and sunstroke, and quinine, whiskey, and arsenic, he can hardly see,
but clings to duty to the last! Finding nothing there, he said the book
was a humbug, and determined on 8000 lbs. The charge was tamped
with twenty-five feet of sand bags." — Lyman's *Journal*.

gallery outside, from which they dug each way, to cut our gallery. But they did not go *deep* enough and so missed their object. The enemy had lately sent a large part of their force to head off Hancock at Deep Bottom, across the James, a movement that had seriously alarmed them. So the forces in our front were much weakened and the moment was favorable. . . .

On the 29th Hancock was ordered to withdraw, hold two divisions in reserve, and relieve the 18th Corps on the line with the third. The 18th Corps was then to move up in the night, and take position to support the 9th Corps in the assault. The 5th Corps was to be held in readiness on its part of the line, and to open with musketry as soon as the mine was sprung, in order to keep down the enemy's fire on the assaulting column. New batteries of heavy mortars and siege guns were put in position and the whole artillery was ordered to open on the enemy's batteries, the moment the mine was blown up. The 9th Corps was arranged to make a rush to the gap, the moment the explosion took place, and then one column was to keep on, and occupy the crest beyond (the key of the whole position), and others were to look out for an attack on either flank. The hour for springing the mine was 3.30 A.M.

General Hunt had been everywhere and arranged his artillery like clockwork; each chief of piece knew his distances and his directions to an inch. We were all up and horses saddled by 2.30. . . . We were to go to Burnside's Headquarters to wait — an arrangement that I regretted, as you can see nothing from there. It was near half-past three when we got there, and only a faint suspicion of daylight was yet to be noticed. It was an anxious time — eight thousand pounds of gunpowder to go into the air at once! I had considered all I had read about explosions and had concluded it would make little noise and be very circumscribed in its effects. Others, however, thought it might be a sort of earthquake, overturn trees, etc., which idea was founded on the fact that even a dozen pounds confined would pretty nearly blow a house down. However, we were something like a mile away and would not be likely to get the *worst* of it. General Burnside with his Staff had gone to the front. Presently General Grant arrived, I think after four o'clock. He said, "What is the matter with the mine?" General Meade shrugged his shoulders and said, "I don't know — guess the fuse has gone out." Which was a true guess. Where the fuse was spliced, it stopped burning; upon which Colonel Pleasants coolly went into the gallery and fired the new end! At ten minutes before five there was a distant, dull-sounding explosion, like a heavy gun, far away; and, in an instant, as if by magic, the whole line of batteries burst forth in one roar, and there was nothing but the banging of the guns and the distant hum of the shells! My back was turned at the moment, but those that had a good view say that a mass of earth about 50 feet wide and 120 long was thrown some 130 feet in the air, looking like the picture of the Iceland geysers. The explosion made a crater some 120 feet long, 50 feet wide, and 25 deep (so it was described to me). The mine blew up about under the bastion and rather on one side of it.

[The description of what followed, is copied from Lyman's "Journal."]

So astounded was the enemy and so covered was their position by our augmented artillery, that their reply was weak indeed and was soon almost silenced. Meantime, after incomprehensible delay (usually described as at least twenty minutes), the assaulting column moved forward, in a loose manner. This was Marshall's brigade of Ledlie's division, a brigade composed of dismounted cavalry and demoralized heavy artillery (!), the whole good for nothing, over which Marshall, a severe, courageous man, had been put, in the vain hope of beating in some discipline! Burnside, with inconceivable fatuity, allowed the troops for leading the assault to be *selected by lot!* The Corps was enough run down to make it hard to get a good forlorn hope with the most careful picking. Then no gap had been made in the parapet, which, next the mine, was at least eight feet high — all in disobedience to orders. All this time there was more or less cannon and musketry. Orders were sent to take the crest: to push on at once! But plainly there was a hitch! Colonel de Chanal, who was standing with me, was frantic over this loss of precious moments. "Mais, cette perte de temps!" he kept saying. In fact Marshall's brigade had gone into the crater and had filled it, and now were utterly immovable and sullen! The supports, brought up by the flank in bad order, crowded into the crater and the neighboring bomb-proofs and covered ways. There was some fighting, and the Rebel breastworks for 200 or 300 yards were taken, with a few prisoners; but advance to the crest the men would not. Our own covered ways were jammed with supporting troops that could do no good to anyone. 7 A.M. A lull. At a few minutes after 8 A.M. the troops of the 18th Corps and the black division of the 9th attempted a charge. Sanders, who saw it, said the troops would not go up with any spirit at all. The negroes came back in confusion, all mixed with the whites in and about the crater. Their officers behaved with distinguished courage, and the blacks seem to have done as well as whites — which is faint praise. This attack was over three hours after the springing of the mine. Meanwhile, of course, the enemy had strained every nerve to hold their remaining works and had made all preparations to retake the lost ground. They got guns in position whence they could play on the assailants without fear of getting silenced; and they brought a heavy musketry to bear in the same direction. The space between our line and the crater now was swept by a heavy fire, and made the transit hazardous. 9.15 A.M. or thereabouts; a charge by a brigade of the 18th Corps and a regiment of blacks; a part of one white regiment got to, or nearly to, the crest, but of course could not stay. During the morning a despatch had come, by mistake, to General Meade. It was from Lieutenant-Colonel C. G. Loring, Inspector of 9th Corps, who reported that the troops jammed in the crater and *could not be made to advance.* Loring had himself gone into the crater. This was the first news from the spot that showed Meade the hitch in affairs; because Burnside's despatches had been of a general and a favorable character. Hereupon Meade telegraphed Burnside that he wanted the full state of the case, which B. took to mean that *he had not told the truth!* and at once flew into one of his singular fits of rage. Grant mounted his horse and rode down towards the Taylor Battery to try and see something. Meade remained, receiving despatches and sending orders. Grant is very desirous always of seeing, and quite regardless of his own exposure. 10.30 A.M. Burnside and Ord came in. The former, much flushed, walked up to General Meade and used extremely insubordinate language. He afterwards said he could advance, and wished of all things to persist; but could not show how he would do it! Ord was opposed to further attempts. Meade ordered the attack suspended. As Ord and Burnside passed me, the latter said something like: "You have 15,000 men concentrated on one point. It is strange if you cannot do something with them." Ord replied angrily, flourishing his arms: "You can fight if you have an opportunity; but, if you are held by the throat, how can you do anything?" Meaning, I suppose, that things were so placed that troops could not be used. Burnside said to one of his Staff officers: "Well, tell them to connect, and hold it." Which was easy to say, but they seem to have had no provision of tools, and, at any rate, did not connect with the old line. Poor Burnside remarked, quite calmly: "I certainly fully expected this morning to go into Petersburg!"[1] At 11.30 A.M. Head-quarters mounted and rode sadly to camp. 3.30 P.M. Har-wood, of the Engineers, said to me: "They have retaken that point and captured a brigade of our people!" Indeed, the Rebels had made a bold charge upon the huddled mass of demoralized men and retaken the crater, killing some, driving back others, and capturing most. And so ended this woeful affair! If you ask what was the cause of this failure to avail of one of the best chances a besieging army could ask for, I could answer with many reasons from many officers. But I can give you *one* reason that includes and over-rides every other — *the men did not fight hard enough.*

August 1, 1864

I waked at about six in the morning and heard the General say, "Very well, then, let the truce be from five to nine." Whereby I knew that Beauregard had agreed to a cessation of hostilities for the burial of the dead and relief

---

[1] "All Burnside's baggage was packed, ready *to go into Petersburg!*" — Lyman's *Journal.*

of the wounded. After struggling awhile with my indo-
lence, I tumbled out of bed, waked Rosencrantz and ordered my horse. We speedily got ready and sallied forth to
look at the field. We rode into a piece of pine woods, at
the corner of which I was during the assault of the 18th of
June. Some of the advanced camps were here, the danger
of their position being plainly marked by the banks of
earth put up by each tent. Getting out of the wood, we
came on an open tract, a good deal elevated. Here, on the
left, and by the ruins of a house was a heavy battery,
known as the Taylor house battery. And here too begins
the "covered way." Before I saw real operations I never
could understand the management of cannon. On the
principle of your battle on "the great white plain," I had
an idea that all the guns were put in the front line: else how
could they hit anybody? But really there are often no cannon at all there, all being placed in a second or a third line,
or in isolated batteries in these relative positions. One of
our heavy siege guns would sometimes have to fire as many
as 1700 yards to hit the enemy's breastwork. You see
that cannon-shot must rise high in the air to go any distance; so they fire over each other's heads. In practice this
system is not without its dangers, owing to the imperfec-
tions of shells. In spite of the great advances, much remains
to be done in the fuses of shells; as it is, not a battle is fought
that some of our men are not killed by shells exploding
short and hitting our troops instead of the enemy's,
beyond. Sometimes it is the fuse that is imperfect, sometimes the artillerists lose their heads and make wrong
estimates of distance. From these blunders very valuable
officers have lost their lives. Prudent commanders, when
there is any doubt, fire only solid shot, which do not explode,
and do excellent service in bounding over the ground.

We got off our horses at the edge of the wood and took to the covered way (we might better have ridden). A covered way is singularly named, as it is open on top. It is simply a trench, about four feet wide, with the dirt thrown up on the side towards the enemy. It should be deep enough to cover a man standing upright. The great thing is, so to run it that the enemy cannot get a sight of it *lengthwise*, as they could then enfilade it. To this end the way is run zig-zag, and advantage is taken of every hollow, or knoll, that may afford shelter. I was not impressed with the first part of our covered way, as it could be shot into in many places, and was so shallow that it covered me no higher than the shoulders. Probably it was dug by a small officer who was spiteful against men of great inches. . . . We scrambled up the opposite steep bank and stood at the high breastwork of Burnside's advanced salient. The parapet was crowded with troops, looking silently at the scene of the late struggle. We got also on the parapet and at once saw everything. Opposite, and a little above us, distant about 350 feet, was the rough edge of the crater, made by the mine. There were piles of gravel and of sand, and shapeless masses of hard clay, all tumbled on top of each other. Upon the ridge thus formed, and upon the remains of the breastwork, stood crowds of Rebel soldiers in their slouched hats and ghostly grey uniforms. Really they looked like malevolent spirits, towering to an unnatural height against the sky. Each party had a line of sentries close to his works, and, in the midst, stood an officer with a white flag, where the burial parties were at work.[1] I jumped down and passed towards the enemy's line, where only officers were allowed to go, with the details for work.

[1] "The Rebels were meanly employing their negro prisoners in this work." — Lyman's *Journal*.

I do not make a practice of describing disagreeable spectacles, and will only say that I can never again see anything more horrible than this glacis before the mine. It did not take long to satisfy our curiosity, and we returned to camp, getting in just as the General was at breakfast. He takes his disappointments before Petersburg in an excellent spirit; and, when the "Herald" this morning said he was to be relieved and not to have another command, he laughed and said: "Oh, that's bad; that's very bad! I should have to go and live in that house in Philadelphia; ha! ha! ha!" The papers will tell you that Grant has gone to Washington. As I don't know what for, I can make Yankee guesses. I presume our father Abraham looks on his election prospects as waning, and wants to know of Ulysses, the warrior, if some *man* or some *plan* can't be got to do some *thing*. In one word he wants to know — WHY THE ARMY OF THE POTOMAC DON'T MOVE. A month since there was a talk of putting Hancock at the head: that is, losing the most brilliant of corps commanders and risking (there is always a risk) the making of a mediocre army commander!

August 4, 1864

This was quite a festal day for us. The General, accompanied by the Frenchies, Rosencrantz, Bache, Biddle and myself, paid a grand visit to Butler. Butler was in high feather. He is as proud of all his "fixin's" as a farmer over a prime potato patch. We first got on the Greyhound, an elegant steamer (Butler believes in making himself comfortable), and proceeded down the Appomattox, past City Point, and then bore up the James, passing Bermuda Hundred, with its flotilla of schooners and steamers. . . . We had got a good bit above Bermuda Hundred and were

paddling along bravely when we came in sight of two gunboats; that is, common steamers with some heavy guns on
board. There are many in the river and they go up and
down to keep it clear. As we drew near, I saw the men were
at quarters and the guns run out. We passed between the
first boat and the high wooded bank, when I beheld the
gunboat captain dancing up and down on the paddle-box
and roaring to us: "The left bank is lined with sh-a-a-rp-
shooters!" It would have edified you to have seen the
swift dignity with which General Meade and his gallant
Staff stepped from the open, upper deck to the shady
seclusion of the cabin! Our skipper jingled "Stop her,"
with his engine-room bell, and stop she did. Here was a
chance for war-god Butler. "Hey? What? Sharpshooters?
Pshaw! Fiddledeedee! Stop her! Who said stop her?
Mr. DeRay, tell the Captain to go on, *instantly!*" And
Butler danced out on the open deck and stood, like George
II at Dettingen, in "an attitude of fence." I, who looked
for a brisk volley of musketry, fully expected to see him
get a bullet in his extensive stomach. Meanwhile the Captain went on, and, as soon as we were clear, the naval party
in the rear (or "astern," we ought to say) let go one big
gun, with a tremendous *whang!* and sent a projectile
about the size of a flour barrel on shore, severely wounding
a great many bushes and trees. The other gunboat went
ahead of us and kept up a little marine combat, all on her
own hook. Whether there really were sharpshooters, I
know not: I only think, if there *were*, it would be difficult
to say which party was the more scared. . . .

Finally we went on shore where our horses were waiting,
for this is not over three and a half miles from the Appomattox, though it is fifteen or sixteen miles round by the
river. From the top of the cliff we had a splendid view of

the cultivated country towards Richmond. And so, after inspecting more of Benjamin's apple-pie batteries, we went home.

August 6, 1864

I took a limited ride along our flank defences, where I discovered a patriotic sentry, sitting with his back to where the enemy might be supposed to come, and reading a novel! He belonged to the 7th Indiana. "What are your instructions?" say I. "Han't got none," replies the peruser of novels. "Then what are you here for?" "Well, I am a kind of an alarm sentinel," said this literary militaire. "Call the corporal of the guard," said I, feeling much disposed to laugh. The sentry looked about a little and then singling out a friend, called out: "Oh, Jim, why, won't you just ask Jeremiah Miles to step this way?" After some delay, Jeremiah appeared. He was in a pleasing state of ignorance. Did not know the sentry's instructions, did not know who the officer of the guard was, did not know much of anything. "Well," said I, "now suppose you go and find the sergeant of the guard." This he did with great alacrity. The sergeant, as became his office, knew more than the corporal. He was clear that the sentry should not read a book; also that his conduct in sitting down was eccentric; but, when it came to who was the officer of the guard, his naturally fine mind broke down. He knew the officer *if he saw him*, but could *not* remember his name. This he would say, the officer was a lieutenant. "Suppose you should try to find him," suggested I. Of course that he could do; and soon the "Loo-tenant" appeared. To him I talked like a father; almost like a grandfather, in fact; showed him the man's musket was rusty and that he was no good whatsoever. Loo-tenant had not much to say; indeed, so to speak, nothing; and I left him with a strong impression that you can't make a silk purse from a sow's ear. It is not ludicrous, but sad, to see such soldiers in this Army of the Potomac, after three years of experience. The man could not have been better: tall, strong, respectful, and docile; but no one had ever taught him. It was a clear case of waste of fine material, left in all its crudity instead of being worked up. And this is the grand characteristic of this war — waste. We waste arms, clothing, ammunition, and subsistence; but, above all, men. We don't make them go far enough, because we have no military or social caste to make officers from. Regiments that have been officered by gentlemen of education have invariably done well, like the 2d, 20th, and 24th Massachusetts, and the 1st Massachusetts Cavalry. Even the 44th and the 45th, nine-monthers, behaved with credit; though there was this drawback in them, that the privates were too familiar with the officers, having known them before. However, perfection does not exist anywhere, and we should be thankful for the manifold virtues our soldiers do pre-eminently possess. I see much to make me more contented in reading Napier, before referred to. After the taking of Badajos, the English allowed their own wounded to lie two days in the breach, without an attempt to carry them off. This is the nation that now gives us very good lectures on humanity. As to old Wellington, I suspect he was about as savage an old brute as would be easy to find.

August 8, 1864

"What do you think of filling up with Germans?" you ask. Now, what do you think of a man who has the toothache — a werry, werry big molar! — and who has not the courage to march up and have it out, but tries to persuade himself that he can buy some patent pain-killer that will

cure him; when, in his soul, he knows that tooth has to
come out? This is what I think of our good people (honest,
doubtless) who would burden us with these poor, poor
nigs, and these nerveless, stupid Germans. As soldiers *in
the field* the Germans are nearly useless; our experience is,
they have no native courage to compare with Americans.
Then they do not understand a word that is said to them
— these new ones. So it has proved with the Massachusetts 20th (which has a perfection of discipline not at all
the rule). Under the severe eyes of their officers the German recruits have done tolerably in simple line, mixed with
the old men; but they produced confusion at the Wilderness, by their ignorance of the language; and, only the
other day, Patten told me he could not do a thing with
them on the skirmish line, because they could not understand. By the Lord! I wish these gentlemen who would
overwhelm us with Germans, negroes, and the offscourings
of great cities, could only see — only *see* — a Rebel regiment, in all their rags and squalor. If they had eyes they
would know that these men are like wolf-hounds, and not
to be beaten by turnspits. Look at our "Dutch" heavy
artillery: we no more think of trusting them than so many
babies. Send bog-trotters, if you please, for Paddy will
fight — no one is braver. It should be known, that ill-dis-
ciplined, or cowardly, or demoralized troops may be useful
behind walls, but in open campaigning they literally are
worse than useless; they give way at the first fire and expose the whole line to be flanked. At the Wilderness the
6th Corps would have been stronger without Ricketts's
division; at Spotsylvania the whole army would have
been stronger without Mott's division. Howland[1] has influence in recruiting; impress upon him, therefore, that

[1] His brother-in-law.

every worthless recruit he sends to this army is one card in the hand of General Lee and is the cause, very likely, of the death of a good soldier. The trouble is *this:* we have not the machinery to work up *poor material.* They won't let us shoot the rascals, and few regiments have the discipline to mould them into decent troops; the consequence is, they are the stragglers, pillagers, skulkers and run-aways of the army. If you had seen as many thousands as I, you would understand what sort of fellows they are. I don't believe in recruiting another man! We have recruited already more *volunteers* than any country ever saw. Volunteers are naturally exhausted; and now we pay huge bounties to every sort of scoundrel and vagabond and alien. These men will *not* fight and you can't make 'em fight. But draft men and you will get good ones, without bounty. They will not *want* to go, but they have the pride of native-born Americans, and they fight like devils. The very men that desert the next day will fight the day before, for sake of avoiding shame. I have written quite a disquisition, but the topic is an important one, and I have the honor, in conclusion, to suggest to the honorable City of Boston that, when the Germans arrive, they should be let out as gardeners, and the poor remnants of the old regiments should be allowed to fight it out alone.

August 9, 1864

In the forenoon, as we were sitting in camp, we heard a noise, like a quick, distant clap of thunder, but sharper. We concluded it must be an explosion, from the sound, and in a few minutes came a telegraph from Grant, at City Point, saying that an ordnance barge had blown up, with considerable loss of life. I think the number of killed will not exceed thirty-five; and, of the wounded, perhaps eighty;

15

at first they thought there were many more. The greater part of the injured were negroes employed as wharf-laborers. To return to the explosion: Rosy, Worth, Cavada, and Cadwalader were at Grant's Headquarters, and they said it perfectly rained shells, shot, bullets, pieces of timber, and *saddles* (of these latter there was a barge load near by). Two dragoons were killed, close to them, and a twelve-pounder solid shot went smash into a mess-chest in the tent. The only man who, at the first shock, ran *towards* the scene of terror was Lieutenant-General Grant, which shows his kind of character very well. We dined very pleasantly with Dalton. You should see his town of tents, with regular streets — accommodation easy for 8000 patients. Everything as neat as a pin. Steam-engine to pump water from the river; every patient of the 4000 on a *cot;* the best of food for all; and the most entire cleanliness. When Dalton heard the explosion, he jumped on his feet, and, true to his instincts, cried out: "Harness the ambulances!"

August 11, 1864

Sheridan has been appointed to command all the upper Potomac forces, which is saying that he is to command all the troops to drive Early out of the Shenandoah Valley. He is a Major-General, and is an energetic and very brave officer. This command, however, is a very large one, larger than he ever before had. I have little doubt, that, for field-service, he is superior to any officer there. Things are cooking, and the Rebels will find they must fag away still, as well as we. I do not exactly know if Meade likes this appointment: you see they have taken one of his corps, added much of his cavalry and many other troops to it, and then given the command to his Chief of Cavalry, while he

[Meade] is left, with a reduced force, at this somewhat negative Petersburg business. I rode out just at dark, and from an "elevated position," as Smith would say, watched the flashes of the sharpshooters, and the fires of the camp.

August 12, 1864

I did not yet mention that I had seen Colonel Thomas, who commands a negro brigade. A singular thing happened to him. He went out during the truce to superintend, and, when the truce was over, he undertook to return to the works, but took a wrong turn, passed inside the Rebel picket line, and was seized. He told them they had no right to take him, but they could not see it and marched him off. But he appealed to the commanding General who, after eighteen hours, ordered him set free. He was in and about Petersburg and told me the flower-patches were nicely cultivated in front of the houses, the canary birds were hung in cages before the doors, and everything looked as if the inhabitants meant to enjoy their property during their lives and hand it quietly down to their children. Little damage seemed to have been done by our shells, which I was glad to hear, for I hate this business of house-burning. Next time, I fancy the warlike Thomas will make no mistakes about turns.

August 13, 1864

. . . I rode over to make some enquiry about Colonel Weld, of Loring, at Burnside's Headquarters. As I drew near, I heard the sound as of minstrelsy and playing on the psaltry and upon the harp; to wit, a brass band, tooting away at a great rate. This was an unaccustomed noise, for Burnside is commonly not musical, and I was speculating on the subject when, on entering the circle of tents, I beheld a collection of Generals — not only Burnside, but also Potter, Willcox, and Ferrero. Speaking of this last, did you hear what the negro straggler remarked, when arrested by the Provost-Guard near City Point, on the day of the assault, and asked what he was doing there. "Well, saar, I will displain myself. You see, fus' I was subjoined to Ginral Burnside; an' den I was disseminated to Ginral Pharo. We wus advancing up towards der front, an' I, as it might be, loitered a little. Presently I see some of our boys a-runnin' back. 'Ho, ho,' sez I, 'run is your word, is it?' So I jes separates myself from my gun and I re-tires to dis spot."

Well, there was "Ginral Pharo" taking a drink, and an appearance was about as of packing. Whereat I presently discovered, through the joyous Captain Pell (who asked me tauntingly if he could "do anything for me at Newport"), that Burnside and his Staff were all going on a thirty-day leave, which will extend itself, I fancy, indefinitely, so far as this army goes. On my return I found two fat civilians and a lean one. Fat number one was Mr. Otto, Assistant Secretary of the Interior; Fat number two, a Professor Matile, a Swiss of Neufchâtel, and friend of Agassiz (you perhaps remember the delicious wine of that place). The lean was Mr. Falls, what I should call Mr. Otto's "striker," that being the name of an officer's servant or hanger-on. Mr. Falls was very chatty and interrogative, following every sentence by "Is it not?" So that finally I felt obliged always to reply, "No, it isn't." I scared him very much by tales of the immense distances that missiles flew, rather implying that he might look for a pretty brisk shower of them, about the time he got fairly asleep. Professor Matile was bright enough to be one of those who engaged in the brilliant scheme of Pourtalès Steiger to seize the château of Neufchâtel on behalf of the

John Grubb Parke

King of Prussia. Consequently he since has retired to this
country and has now a position as examiner at the Patent
Office. Mr. Otto was really encouraging to look at. He
did not chew tobacco, or talk politics, or use bad grammar;
but was well educated and spake French and German.
General Butler, having a luminous idea to get above the
Howlett house batteries by cutting a ship canal across
Dutch Gap, has called for volunteers, at an increased rate
of pay. Whereupon the Rebel rams come down and shell
the extra-pay volunteers, with their big guns; and we hear
the distant booming very distinctly. I think when Butler
gets his canal cleverly through, he will find fresh batteries,
ready to rake it, and plenty more above it, on the river.
The Richmond papers make merry, and say it will increase
their commerce.

August 14, 1864

. . . General Parke got back from his sick leave and took
command of the 9th Corps. He is a very pleasant-looking
man and liked apparently by everyone. He has been
obliged twice to return to the North by reason of malarial
attacks, which is a pity, as he acted usually as adviser to
General Burnside and had an excellent effect on him. He
cured himself twice of malarial fever by accidentally taking an overdose of medicine. The last time, he had been
told to take one pill, containing something very strong;
but made a mistake and took *four*. After which he was
somewhat surprised to find his face making a great many
involuntary grimaces, and his body feeling uncommonly
uncomfortable. However, next day he was all well, and
the doctor told him it was a good dose to take, provided it
did not unfortunately happen to kill him. Captain Fay
took out the cits to-day, in an ambulance, and showed them

the lines. After which the youth Falls was seized with a
noble ambition to ride on horseback in company of Captain Guzman. Being provided with a hard trotter, he
came near tumbling off, at the first start, and was obliged
to change horses and perform the rest of the journey at a
mild pace.

August 16, 1864

I have been well content to get your letter this afternoon. In regard to what you say for the troops for the
assault,[1] it is true that General Meade should have ordered in the best — and so he *did*. Express orders were
given to put in the best troops and have the division generals lead them if necessary. General Meade made exam-
inations in person of the enemy's lines, and the orders
drawn up by General Humphreys were more than usually
elaborated. People have a vulgar belief that a General
commanding a great army can, and ought to arrange in
person every detail. This is not possible, nor is it desirable;
the corps and division commanders would at once say:
"Very well, if you have not enough confidence in me to let
me carry on the ordinary business of my command, I
ought to be relieved." I see great discussion in the papers
as to the conduct of the negroes. I say, as I always have,
that you never, in the long run, can make negroes fight
with success against white men. When the whole weight
of history is on one side, you may be sure that side is the
correct one. I told General Meade I had expressed myself
strongly, at home, against the imported Dutchmen, to
which he replied: "Yes, if they want to see us licked, they
had better send along such fellers as those!" As I said
before, the Pats will do: not so good as pure Yanks, but

[1] When the mine was exploded.

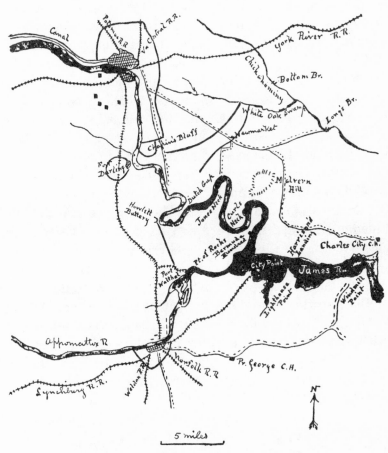

BETWEEN PETERSBURG AND RICHMOND

they will rush in and fight. There was a report at first that Colonel Macy of the 20th Massachusetts was mortally wounded, but I have since heard that it is not so. On Sunday, he had command of a brigade, and had his horse killed: he then came back, got another horse from Barlow and returned to the front. This horse either was shot or reared over with him, frightened by the firing, and crushed him badly. Let me see, I told you this before; never mind, you will be sure now to know it. Sometimes I get rather mixed because I write often a few words about a day, on the eve of the same, and then detail it more at length afterwards. The Rebels got well alarmed about Hancock and sent reinforcements, recalling troops that had started to help Early in the valley; an important point gained. Hancock had some hard fighting to-day, with considerable success, taking several hundred prisoners and driving the enemy. The Rebel General Chambliss was killed, and we found on him a valuable map containing the fortifications of Richmond. They also are said to have killed a General Gherrard; but I have an idea there is no such General in their service.[1] Perhaps he was a new appointment, or a colonel commanding a brigade. As to giving you an account of the engagement, it would be out of the question; as it is a perfect muddle to me. I only know that Gregg, with a cavalry division, went out on the Richmond road, to within six and one half miles of the city, and encountered a big crowd of infantry and had to come back. Barlow had to leave his division, sick, and go to friend Dalton, at City Point.

August 18, 1864

Last night I had got well into the first sound sleep, when images of war began to intrude on my dreams, and these, taking on a more corporeal form, gradually waked me enough to prove to my mind that there was a big racket going on. The noise of a few shells and many muskets I don't mind, as I am used to it, but, when it comes to firing heavy mortar shells in salvos, one is authorized to sit up in bed, even if it is one in the morning. Once awake, I recognized the fact that the largest kind of a cannonade was

[1] It was Brig. Gen. Victor J. B. Girardey.

going on. The still, damp air was filled with the detonations of all sorts of big guns and projectiles. It was quite as extensive as the firing on the morning of the mine and sounded very much louder, in the night. Our side replied rather moderately, but the enemy kept up one roar of batteries for some two hours, and the air was full of the humming and bursting of the shells. At the end of that time they stopped, rather suddenly. We expended some 1500 rounds of ammunition and they must have fired much more, and all to kill and wound thirty men. . . . The great joke of the matter was, that General Meade (who is a sound sleeper, and was a little deaf from a cold in the head) remained calmly in the arms of Morpheus, till a telegraph from *Grant* at *City Point*, came in, asking what all that firing was about! It so happened that the General woke just at a lull in the cannonade; so he didn't understand the despatch, but called the officer of the night to know if he had heard any more firing than usual! You should have seen the deshabille parade of officers in the camp: such a flitting of figures in a variety of not much clothing! General Humphreys said: "Yes, perhaps it would be well to have the horses saddled; for," he added with a hopeful smile, "we may have a scrimmage, you know." But he was disappointed, and we all went to bed again.

August 19, 1864

To-day I have been with the General to General Warren, who with the 5th Corps seized the Weldon railroad yesterday. It is touching a tiger's cubs to get on that road! They will not stand it. Warren had a severe fight yesterday at midday, but they could not get him off. All was quiet this morning towards the railroad. Mott[1] got in,

[1] Ordered back from Deep Bottom.

JERUSALEM PLANK ROAD AND WELDON RAILROAD

through the mud, about seven, and began at once to relieve the 9th Corps, which was not an easy matter, for the
covered way was, in many places, waist-deep in water, so
the troops had to march up as well as they could, keeping
behind hills, etc. The enemy opened on them with artillery
but it was rather too late, and the columns were already
pretty well out of reach. At noon the General started to
go out to visit the scene of action. It was raining steadily,
and we went *slop, slop* along. Near the Cheever house
was a damp brigade of Potter's division, halted. The
General ordered me to tell it to move on, as it might be
needed. General Potter himself was near by at General
White's Headquarters. . . . After which I was fain to
gallop briskly to catch up with the Staff, which was jogging
along the Williams house road. . . . Cutting through a
skirt of wood, we came on a very large, flat, open farm, on
which is the Globe Tavern,[1] and through which runs the
railroad. . . . General Warren had a narrow escape in
the fight of yesterday. His horse was struck directly between the eyes by a minié ball. If his head had been
down, there would have been nothing to save the General's
body. The Corps [Warren's] was then formed in form of
two sides of a rectangle, the longer arm lying across the
railroad, the shorter parallel to it. It could scarcely fail
to strike me that, while his left flank was well protected,
his right was "in the air," having nothing in connection with
it but the picket line. However, as I am not a military
critic, I thought no more of it. The enemy *did* think a
good deal of it. In front of the position were dense woods,
on its left a fine open tract, and, on the right, a wood separated it from the open farm of the Aiken house. We left at
3.30, and returned by the way we came. Both going and

[1] Where they found Warren.

coming I quite expected to see the picket line tumbling in on top of us, and was not surprised, as we rode along near the Aiken house, to hear a number of dropping shots to our left. Just after we got to the plank road, we could hear the cannon opening, which continued a short time and then ceased. During the said short time was enacted one of those disgraceful surprises which we have in such perfection. The enemy, making a front attack, at the same moment threw a strong column down a road leading past the Linear house and outside our right flank. They smashed through the picket line, passed down the road, faced to their right, and rushed, yelling and firing, into the open fields, in rear of our right wing. Met here by a fire of artillery and reserve troops, they themselves fell into confusion, and rushing back through our lines, like a great tide, carried out to sea at least 2000 of our men, including most of our gallant little regular brigade with its commander, General Hayes. To be sure we drove them off and held the railroad, but we *ought* to have taken all that flanking column.[1]

August 20, 1864

A brigade of cavalry passed last night, coming from Deep Bottom, and reported this morning to General Warren, to cover his flank and rear, and help destroy the railroad. A Lieutenant McKibbin, who once went out with me on a flag of truce, was badly hit in the shoulder yesterday. He is a curious young man and belongs to a very fighting family. Being the son of a hotel-keeper, he joined the army as a sutler; but, at the battle of Gaines's Mill, as soon as the musketry began, he deliberately anointed his tent with butter, set the whole shop on fire,

[1] "The position was faulty! Warren should have corrected it, and Meade should have known it!" — Lyman's *Journal*.

took a gun and went into the fight, where he presently got a bullet, that entered on one side of his nose and came out under his ear! Thereupon he received a commission in the regulars, where he still remains. . . . There was rain still to-day, making the ground so bad that orders were finally issued that no waggons should go west of the plank road, all stores being sent thence on pack mules. In the morning came a couple of hundred Rebel prisoners, taken yesterday. Among them were a number of *their* Maryland brigade, quite well dressed and superior men, many of them. They were very civil, but evidently more touchy than the extreme Southerners, who exhibit no feeling at all. These Marylanders, however, were very anxious to say they were fighting hard when taken, which I don't doubt they were. They had the remains of fancy clothes on, including little *képis*, half grey and half sky-blue. There was one officer who was next-door neighbor of Dr. McParlin, our Medical Director, and the Doctor went to see him. General Williams has just been in. His great delight is to rub the fuzz on top of my head with his finger, and exclaim: "Wonder what color the baby's hair is going to be!"

August 21, 1864

Last night, Hancock, with his two remaining divisions, marched from Deep Bottom and took position on our left, ready to support Warren. The long, rapid marches of this Corps have given it the name of "Hancock's cavalry." When a halt was ordered, one soldier said to the next: "O Jim, what er we a-stoppin' for?" "The Staff is getting fresh hosses!" replied James. At 9.30 in the morning we again heard Warren's artillery opening very heavily. I felt anxious on account of the nature of the last attack. This, however, turned out a very different thing. You saw my diagram of his position in my last letter. In addition he now had made a short exterior flank line. The enemy formed in the woods, out of sight, so as to envelop his flank defence, and coming partly in rear; the troops were those of Beauregard and A. P. Hill, many of which had been concentrated from Deep Bottom. They first opened a heavy artillery fire from behind the woods, throwing most of the projectiles into the angle of the line. Then their infantry advanced, in three lines of battle, and attempted to charge, but were received by such a discharge of all sorts of things that they broke and ran back before getting anywhere near. A South Carolina brigade coming out of the woods, saw that they were on the prolongation of our *front* flank line, and, thinking they had us foul, immediately charged, and caught an awful musketry fire on their flank, from our *rear* flank line, which they had not noticed. Immediately they began throwing down their arms and shouting, and an officer and some men from our front ran out to accept their surrender. The officer approached General Hagood and either demanded or seized the flag he held in his hand, when Hagood shot him mortally with a pistol, and shouted to his men to run. Some did so, others (about 300) gave themselves up, and others were shot down as they ran. The conduct of Hagood is denounced as treacherous, but this all depends on the details of the affair, which remain to be proved. The *next* time I think we shall go on shooting till some official announcement of surrender is made! Hagood's flag we got, a new one, with fifty-seven bullet holes through it! Also three or four other flags, and some 400 prisoners in all. The total loss of the enemy in the day's work must have been from 1500 to 2000.

We left at about one o'clock, and rode down, first to the

stalwart Hancock, who was just then at the Jones house, and then kept on and saw Warren; for we expected another heavy fight, and General Meade wished to be present and see all the troops worked to proper advantage. Warren proposed to attack in his turn, but I am glad he did not, for there was no advantage to be gained that I could see, and we had all we could desire, the possession of the railroad. . . .

August 23, 1864

Major Duane, who visits me much of evenings, because he can't use his eyes, told me a story of Captain Cullum (now General Cullum) that I thought eminently Cullumish. Cullum was building a small fort at New London and was visited by a country editor, whom he received with high state and gave a lecture on the principles of fortification, after showing the small work on which he was engaged. He took as an example a large bastioned fort, and showed how it could be breached in forty days; and how the defenders would then make an interior line and drive out the stormers when they got inside the first. The editor, taking all this as applicable to the New London work, went home and published a tremendous leader, in which he said that the talented Captain Cullum was erecting the largest bastion fort in the world; that it would take you forty days to get inside it, and, when you *were* inside, you were *worse off than you were before!* The General rode along a new line we had been making, principally the work of the nigs, who are very faithful at making a breastwork and slashing the timber in front. A colonel or two got well pitched into for not having their men with their belts on and ready for action. I do believe our soldiers would sooner run the risk of getting shot twice a day, than take any little precaution. To-day I performed an act of military charity, by sending, per flag-of-truce boat, some coffee and sugar to Joe Hayes and Arthur Sedgwick.

August 24, 1864

What you say of Meade's want of success is, as a fact, true; but what I don't understand is, that the successes are Grant's but the failures Meade's. In point of reality the whole is Grant's: he directs all, and his subordinates are only responsible as executive officers having more or less important functions. There have been cases where they might be said to act alone; for instance, the assault of the 18th of June, though under a general permission from Grant, was strictly an operation of Meade. He felt badly about that failure, "Because," said he, "*I* should have taken Petersburg. I had reason to calculate on success. The enemy had no defences but what they had thrown up in a few hours; and I had 60,000 men to their 25,000." All of which was true and the result showed the difference of morale. The men who stormed the Rappahannock redoubts in November '63 would have walked over the breastworks and driven Beauregard into the Appomattox; but those men are on the ground between here and the Rapid Ann, or fill the hospitals in the North. Put a man in a hole and a good battery on a hill behind him, and he will beat off three times his number, even if he is not a very good soldier.

August 25, 1864

There has been more fighting to-day. Hancock, at Reams' station, was destroying the railroad (Weldon) and holding a position, also, for defence, having two of his divisions of infantry, besides Gregg's cavalry. The Rebels sent down a large force to drive him off. They began attacking say about one o'clock and were severely repulsed, till evening; but the last news is, that they made a desperate attempt on all sides and broke through a part of our right, just at nightfall. Hancock hoped to retake the part of the line lost, with the reinforcements coming up; but we have not yet heard the result. I feel rather anxious, though I don't fear for Hancock's safety; but I like to see him fully successful. Oh, bah! Captain Miller is just in (this is eleven o'clock at night). Hancock has lost eight guns — among them, I am told, Sleeper's battery. Poor Sleeper was here this afternoon, wounded in the arm. It is too much all one way in this business, it really is! I don't like to complain, because it troubles you, but it must break out occasionally. I get so mad and so bothered. For, when we have no good chance, or almost none, when our best undertakings fall through, I lose confidence in each move, and, when I hear the cannon, I look for nothing but our men coming back and a beggarly report of loss of prisoners. It is not right to feel so, but I can't help it. When a man gets knocked down every time, he expects to go down the next. Well, well, well, I feel already a little better at this grumbling. I must be a sorry eel if I am not yet used to this sort of skinning. I like to see General Meade. I think these *contretemps* rather rouse and wind him up; he doesn't seem to be depressed by that sort of thing; perhaps three years of it have made it necessary to his life, just as some persons enjoy a daily portion of arsenic.

August 26, 1864

It may be laid down as a general principle, that it is a bad thing, in a musket or a man, to go off at half-cock. In some respects I may be said so to have done in my letter last night. Our information this morning shows that, after dark, while we marched off the ground *one* way, the enemy

marched off the *other*, leaving their dead unburied and some
wounded. Accounts of the field show their loss to have
been fearful, much greater than ours, which was not serious either in killed, wounded or prisoners. Thus, all the
strategic results lie with us, and we hold the Weldon road.
But I would not have you believe I was disposed to turn
about and crow. No! I do not so much mind the loss of
the guns — a mere matter of prestige — but I *do* mind the
fact that the 2d Corps men did not all fight as they should
have fought; had they done so, the Rebels (who I suppose
were about as three to two) could never have budged
them. As Major Mitchell observed: "The Rebels licked us,
but a dozen more such lickings and there will be nothing
left of the Rebel army!" My gracious, what a donkey am I
to be solemnly sending a telegraph, when I have not been
in a single fight. I felt like a donkey at the time, but I
thought you would be fussing and imagining, because there
had been fighting in various directions. But I will not be
so silly in future. And there is your mother, bless her
heart! thanking God I am safe out of it, when I have not
been *in* it! Really, I feel it almost my duty to go on the
picket line and get shot at by a grey-back, for the sake of
doing something! Yes, ma'am, thirty-one *is* quite an old
man, but I am "so as to be about," can ride a horse and
hold up my head; and, as the late T—— remarked, when
he proposed, "I am good for ten years," which turned out
to be true (to the regret of Mrs. T.), for he lived twenty-
five years after and begat sons and daughters. You must
thank Madre[1] from me for the present of "Forbes's Naked-
eyed Medusa." Tell her, also, that, having neglected my
natural history for three years, [much] of which has been

[1] His mother-in-law.

devoted to becoming semi-idiotic from having nothing to do but listen to cannon and mortars and rifles, and associate with young gentlemen still further advanced in semi-idiocy, I have not a clear idea of what a Medusa is; but am impressed with the notion that it is something flabby that lives in the sea.

VI

THE SIEGE OF PETERSBURG

[THE next day Lyman was surprised to have Meade say to him. "I think I must order you home to get me some cigars, mine are nearly out!" But, as the former remarked, "It's hard to surprise a man out of going home, after a five months' campaign."

General Williams gravely prepared a fifteen-day leave, and the aides tendered their congratulations. Lyman was bound for Richmond on secret service! So the Staff persuaded the inquisitive Biddle, who talked about it all over camp, and got very mad when undeceived. He recovered, however, when tendered a cocktail as a peace offering.

Lyman's visit to the North proved longer than he expected. For, shortly after his arrival in Beverly, where Mrs. Lyman was passing the summer, he had an attack of malaria which kept him in bed for some time. According to the doctors, "The northern air, with the late cool change, had brought to the surface the malaria in the system." Consequently, he was not able to rejoin the army until the end of September.

Meanwhile, the gloom was lifting, that had settled on the North after the failure to take Petersburg. For Sherman's capture of Atlanta, and Sheridan's victories over Early in the Shenandoah, had somewhat changed the situation, although the Army of the Potomac still lay before Petersburg, where it hovered for many weary months.]

228

HEADQUARTERS, ARMY OF POTOMAC
September 28, 1864

It is late; I am somewhat tired and sleepy; I must be up early to-morrow, and many friends keep coming in to say "How are you?" So you will let me off from a long letter till to-morrow. It is as "nat'ral as the hogs" here. I have just taken my supper in a tent as gravely as if I never ate in a room. I got here without delay or accident and am stronger than when I started.

HEADQUARTERS, ARMY OF POTOMAC
September 29, 1864

The 6.45 P.M. train, which bore me, on Monday, from the ancient town of Beverly, did arrive in very good season in Boston, where I hired a citizen, in the hack line, to convey me with speed and safety to the Worcester depot. With an eye to speculation the driver took in also a lone female, who looked with a certain alarm on me, doubtful as to whether I might not be in the highway-robbery line. She had evidently been on a sea-shore visit, and bore a small pitcher with a bunch of flowers therein. By a superior activity I got a place in the sleeping-car, for it seems to be the policy to have about half room enough for the sleepy passengers, so that those who don't get places may look with envy on t'others and determine to be earlier next time. Geo. D—— was along. The canny man had got a good berth, in the middle of the day, and you should have seen his traveller's fixings: a blanket, a sort of little knapsack, and finally a white handkerchief to tie over his head; "For," said he, "perhaps the pillows are not very clean." With martial indifference I took off boots and blouse, got on an upper shelf (not without convulsive kicks), and composed myself to the fitful rest which one gets under such circumstances. There was, as the conductor truthfully observed, "a tremendous grist of children in the car" — of all sizes, indeed, from a little one that publicly partook of its natural nutriment, to youths of some twelve summers. The first object I saw, on wakening in the morning, was an attentive Ma endeavoring to put a hooped skirt under the dress of a small gal, without exhibiting to a curious public the small gal's legs; which attempt on her part was a lamentable failure. I was glad to get out of the eminently close locomotive dormitory and hop with agility on the horse-car, which landed me, a little before seven A.M., at the Astor House. Here I partook of a dollar and a quarter's worth of tea and mutton-chop, and stretched my legs by a walk to the Jersey ferry, and there, as our pilgrim fathers would have said, took shipping for the opposite shore. I should not neglect to say that at the Astor I had noticed a tall man, in the three buttons of a Major-General, whom I at once recognized as the original of the many photographs of General Hooker. I was much disappointed in his appearance: red-faced, very, with a lack-lustre eye and an uncertainty of gait and carriage that suggested a used-up man. His mouth also is wanting in character and firmness; though, for all that, he must once have been a very handsome man. He was a passenger for Washington and sat near me. Next me was a worthy minister, with whom I talked; he, I do remember, delivered a prayer at our chapel last winter, at Headquarters. He was like all of that class, patriotic and one-sided, attributing to the Southerners every fiendish passion; in support of which he had accumulated all the horrible accounts of treatment of prisoners, slaves, etc., etc., and had worked himself into a great state. Evening. 10 P.M. I have got to Baltimore and can't go a step farther; for all

day have I been on the Weldon railroad with General
Meade, and I must slap to bed, for I am most sleepy,
though all right.

September 30, 1864

If the General *will* ride out at 8.30 A.M., and get back at
10.30 P.M., and fight a good part of the day, *how* am I to
feel wakeful and lively to write to you? I am very well and
getting stronger; was in part of the battle beyond the railroad; but only had a few bullets and one solitary cannon-
ball in my neighborhood. This going from Beverly to
battle is quite a sharp contrast. Our advantage was signal
and important if we have good luck in holding on, which I
think we shall. There may be fighting to-morrow, but I
incline to think not.

October 2, 1864

. . . The Washington boat was much in the style of
the other — rather worse and more crowded, people and
freight similar. There were more Christian Commissioners, who were joined by those who had come with me. The
funniest people you ever saw! Their great and overshad-
owing anxiety was *dinner;* that was the thing. Accordingly
they had deputed the youngest — a divinity student, and
supposed to be a terribly sharp fellow — to lie in wait at
sundry times and secure tickets for the meal. "I have
arranged it all with the steward; we shall sit together,"
said this foxy one. Long before the hour, they all went
down and stood against the door, like the queue at a
French theatre. One of them came up, a little after, wip-
ing his mouth; and asked me with surprising suddenness,
if I "was on the side of the Lord." They were mostly
Methodists, and of course very pious. One of the soldiers
on the lower deck, suddenly cried out: "Oh, H——!" upon

which a Christian Commissioner said: "Mr. Smith, did
you think to bring a bundle of the tracts on swearing?" I
told him I hoped he had brought a good many, and of
several kinds, as there was a wide field in the army. All of
which reminds me of an anecdote. A group of these gentlemen, going on foot and with their carpet-bags towards the
front, were addressed by a veteran with "Hullo! got any
lemons to sell?" "No, my friend, we belong to the army
of the Lord." Veteran, with deep scorn: "Oh, ye—es;
stragglers! stragglers!" I respect these Christian Commissioners, though they are somewhat silly often. Some of
them had come all the way from Wisconsin. I arrived in
camp somewhat after dark and was tenderly welcomed by
all, from the General down. Barstow and Humphreys
were highly pleased with their gifts. To-day a curious
thing occurred. While I was away, looking for a place for
the new camp, General Meade rode out with the Staff.
There came a conical shell, which shaved a patch of hair
off the tail of General Humphrey's horse, scraped the leg
of General Meade's boot, passed between General Ricketts
and Griffin who were standing within a foot of each other,
and buried itself in the ground, covering several officers
with sand and dirt. Four Generals just escaping by a turn
of the head, so to speak! I got this shell and shall send it
home as a great curiosity.

October 3, 1864, to-wit *Monday*

The night of my arrival, curiously enough, was the eve
of a grand movement.[1] I never miss, you see. Rosey drew
me aside with an air of mystery and told me that the whole
army was ordered to be packed and ready at four the next

[1] "The move now proposed consitsted of an advance both on the right
and the left flanks. On the right, towards Richmond, taking the north

morning, all prepared to march at a moment's notice.
Thursday, September 29. Headquarters contented itself
by getting up about half-past five, which was plenty early
enough, as turned out. We rode down to General Hancock's about 9.30. He was camped not far from us, or *had*
been, for now his tents were struck and packed, and there
lay the familiar forms of Lieutenant-Colonel Morgan and
Major Mitchell, on some boards, trying to make up for
their loss of sleep. The cheery Hancock was awake and
lively. We here were near the point of the railroad, which
excited General Meade's indignation by its exposure.
Now they have partly sunk it and partly built a bank, on
the enemy's side, so that it is covered from fire. Here we
got news that Ord and Birney had crossed the James, the
first near Dutch Gap, the other near Deep Bottom, and
advanced towards Richmond. Birney went up the New-
market road, took a line of works, and joined Ord, who
took a strong line, with a fort, on Chapin's farm, which is
before Chapin's bluff, which again is opposite Fort Dar-
ling. We got sixteen guns, including three of heavy calibre,
also some prisoners. General Ord was shot in the thick of
the leg, above the knee. There was another line, on the
crest beyond, which I do not think we attacked at all. We
went down then to the Jones house, where were Parke's
Headquarters, and talked with him. I saw there Charlie
Mills, now on his Staff. Finally, at 1.30 we got to Globe
Tavern where was the astute Warren. Everything was
"set," as he would say, for an advance by Griffin's and

---

side of the river; on the left towards the Boydton plank road and south-
side rail. The strategic object was two-fold: first, to effect threatening
lodgments as near as possible to these points, gaining whatever we
could by the way; and, secondly, to prevent Lee from reinforcing
Early." — Lyman's *Journal.*

Ayres's divisions, while Willcox's and Potter's divisions of the 9th Corps were massed at the Gurley house, ready to support. General Gregg made an advance west of Reams' station, and was heavily attacked about 5 P.M., but repulsed them. Their artillery blew up one of his caissons and we could see the cloud of smoke suddenly rise above the trees. This was all for that day in the way of fighting.

[Colonel Lyman wrote on October 4 the following paragraph:]

October 4, 1864

To-day I have ridden along the new lines with the General, no fighting but a picket skirmish. I see by the papers funny accounts of the operations on the left; "desperate fighting," when there was only some trifling skirmish; "our troops going to take Petersburg next morning," which indeed didn't enter their minds. Mr. Stanton (who, I will confess, beats everybody for inaccuracy) puts our forces on the south-side railroad! Even the Associated Press man, McGregor, makes such a hopeless muddle, that I despair of seeing any common observation in any one of them. However, here *is* your accurate account.

Friday, September 30. At 8.30 in the morning, the General, with the combative Humphreys and all the Staff, rode towards the left, stopping of course at the irresistible Hancock's. At noon we got to Globe Tavern, which is some six miles from our old Headquarters. Crawford's division still held the works on the Weldon road, while Warren, with two divisions, followed by Parke, with two divisions of the 9th Corps, had moved out to the west, and already we could hear the Rebel artillery shelling our advance. . . . At the Poplar Grove Church the Rebels began to throw shells, with a good deal of accuracy, into the road; for they had the range, though they could not see for the woods. Near here was a swampy run, where our skirmishers drove those of the enemy across, and the division then got over and kept ahead. General Meade, meantime, staid at the Globe Tavern, waiting for the movement to develop. He sent out an aide or two, to tell Warren he was there and to bring news of the progress. Warren sent in word that, having got across the run, he would soon see what could be done. At 12.45 we could hear pretty brisk musketry, which continued a short time and then ceased. Some time after, an aide came in from General Warren, with news that Griffin had captured a strong line and a redoubt, in handsome style. Not long after, the General rode to the front, where we arrived at 2.45. Most of the road was through a pleasant wood, chiefly oak. Passing the "church" (a little, old, wooden building that might seat forty persons), we turned to the right and came out on a large, open farm. On a roll of land, just ahead, was the Peeble house (pretty well riddled with bullets), and hence you looked over more open land ending in a fringe of wood. Perhaps 400 yards in front was the captured line and the redoubt: the former very strongly and handsomely made; the latter not quite finished inside, wanting still the platforms for the guns; otherwise it was done, with a ditch outside and an abattis. So far as I can learn, the occupying force was about equal to the attacking; but they did not make as good a fight as usual. The two assaulting brigades advanced very handsomely and rushed over the works. The enemy began at once to draw off their cannon, but the horses of one piece were shot, and it fell into our hands. The loss was very small in the assault, not over 100, which shows how much safer it is to run boldly on: the enemy get excited and fire high. I went into the redoubt. A Rebel artillery-man lay dead on the parapet, killed so instantly, by a shot through the head, that the expression of his face was unchanged. In front they were burying two or three of our men and a corporal was marking their names on a headboard, copying from letters found in their pockets. Parke was now ordered to form on the left of Warren (Ayres being on the right of Griffin), and it was understood that the whole line would then advance from its present position, near the Pegram house, and see if it were practicable to carry the second line, which lay perhaps three fourths of a mile beyond. As I understand it, General Meade's orders were not properly carried out; for Griffin did not form, so as to make an extension of Parke's line. At 5.30 we were sitting in the Peeble house, waiting for the development of the attack, when we heard very heavy musketry beyond the narrow belt of the woods that separated us from the Pegram farm; there was was cheering, too, and then more musketry, and naturally we supposed that Parke was assaulting. But presently there came from the woods a considerable number of stragglers, making their way to the rear; then came even a piece of a regiment, with its colors, and this halted inside the captured works. The musketry now drew plainly nearer, and things began to look ticklish. I watched anxiously a brigade of the 5th Corps that stood massed in the edge of the wood, beyond the redoubt. Suddenly it filed to the left, at a double-quick, the brigade colors trotting gaily at the head, then formed line and stood still. In another moment the men leveled their muskets, fired a heavy volley and charged into the wood. The musketry receded again; a battery went forward and added itself to the general crash, which was kept up till darkness had well set in;

while we sat and watched and listened, in comparative safety, just beside the captured redoubt. Potter had been taken in the flank by the Rebels charging, and had been driven back in confusion. Griffin had advanced and restored the retired line. And who rides hither so placidly? It is General Humphreys: he has stolen off and, bless his old soul, has been having a real nice time, right in the line of battle! "A pretty little fight," said he gingerly, "a pretty little fight. He! he! he!" Poor Potter! it wasn't his fault. Our extreme advance was driven back, but the day was a great success, with important strategic bearing.

October 2,[1] *1864*

Abou Ben Butler had quite a stampede last night. Having got so far away from home, he conceived that the whole southern host was massed to crush him, and communicated the same with much eloquence, by the instrumentality of the magnetic telegraph; whereat Major-General Humphreys, Chief-of-Staff, had the brutality to laugh! We made our usual peregrination to Globe Tavern, where we got about 10 o'clock. Here General Meade sent me to look for a new camp, first enquiring if I felt well enough for that arduous service, as he looks on me as a tender convalescent! It was a tedious business getting a spot; for the whole country was either occupied, or was very dirty from old camps. At quarter to eleven, as I was poking about, I heard firing to the left, pretty sharp for a few minutes, and supposed there might be quite a fight; but it died away, shortly, except the cannon, which were not frequent. I got to the front about one, and met Gen-

[1] Taking up the narrative of the events of this day. The letter was written on the 6th.

eral Meade at the Peeble house. He had been to the Pegram house and it was near there he had such a narrow escape from a shell. I told them that, had I been there, I should have been the odd man that would have been hit; for they all said that the Staff could not well have been arranged again so that there would have been room for a three-inch shot to pass without hitting somebody. The cause of the firing was, that the whole line advanced, except the right division, and established a front position at the Pegram house. . . .

The engineers were trotting round briskly, you may depend, ordering a redoubt here and a battery there, all intent on fencing in our new property. Luckily, the soil is very light and easy to dig, for our earthworks have now to be measured by miles. Not only must the front be protected, but the exposed flank and the rear. With what men we have, we do a great deal. Since we left Culpeper, I have not seen the troops look so healthy. If we could work a little more backbone into that 9th Corps, it would help wonderfully; but they started green and that is no way to ripen men. Many faults there have been also in the command. The men are in good spirits, I think, and well conditioned for the prosecution of the campaign. The evening of Sunday we went to our new camp, having lived nearly three months in the old one. It seemed quite like leaving home; for you get used to your little canvas house, pitched in a particular spot. The new camp is well enough placed, but in a region of evil savors. There is a timber bridge near by, and, every waggon that went over it, the General would jump and say, "By Jove, there is heavy musketry!" Gradually he learned the difference of sound and settled down quietly. The weather has been very warm the last day or two.

October 3, 1864

Yesterday afternoon arrived Lieutenant-Colonel Loring and Major L——. The former looks in better health and immediately set to work on the duties of his office, as Inspector-General, under the easy rule of General Parke, who succeeds the rule of Burnside the Fat. L——, always fancy, comes in much store clothes, a new shell jacket, double-breasted, and a pair of cerulean riding tights with a broad gold band, into which, according to report, he must be assisted by two strong men. Also his sabre newly burnished, and the names of the battles engraved on it, with other new and elegant touches. He was the young gentleman, you know, of whom the Reb paper said it was unworthy an honest officer to clasp the hand dipped in the gore of their brethren, even though cased in a glove of delicate kid!

This was a quiet day, wherein we lay still and made ourselves comfortable. The "comfortable" meant, with many of the officers, lying abed till the classic hour of Richard and Robin; for the General, these last days, has been getting up and riding out at fitful and uncertain hours. I think, when he feels anxious and responsible himself, that he likes to keep others a little on the stretch also. So he would give no orders overnight, but suddenly hop up in the morning and begin to call for breakfast, orderlies, aides, horses, etc. I am sharp, and, at the first sound he makes, I am up and speedily dressed; whereas the others get caught and have to leave suddenly. Biddle is the funniest. There he was, trotting along, the other morning, talking away, like a spinster who had lost her lap dog. "Well, I *do* think it is too bad! The General never tells anyone when he is going out, and here I am with no breakfast — no breakfast at all!" And here B. opened his fingers and disclosed *one boiled egg!* To think of a Major on the

General Staff riding after his General, with the reins in one hand and a boiled egg in the other!

October 4, 1864

The General rode along the whole front of the new line and carefully examined it, accompanied by his Staff and by the taciturn Roebling. R. is a character, a major and aide-de-camp and engineer, and factotum to General Warren. He is a son of the German engineer, Roebling, who built the celebrated suspension bridge over the Niagara River. He is a light-haired, blue-eyed man, with a countenance as if all the world were an empty show. He stoops a good deal, when riding has the stirrups so long that the tips of his toes can just touch them, and, as he wears no boots, the bottoms of his pantaloons are always torn and ragged. He goes poking about in the most dangerous places, looking for the position of the enemy, and always with an air of entire indifference. His conversation is curt and not garnished with polite turnings. "What's that redoubt doing there?" cries General Meade. "Don't know; didn't put it there," replies the laconic one. The Chief growled a little while at the earthwork, but, as that didn't move it, he rode onward. We passed at a clever time, for, a few minutes after, the Rebel skirmishers made a rush, and drove ours out of a house, and their bullets came over the corner of a field where we had been. Thereat our skirmishers made a counter-rush and drove theirs again away from the house, and our cannon fired and there was a small row generally. Some of our earthworks were really very workmanlike, handsomely sloped in front, and neatly built up with logs in the rear. It is really a handsome sight to get a view of half a mile of uniform parapet, like this, and see the men's shelter-tents neatly pitched in the pine woods, just in rear, while in front a broad stretch of timber has been "slashed," to give a good field of fire and break up any body of troops advancing to attack. It is quite interesting, too, to see a redoubt going up. The men work after the manner of bees, each at the duty assigned. The mass throw up earth; the engineer soldiers do the "revetting," that is, the interior facing of logs. The engineer sergeants run about with tapes and stakes, measuring busily; and the engineer officers look as wise as possible and superintend. . . .

October 6, 1864

Poor Biddle! I always begin his name with "poor." He was detailed to examine the trenches occupied by the 2d Corps, and see that the pickets were properly arranged. This part of the works is much exposed to fire in many parts, being near the enemy; so that you have to stoop a good deal of the way. What did Biddle do but ride out by a road to the works, on horseback! In consequence of which the whole skirmish line opened on him, and he returned, after his inspection, quite gasping with excitement. As he was not hit, it was very funny. If there is a wrong road, he's sure to take it. Lord Mahon (son of the Earl of Stanhope, who presided at that literary dinner I went to at London) and Captain Hayter, both of the Guards, were down here — Spoons rather, especially the nobil Lord.

October 7, 1864

There is a certain General Benham, who commands the engineers at City Point, and was up about laying out some works. Channing Clapp is on his Staff. You ought to see this "Ginral." He has the face and figure of Mr. Briggs and wears continually the expression of Mr. B. when his horse sat down at the band of music. When he had got through all the explanations, which were sufficient to have laid out a permanent work of the first class, the Meade rose with weariness, and eased his spirit by riding out and looking at my new camp-ground, and inspecting those everlasting redoubts. Now that the camp is arranged, the Meade is dubious about moving: that's like him! When we got to the extreme left, he thought he would go out and take a peek at the picket line. First there was a little bunch of cavalry. They were of a jocose turn; they had found an old pair of wheels whereon they had mounted a keg, making a very good cannon, which pointed, in a threatening manner, down the road. Its ensemble was completed by a figure, closely resembling those that defend cornfields, and which was keeping steady guard with a small pole. A hundred yards beyond was the picket reserve, behind a barricade. Then, beyond, a couple of hundred yards more, the sentries, each standing and looking sharply to the front. The one in the road was a half-breed Indian, though he looked more like a Neapolitan. He had that taciturnity that clings to the last drop of blood. "Are you a picket here?" asked the General. "Yes." "Is there anyone on your right and left?" "No." "You are an Indian, are you not?" "Part." All of which the red warrior delivered, without turning his gaze from the vista before him. Beyond this gentleman was a post of two cavalry videttes. From this place we could get a very good view of one of the Rebel lines of earthworks; but there seemed very few men behind it. I could only notice one or two. And so we rode back again past the perils of the keg cannon. General Warren has a short leave, and General Crawford commands the Corps, to the indignation, I presume, of old cocks like Griffin and Ayres; for C. was doctor in Fort Sumter, and thus got a star, and thus is an old brigadier, and thus ranks the regulars G. and A.

General Grant was on a flying visit to Washington to-day. I like to have him down here: first, he gives a general balance and steadiness; then, what is most important, he can order — just order what groceries he pleases, and no questions asked behind the counter!

October 10, 1864

General Humphreys deserted us to-night, for a brief leave — no, of course I mean he went early this morning, having taken his breakfast before us. The good General is fond of sitting awhile and talking after meals. He discourses sometimes on the art military and said it was "a godlike occupation"! "Ah," he said, "war is a very bad thing in the sequel, but before and during a battle it is a fine thing!" (*Note by T. L.* — I don't see it.) The Commander has been death on riding round lately on his jogtrotter, to inspect and mouse over works. He is mighty smart at such things, and if a line is run fifty feet out of position, he sees it like a flash. It is very creditable to our engineers, that, though a part of our works were laid out after dark, no corrections have been made in the general position. I had the honor to follow George about, as he rode round the country. In the camps, one sees the modes of punishment adopted. One ingenious Colonel had erected a horizontal bar, about a dozen feet from the ground, and supported at each end by a post. On this elevated perch he causes malefactors to sit all the day long, to their great discomfort and repentance. In the 9th Corps, they had put some barrels on the breastworks, and, on these high pedestals, made the men stand. They had run away in the fight and had great placards of "Coward" on them. A pretty severe punishment if they had any shame left. This is a grubby little letter, for my tent has been invaded by various silly, chattering, idle officers.

October 11, 1864

Did I tell you of the two spies, last night? There is a redoubt on our line which had no garrison except a sergeant and two or three men. Towards sunset appeared two officers, who attracted attention, the one by having three stars on his coat arranged somewhat like those of a Rebel colonel, the other by being much concealed by a high collar and a flap hat. They asked a number of questions about the work, which so increased the suspicion that word was sent to General Meade, who ordered a regiment at once to proceed to the spot, and the sergeant to be arrested for not seizing the persons. Who do you think they were? Why, Captain Craig and Rosencrantz, taking an evening stroll! Craig has no circulation and turns up his collar whenever the mercury falls below 70 degrees. Rosie has a Swedish coat with three stars indicating a captain; hence the alarm! This morning arrived a passing visitor, Major-General Doyle, commanding in Nova Scotia. He is a Pat and is favorable to us, for a wonder; gave up the Chesapeake to us, you know. He looks as funny as Punch; indeed just like Punch — a very red edition of him, with a stiff throttled aspect, caused by an apoplectic stock, five inches high. He was a jolly old buck and much amused by a lot of civilians, who also had come up from City Point. He called them T.G.'s, signifying "travelling gents," and, whenever we came on a redoubt, with a good abattis, he would say to the T.G's: "What do you think, hey? How would you like to attack *that*, hey?" Upon which the T.G's, whose pantaloons were somewhat up their legs, would look dubious. As he beheld the wonders of the land, he would exclaim: "Oh, bless my soul! why, you know, we have no idea of this at home. Oh, bless my soul!" On the road we met a Rebel deserter, who chanced to be an Irishman,

whereat the Doyle was highly delighted and asked him if
he got much whiskey the other side. To which Pat replied
with regret, that that strengthening beverage cost $30 a
quart in Secessia. After trotting him all over creation and
giving him a lunch, we put him on top of the Avery house,
and let him look at Rebs through a telescope; but I am sure
he saw nothing, though he exclaimed, "Bless my soul!" a
great deal.

October 14, 1864

How shall I vote? I don't know that I shall be given the
chance; but, if I am, I shall vote for the blue-blooded
Abraham. It was with a feeling of depression that I heard
the first rumors that the Dems had carried Pennsylvania,
Ohio, and Indiana; and when the truth came out, I felt
glad. This proves to me that I look on the Mac party with
misgiving. The soldiers' vote is an unexpected one; they
are said to show five to one for the Administration, which
tells me that they identify it with the support of the war;
for the troops in their private thoughts make the thrashing
of the Rebs a matter of pride, as well as of patriotism.

I venture to say that at no time during the war have the
Rebel papers talked so desperately; they speak of the next
month settling the question, and of arming the negroes.
If they do this latter, the slavery candle will burn at both
ends. I have no idea that the next month will settle it,
though, of course, there is a chance for important movements during the autumn, as at other seasons of good
weather. We must keep at them — that is the only way;
no let up, no armistice. They perfectly hate what we are
doing now, going a couple of miles and fortifying, then
going two more and fortifying again; then making a sudden rush, taking a position and a lot of cannon, and again
fortifying *that*. All these moves being a part of what we

may call a throttling plan. Their struggles, though often apparently successful, do them thus far no good. They flank us on the Weldon railroad and brush off 2000 prisoners: no use! we hold the road. They flank us again at the Pegram house, and capture 1000 more: no use; we hold the Pegram position and add it to former acquisitions. Then they flank Butler and get eight of his guns; but they have to go back, and Benjamin remains in what General Halleck terms a "threatening attitude." . . . Yesterday, Loring, whom I saw over at General Parke's Headquarters, was speaking of the quaint ways of talking among soldiers. Their lines are at peace out there, and the soldiers don't fire; notwithstanding, some sharpshooters, with telescopic rifles, are posted here and there. As he rode along, he met two of these gentry coming with faces as of men who had labored in a good cause, without profit. "Hullo!" said L., "did you get good places out in front?" "Yes, fust-rate places: but no shooting, no shooting!" General Meade rode to Parke's on account of a statement from a deserter, that the enemy would attack our left. "If they *do*," quoth the General, proud of his engineering skill, "if they do, they'll get into a nice hornet's nest." It is funny to see two engineers, like Meade and Parke, ride along works and pleasantly discuss them. In their enthusiasm, they always personify redoubts as far as to give them eyes, and speak of their "looking" in sundry directions, meaning thereby that they can fire there. "Here is a nice swallow-tail lunette," says Parke as if introducing a *pâté de foie gras;* "these two faces, you see, look down the two roads of approach, and here is a face that looks into that ravine: nothing could live in that ravine, nothing!" This last he emphasizes, as if the presence of life in the ravine aforesaid was a thing in the highest degree sinful, and this redoubt was virtuously bent on preserving the public morality. "Yes," replies Father Meade, "that seems all right; now you want to slash out, about 300 yards further, and get a good field of fire so that the enemy's sharpshooters can't annoy your gunners." The use of the word "annoy" is another military eccentricity. When half the men are killed or wounded by the enemy's riflemen, an officer will ride pleasantly in to the chief of artillery, and state that the battery is a good deal "annoyed" by sharpshooters, giving to the novice the impression that the sharpshooters complained of have been using provoking and impertinent language to the battery. To-day I was the sole companion of the General on his exercise ride, on which occasions, instead of riding behind him, I ride beside him, but keep as it were a little back of his horse's head. When we approach any body of troops, I fall entirely to the rear — strong on etiquette *we* are! For two or three days he has been in the best of humors and sits in the evening by the camp-fire before my tent, talking familiarly with all the aides; a rare thing with him. . . .

October 17, 1864

It is indeed not difficult to get material for a grumble, if one will but look about in this world. You see I can't be enthusiastic about such a government as Lincoln's, when I see, under my nose, the petty tyranny and persecution they practise against subordinate officers. Now there is Colonel Collis, a petty, scheming political officer; he sends letters to newspapers and despatches to Mr. Stanton about the enthusiasm for Lincoln in the army, etc., etc. Nothing is said to him; *that* is all right; he has an opinion, as he ought to have. *But* there is Lieutenant-Colonel McMahon, lately Adjutant-General of the 6th Corps, an excellent soldier, whose brother fell at the head of a charge at Cool Arbor, and who himself had been in all the battles: *he* is a McClellan man, as was natural in one of General Sedgwick's Staff. He talks very openly and strongly about his side, as he has a right to do. What is the consequence? He is, without any warning, mustered out of the service! That is to say, a soldier who don't agree with the Administration must be got rid of; it is nothing in his favor that he has exposed his life in twenty different actions. You would scarcely credit the number of such cases as this, cases of petty spite, fitting rather to a bad-tempered child than to a great and dignified cabinet minister. They suffer chances of victory to pass, rather than take voters from states. They send down three brevets of brigadiers, only one of which has been recommended by General Meade; and all three are men from the much dreaded and uncertain state of Pennsylvania. Don't think I am a grumbler; all this wickedness and smallness and selfishness is a part of humanity, and to be expected; but don't ask me to be enthusiastic for such people. There were a parcel of them down here to-day; bah! the sight of them is enough!

As we sat at breakfast there came a despatch saying that Hon. Secretary Stanton, with a long tail, might be looked for, per rail, very presently. It is an historical fact that General Meade expressed his gratification at this deep honor, in the following terms: "The devil! I shan't have time to smoke my cigar." Immediately I got on my double-barreled coat, with a sash withal, and a pair of white cotton gloves; but there was plenty of time to smoke a cigar, for they didn't get along for an hour or two, and then the greatest posse of large bugs! First, on horseback, Generals Grant, Meigs (Quartermaster-General), Barnard, Eaton (Commissary-General), Barnes (Surgeon-General), Fessen-

den (with a Palmer leg). Then, in ambulances, Fessenden's
papa, the Secretary of the Treasury, a sharp, keen, quiet-
looking man; Hon. Secretary Stanton, who looks like his
photographs, only more so; Hon. Sim. Draper and Mr.
Barney, twin New York politicians. The former had a very
large, long nose, and a very round and abrupt waistcoat,
so that he resembled a good-natured pelican, just after a
surfeit of sprats. General Meade received them with his
usual high ceremony. He walked out of his tent, with his
hands in his pockets, said, "Hullo, how are you?" and removed one hand, for the purpose of extending it to Grant,
who lighted down from his horse, put his hands in *his*
pockets, and sat down on a camp chair. The pelican came
up and bobbed at the Meade, as did his friend. We carted
them all to see Fort Wadsworth, where Rosencrantz
swears that Mr. Stanton, on being informed that there was
only a picket line between him and the enemy, pulled out
his watch and said they really must be going back! which
indeed they did. When the train started with its precious
freight of military and diplomatic jewels, General Meade
accompanied it, with Biddle, Mason and Rosencrantz.
It would appear that they encountered, at City Point,
Admiral Porter with Mrs. P. and another lady, who came,
on their return, as far as Hancock's Headquarters. The
hospitable H. did thereat cause supper to be set forth, for
it was now dark, and the General, with much talk and
good humor, took root there; for he is death to hold on,
when he gets talking and in company he likes. At nine
o'clock came the galliant Generale, with his aides, whereof
Rosencrantz and Mason were bursting to tell something
good; whereas Biddle had a foolish and deprecatory air.
It immediately was related, midst loud shouts, how, at
City Point Grant had given General Meade a bunch of

cigars to beguile the way of himself, Admiral Porter, and
some other guests going to the front. The Chief handed
them to Biddle, asking him to take charge of them for the
present. Now B. has few equals in the power of turning
things end for end; and so he at once and clearly understood that he [was] made a sort of almoner of tobacco, and
proceeded to distribute the cigars in the most liberal manner, to everybody who would either smoke or pocket them!
The Staff and bystanders asked no questions, but puffed
away at Grant's prime Havanas. Arrived at Hancock's
and supper done, the General said to Porter: "I think *now*
is the moment to enjoy those good cigars!" Out comes
"Shaw," the faithful servitor. "Oh, if you please, Major,
the Gen'ral sends his compliments, sir: and would like that
bunch of cigars, sir." Biddle immediately assumed the
attitude indicated in the accompanying drawing! and the
curtain dropped. . . .

October 27, 1864

I won't write at length till I get a decent chance. I
caught the greatest pelting with all sorts of artillery projectiles to-day, you ever saw, but no hurt therefrom. I
could not help being amused, despite the uncomfortable
situation, by the distinguished "queue" of gentlemen, behind a big oak! There was a civilian friend of Grant's, and
an aide-de-camp of General Barnard (a safe place to hold),
and sundry other personages, all trying to giggle and all
wishing themselves at City Point! As to yours truly, he
wasn't going to get behind trees, so long as old George G.
stood out in front and took it. "Ah!" said Rosey, with the
mild commendation of a master to a pupil: "oh! you did
remember what I did say. I have look at you, and you
did not doge!" It don't do to dodge with Hancock's Staff

about; they would never forgive you. At length says the General: "This is pretty hot: it will kill some of our horses." We came out on a big reconnaissance, which may be turned into a move or not, according to results. I rather fancy the enemy's line is too long to be turned by what troops we have to dispose.

October 28, 1864

Where do you think I am? Why, right by my dear chimney! All camped just where we were! I called our movement a grand reconnaissance in force; it would be more fair to call it an "attempt," whose success depended on the enemy not having certain advantages of position. But they were found *to have* these advantages, and so here we are back again, nobody having fought much but Hancock, who had a most mixed-up and really severe action, on the extreme left, in which the Rebels got rather the worst of it; but Grant ordered Hancock to withdraw during the night, or early in the morning, by which he was compelled to leave some of his wounded in a house on the field. Warren would fain fight it out there, for the name of the thing; but that would have been bad strategy, though I do confess that (albeit not a fire-eater) I would sooner have seen it through the next day, by reinforcing the left. This, however, is a mere matter of sentiment; certainly I don't set up *my* wisdom. As the Mine was to be termed an *ill*-conducted fizzle, so this attempt may be called a *well*-conducted fizzle. The Rebs are good engineers and had thrown up dirt scientifically, I can tell you. We got a pretty good handful of prisoners; I dare say 800 or so, and lost, including stragglers, I fancy as many, though they say we did not. The killed and wounded about equal; perhaps the enemy lost rather more than we; but the honors

of the left lie with the enemy, for we abandoned the field
in the night. To-day we marched back scientifically (we
are hard to beat on a retreat I can tell you). The 9th and
5th Corps withdrew by successive lines of battle, one behind the other, and alternately marching to the rear, the
front line passing through that behind. A very handsome
manœuvre; and the enemy, with relief, said good riddance.
I do not feel anywise down in spirits, for we gave blow for
blow, and came back when we saw the positions would not
admit of the plan proposed. There was no blunder or disaster, but it was soldierlike. The General kept a good temper throughout, so that it was quite pleasant all round.

[In writing some days later, Lyman thus describes the
country over which this engagement was fought:] The
tract marked "dense wood" on my map beggars description. It is a wood, with a tangled, thick undergrowth that
almost stops the passage of a man. The rest of the country
is also much wooded, but wherever you see a house, there
is a farm of greater or less size. [After a more detailed
description of the fighting, he continues:] Mott's men
give way, the Rebels yell and their batteries open a cross-
fire, and the enemy the other side of the run make as
if to attack the 2d division in front. But the valiant
Egán faces his line to the rear and charges the flank of
the Rebels rushing from the woods; they are in turn
smashed up and run back again, and a grand mixed-up
fight takes place, in the midst of which Hampton's cavalry falls furiously upon Gregg, who falls furiously upon
him, and won't budge an inch. The most singular things
happened here; for, as the woods were full of broken
bands of both parties, everybody captured everybody else,

and was in turn captured! A good many parties of Rebels, carrying our prisoners to the rear, took wrong direction and fell into the open maw of Crawford. Lieutenant Woolsey, General Williams's aide, in such an affair, showed a valor little to be looked for in so mild a youth. He was going along a wood road and came directly upon twelve Rebel cavalry; all cried "Halt! surrender!" to him, and two fired their carbines at him; Woolsey snapped his pistol at them, when one seized him round the waist; whereat W. hit him a back-handed blow on the bridge of his nose, put in the spurs, and actually broke away from the whole of them! When I asked him why he didn't give up, he replied in a simple manner: "Why, I thought my mother would be much distressed if I was taken prisoner, so I thought it would perhaps be better not to surrender." General Williams was in the greatest state of chuckle over his aide's conduct, and kept asking unwary persons: "Do you know how Mr. Woolsey escaped from guerillas?" and, being answered "No," would say: "Why, thus!" at the same time giving the unwary one a punch in the stomach, with his elbow. Then Major Roebling rode into a Rebel line of battle and had his orderly killed in his escape; Major Bingham was captured, but scared his guard so by telling him he was within our lines, that the man took to the bushes and left him. Lieutenant Dresser rode into the midst of a Rebel brigade, thinking they were prisoners. "Where is the Provost Guard?" asked D., who luckily had a gray rubber coat on. "Hain't got none." "What troops are these?" "Fourth Alabama." "Oh, all right," says Dresser, with presence of mind, and rides off, very slow at first, and *very* fast as soon as out of sight! The best feat was that of Major Mitchell (he always does perform feats). He rode into the woods, saw 200 Rebel infantry who had got lost, and were drawn up in line; came back, got a regiment, went out again and gobbled them all up. . . .

[The letter finishes with a lively description of some curious visitors to Headquarters.]

I had got safely to the Peeble house and was watching the columns as they marched in. I was still watching when suddenly there appeared a new comico-military procession: to wit, a venerable Brigadier, of a diluted visage, followed by two or three officers, *and* by two beings calculated to astonish the uninitiated. The first was simply gorgeous, not of dubious character, but evidently an officer of one of those theatrical French *indigène* regiments. He was tightly done up in a black jacket, all over which five hundred yards of fine black braid had gone into spasmodic convulsions; then black trousers with a wide scarlet stripe, morocco knee-boots, and a light blue képi. To complete his costume, a row of medals stretched from his central buttonhole to the point of his shoulder! The second stranger was utterly incomprehensible. He had on a pair of red, military trousers, a red fez with a blue tassel, and a *black dress-coat!* In order to mark this simple costume, he had, with admirable taste, suspended a small stiletto from the lower buttonhole of his waistcoat. The képi was presented as Chef-de-bataillon de Boissac; the fez as Vicomte de Montbarthe. Upon which, to myself within myself said I: strike out the "de" and Boissac is correct; strike out "Vicomte" and substitute "Corporal" and we shall be pretty near Mr. Fez. He was one of the vulgarest of vulgar Frenchmen, and a fool into the bargain. De Boissac was a type, and I fancy the real thing; a regular, chatty, boastful, conceited, bright little Gaul, who had been in China, the Crimea,

Italy, Japan, and Africa, and had worn the hair off his little bullet head with serving in various climes. "I was promoted to be Chef-de-bataillon," said képi (just as if I had asked anything about it), "for having planted the flag, alone, on the rampart! My comrades cry to me, 'Descend! descend!' I reply, 'Non! j'y suis!'" "And I," chimed in fez, "received the cross for repelling, with forty men, four hundred Austrians: wounded twice in the leg, I lay on the field and the Emperor himself pinned the cross on my breast!" I could not help thinking what a pity it was that the wounds had not been higher up, whereby the Emperor would have been saved the expense of a cross, and I the trouble of listening to his stories. These two brave bucks were travelling on their good looks, having got down, the Lord knows how, with no letters to anybody; yet they dined with General Meade, and passed the night in camp; passed another night at General Davies', and, the last I heard of them, were pledging General Hancock in the national whiskey! . . . I omitted to mention a third ornament to military life, a gent with eagles on his shoulders, who, on enquiry, turned out to be a brother militia man, and a great credit to the service, as he perilled his life daily in the state of New York, as General Sanford's aide (commanding state militia), and now was visiting the army to see that justice was done to deserving non-commissioned officers in the way of promotion. *Et puis?* — thought T. L. Yes, *that* was to electioneer the regiments in favor of the Republican candidate for governor, in case of whose election, he, Colonel D——, was to be Quartermaster-General! He had not only cheek enough for this, but enough to spare to come and stay all night at Headquarters, and take his meals there, without the breath of an invitation!

October 29, 1864

Having been seized with a powerful suspicion that the valiant Frenchmen would fain squat, to speak in Western phrase, at our Headquarters, I applied my entire mind to shipping them; for, as a travelled man, it was a matter of pride not to be put upon by a brace of such chaps. So I lay [in] wait till they said they would like to see General de Trobriand, and then I hastened to place them on horseback and give an orderly as a guide and tenderly shake hands with them, grieving I should not have the delight of seeing them again! There was a look about their intelligent countenances that seemed to say: "Ah, you are not so soft as we thought," as they bid me a tender adieu.

October 30, 1864

"Grant says I must write a report of the whole campaign," says the General, in the discontented voice of a schoolboy who has been set a long exercise. "I can't write a report of the whole campaign. I don't remember anything about some of it. I'm all mixed up about the Tolopotomoy and the Pamunkey and the what-do-you-call-'em Creek." Hence it came that I was requested to give him some extracts from my valuable archives, and I since have written a lot of notes for him, extending from May 4th to August 28th. He is very quick with his pen, is the General, and possesses a remarkable power of compressing a narrative and still making it clear and telling.

November 6, 1864

I was remarking in my last, a week ago to-day, that General Meade spoke of being obliged to write his report. Yes! as you say, it is a pity he can't have some signal success. The Shaws need not be against him on the negro-soldier question, for if he has a bias, it is towards and not against them, and indeed it would go to the heart of the best Bob[1] to see the punctilious way in which he returns their salutes. I can say with certainty that there is not a General in this army from whom the nigs might expect a judicious helping hand more than from Meade. As to his being slow, it may be so; but I can't see that Grant, on whom rests this entire campaign, is any faster; yet he is a man of unquestioned military talent. If you knew, as I do, the number of men killed and wounded in this campaign from the Potomac Army alone, you would think that a strong opposition from the enemy had as much as anything to do with the want of crowning success thus far. To show what sort of work we have been through: at the assault of June 3d, at Cool Arbor, we lost, in four or five hours, 6000 men, in killed and wounded only. That is a specimen. Even in our move to the left, the other day, which some would call a reconnaissance, and others heavy skirmishing, we had a list of killed and wounded of not less than 1200. In fact, we cannot stir without losing more men than would make a big battle in the West, and the Rebels, if we have any chance at them, lose as many.

Last Sunday, which I was just speaking of, was marked by the arrival of one Alden, a rather dull Captain of the Adjutant-General's Department, who was however a welcome bird to the army, as he brought a large number of brevets for many deserving officers. . . . To my surprise there did appear, or *re*appear, Major Duane, who has taken to visiting me as usual. He is better, but not well. To celebrate his arrival, and to retaliate for our rush into the Mine, the Rebs made a dash on our picket line, gobbled up some fifty stupids, who (being recruits) thought it

[1]Col. R. G. Shaw, who commanded the first negro regiment sent to the war.

was the relief coming round, and were then driven back; upon which, of course, every man fired off his musket a few times, to show how alert he was, the artillery threw all the shells whose fuses happened to be ready cut, and then all went to sleep again.

VII

ANOTHER WINTER

[SOME parts of the following letter make curious reading now. They are, however, interesting, not merely as an individual opinion at that time, but as reflecting the contemporary sentiments of a large body of intelligent men.]

HEADQUARTERS ARMY OF POTOMAC
November 10, 1864

They have been singularly niggardly to us about election returns; but we have reliable intelligence to-night that Lincoln is re-elected, the coarse, honest, good-natured, tolerably able man! It is very well as it is; for the certainty of pushing this war to its righteous end must now swallow up all other considerations. I am still more content that there has been a powerful opposition to him, even from respectable men, an opposition strong enough to carry several states. This will caution him, or better, his party, to proceed cautiously and to make no fanatical experiments, such as we too often have seen, but to proceed firmly, and according to rule and law. Lincoln has some men of ability about him — pre-eminent, Mr. Seward, whom the ultras have thrown over, but whom I think the strong man of the cabinet. Mr. Fessenden is said to be a very superior person, and his face is certainly a bright one, very. There is another important advantage in keeping on as we are: the machine is in running order and it is always a drawback to change midst a season of public trial. And again we have done with Lincoln what the Rebels have successfully done with their generals, let him learn from his own misfortunes

259

and mistakes; not a bad school for a sensible man. So you see, I am inclined to make the best of what I deem *is* the best, albeit not very good. . . .

Have you read an article from Fraser, in *Littell's*, called "Concord Transcendentalists." It is a singular production, rather entertaining some of it, and interspersed with the weakest, sweetened warm milk and water. The place where it says that Theodore Parker hid two slaves in his study, and nightly sat writing at the door of it, with *several* pistols and the *gun that had belonged to his grandfather*, would be a funny passage at any time, but, written so gravely in these war days, it is quite irresistible! If you see any number, in future, containing the tale of Tony Butler,[1] you might send it to me, though it is no great matter. I have read a number or two, the last chapter being in this very number where the Transcends flourish. Which reminds me of what a West Point professor said, according to the solemn Duane. He was hearing a recitation in philosophy, and would fain illustrate how the body might slowly change, yet the individual remain the same. "Now," said he, "if I have a knife and lose a blade and get it replaced, it is still the same knife." "Well," said a stupid-looking cadet, "and suppose you lose the other blades, one after another, and get them replaced, is it the same knife?" "Certainly," replied the Professor. "And suppose the handle should get rather ricketty and you replaced that?" "Yes, it would be the same knife." "Well, now," cried the stupid one, suddenly brightening up amazingly, "suppose you took the old handle, and found the old blades, and put 'em all together, what would you call *that*, hey?" Poor Major Duane! he can't do much but talk and

[1] By Charles James Lever, and then running in *Blackwood's Magazine*.

tell stories, for he is quite miserably yet and is not fit for duty, though he is improving. . . .

Last night, with a mild south wind, we had a singular example of the stopping of sound. Our batteries near the plank road, some three miles off, may usually be heard with perfect distinctness; not only the guns, but the explosion of the shells; and the replies of the Rebels also. At night we can see the shells going over, by the burning fuse, that looks like a flying spark. The deception is very singular in the dark, for, though the shell may be passing at the rate of 1200 feet a second, in the distance the fuse seems to go slowly and in a stately curve. This is because 1200 feet looks very small, three miles away, and the eye gets an idea of rapidity by the space travelled over in a given time. Well, last night, they opened a somewhat brisk discharge of mortar shells from both sides; but though we could see them go through the sky and burst below, not the faintest sound reached the ear! At other times these same guns will sound quite close to us. I could cite many such contrasts.

I rode forth with good Duke Humphrey, to see the dress-parade in the 9th Corps. That and the 5th, not being in the immediate presence of the enemy, have a good chance for drill. The 9th Corps, in particular, have gone into the evolutions to an alarming extent, an exercise which, like Wistar's balsam of wild cherry, can't do harm and may do good. Around General Parke's Headquarters there is a chronic beating of drums and fifing of fifes and playing of bands. We sat some time and watched the drilling; it was quite fun to see them double-quicking here, and marching there, and turning up in unexpected positions. At last the gallant Colonel McLaughlen, after many intricate manœuvres, charged and took a sutler's tent, and the brigade was then marched to its quarters. As we returned, there was a nig brigade, having its dress parade in fine style. They looked extremely well and marched in good style. The band was a great feature. There was a man with the bass drum (the same I believe that so amused De Chanal) who felt a *ruat-coelum-fiat-big-drum* sentiment in his deepest heart! No man ever felt more that the success of great things lay in the whacking of that sheepskin with vigor and precision! *Te-de-bung, de-de-bung, bung, bung!* could be heard, far and near. . . . The nigs are getting quite brisk at their evolutions. If their intellects don't work, the officers occasionally refresh them by applying the flats of their swords to their skins. There was a Swede here, who had passed General Casey's board for a negro commission. He was greatly enraged by a remark of the distinguished Casey, who asked him what Gustavus Adolphus did, meaning what great improvements he introduced in the art of war. To which the furriner replied: "He was commander-in-chief of the Swedish army." "Oh, pooh!" said Casey, "that's nothing!" Which the Swede interpreted to mean that Gustavus was small potatoes, or that the Swedish army was so. Really, most foreign officers among us are but scapegraces from abroad. The other day the Belgian Minister Sanford sent a letter asking for promotion for private Guatineau, whose pa had rendered us great service by writing in the French press. The matter being referred to his commander, the reply was: "This man *deserted to the enemy* from the picket line."

November 11, 1864

The McClellan procession might have spared their tapers, as he has gone up, poor Mac, a victim to his friends! His has been a career *manqué*, and a hard time he has had,

and low he has fallen.   The men who stood, as green soldiers, with him in front of Yorktown, where are they?
Many thousands lie in the barren land of the Peninsula
and the valley of Virginia; thousands more in the highlands
of Maryland and Pennsylvania and in the valley of the
Shenandoah. Many are mustered out — their time ex-
pired — or sick, or crippled. The small remnant are
sifted, like fine gold, through this army, non-commissioned
officers, or even full officers. What an experience it is for
an infantry soldier! To have carried a musket, blanket,
and haversack to the Peninsula, and to the gates of Richmond, then back again to the second Bull Run; up to
Antietam in Maryland; down again to Fredericksburg;
after the enemy again to the Rappahannock; and at last,
the great campaign, like all others concentrated in six
months, from the Rapid Ann to Petersburg! All this alone
on foot, in three long years, at all seasons and all hours,
in every kind of weather, carrying always a heavy load,
and expecting to fight at any moment; seeing so many men
shot in each fight — the great regiment dwindling to a
battalion — the battalion to a company — the company
to a platoon. Then the new men coming down; they shot
off also. Till at last the infantry-man, who left Boston
thinking he was going straight to Richmond, *via* Washington, sits down before Petersburg and patiently makes his
daily pot of coffee, a callous old soldier, who has seen too
many horrors to mind either good or bad. It is a limited
view of a great war, but, for that very reason, full of detail
and interest.

Of course we might have known that this pack of political "commissioners" could not get down here without a
shindy of some sort. The point they brought up was
fraudulent votes. A long-haired personage, fat and vulgar-

looking, one of that class that invariably have objection-able finger-nails, came puffing over to General Meade's tent, with all the air of a boy who had discovered a mare's nest. He introduced himself as a Mr. Somebody from Philadelphia, and proceeded to gasp out that a gentleman had been told by an officer, that he had heard from some-body else that a Democratic Commissioner had been distributing votes, professedly Republican, but with names misspelled so as to be worthless. "I don't see any proof," said the laconic Meade. "Give me proof, and I'll arrest him." And off puffed Mr. Somebody to get proof, evidently thinking the Commanding General must be a Copperhead not to jump at the chance of arresting a Democrat. The result was that a Staff officer was sent, and investigation held, and telegraphs dispatched here and there, while the Somebody puffed about, like a porpoise in shallow water! Finally, four or five people were arrested to answer charges. This seemed to please Stanton mightily, who telegraphed to put 'em in *close* arrest; and, next morning, lo! a lieutenant-colonel sent, with a guard of infantry, by a special boat from Washington, to conduct these male-factors to the capital — very much like personages, con-victed of high treason, being conveyed to the Tower. Were I a lieutenant-colonel, I should feel cheap to be ordered to convey a parcel of scrubby politicians under arrest! But that is the work that Washington soldiers may expect to spend their lives in. General Meade, I fancy, looked with high contempt on the two factions. "That Somebody only does it," he said, "to appear efficient and get an office. As to X——, he said he thought it a trying thing for a gentleman to be under close arrest; and I wanted to tell him it wasn't so disgraceful as to have been drunk every night, which was his case!" That's the last I have heard of the culprits, who, with their accusers, have all cleared out, like a flock of crows, and we are once again left to our well-loved ragamuffins, in dirty blouses and spotted sky-blue trousers.

The day was further marked by an *émeute* in the culinary department. I would have you to know that we have had a nigger boy, to wait on table, an extraordinary youth, of muscular proportions and of an aspect between a drill sergeant, an undertaker and a clergyman — solemn, military and mildly religious. It would, however, appear, that beneath this serious and very black exterior worked a turbulent soul. The diminutive Monsieur Mercier, our chef, had repeatedly informed me that "le petit" (the unbleached brother is about a head taller than Mercier) was extremely indolent and had a marked antipathy to washing dishes — an observation which interested me little, as *my* observation went to show that the washing of dishes by camp-followers tended rather to dirty than to cleanse the platter, and that the manifest destiny of the plate military was to grow dirtier and dirtier, till it at last got broken. However, Anderson was reproved for not washing his crockery, and replied with rude words. On being reproved again, he proposed to smite Mercier, remarking, he "would as soon knock down a white man as a nigger."

At this juncture the majestic Biddle interfered and endeavored to awe the crowd; but the crowd would not be awed, so Biddle put Anderson at the pleasant occupation of walking post with a log on his shoulder. Upon being liberated from this penalty, he charged upon Mercier, giving him the dire alternative of "Pay me mer wages, or *I'll smash yer crockery!*" This being disorderly, I allowed him to cool his passions till next morning in the guard-house, when he was paid off.

November 12, 1864

We have the usual play of rumor about cabinets — everybody seems inclined to heave out Stanton: some to heave him *up* to the Supreme Court — some to heave him *down* to unknown depths of nothingness. Many would fain fancy Ben Butler in the chair of War, where he would be certain to make things spin either for good or for bad. How he will get on, across the James, I know not. He lost a strong man in Ord, wounded; and in Birney, dead, also: Birney was one who had many enemies, but, in my belief, we had few officers who could command 10,000 men as well as he. He was a pale, Puritanical figure, with a demeanor of unmovable coldness; only he would smile politely when you spoke to him. He was spare in person, with a thin face, light-blue eye, and sandy hair. As a General he took very good care of his Staff and saw they got due promotion. He was a man, too, who looked out for his own interests sharply and knew the mainsprings of military advancement. His unpopularity among some persons arose partly from his promotion, which, however, he deserved; and partly from his cold covert manner. I always felt safe when he had the division; it was always well put in and safely handled. The longer I am in the army, the more I see that great bodies of men take their whole tone from a few leaders, or even from one. I climbed on a horse and took a ride to visit Captain Sleeper, whose camp I easily recognized by its neat appearance. He always has things in a trig state about him. His own domicile was a small log cabin, with a neat brick chimney, very smooth-looking, but made in truth of only odd bits of brick, picked up at random and carefully fitted by a skilful Yank. The chimney-piece was of black walnut, made indeed from the leaf of an old table, discovered in the neighborhood. As to his tongs, a private, of prospective views, picked them up sometime last summer, and had carried them, ever since, in waggon! For arras he had artillery horse-blankets. The Sleeper is now more content, having his battery full, new sergeants appointed, and a prospect of officers. His only grief is that with three years' service and many battles he is only a captain. You see Massachusetts has not her batteries in a regiment and can't have field officers. So Sleeper's only hope is a brevet.

November 13, 1864

We had a Lieutenant-Colonel C——, a Britisher, up for a visit; he is commander of the forces in that tropical climate of New Brunswick. In aspect Colonel C—— was not striking; he had done injustice to what good looks he had by a singularly shapeless suit of city clothing, which I judge must have been purchased ready made from a village tailor in New Brunswick. He had a sort of soft cloth hat, an overcoat of a grey-rhubarb tint and trousers which once might have had a pure color, but seemed to have become doubtful by hanging in the sun outside a shop. I don't think the gallant Lieutenant-Colonel was much interested in matters military. Perhaps he had read out, perhaps he had no natural taste that way, or perhaps he felt cold and uncomfortable. At any rate he looked bored, and his only military remark did not indicate deep reflection. "This," said I, "is what we call a corduroy road." "Oh! ah! Indeed; yes, well, it's very well *now*, you know, but what will you do when it *comes wet weather?* " I was too much overcome at this putting the cart before the horse, to inform him that the corduroy was built for no other purpose *than* for wet weather. After this I confined myself to considerations of the state of health of the Hon. Mr. Yorke (he who came back with us from Liverpool). He is under the command of the Colonel, it would appear, and afforded an innocent topic of conversation. Since then two other English officers have been entrusted to the fatherly care of Rosencrantz, and diligently shown round. When they got near the end, they said: "Now we are much pleased to find you are a foreigner, because we can frankly ask you, what you consider the general feeling towards the English in this country." To which Rosie (who don't like to miss a chance) replied: "Vell, I can tell you that, so far as I have observed, some Americans do just care nothing about you, and many others do say, that, when this war is over, they will *im*mediately kick you very soon out from Canada!" When the horrified Bulls asked: "Aw, aw, aw; but why, *why?*" Rosie replied in the following highly explanatory style: "Be-cause they say you have made for the Rebs very many bullets."

General Gibbon dined with us and was largely impressed by our having oysters on the shell, which he pitched into with the fervor of a Baltimorean long separated from his favorites. Gibbon is by birth a Pennsylvanian, but lived, since boyhood, in North Carolina. When the Rebellion broke out, two of his brothers went into the Rebel service, but he remained loyal. One of his sisters was in the South but could not escape, and it was only the other day that they allowed her to come on board the flag-of-truce boat and come down the river to our lines, where her brother met her and took her North. He had sent word to his younger brother to meet him on the same occasion, but the young gentleman sent word, "It would not be agreeable"; which shows they are pretty bitter, some of them. Gibbon has an Inspector named Summerhayes, who is of the 20th Massachusetts, and who has got so used to being

FREDERICK ROSENCRANTZ
Aide-de-Camp

shot at, that he seems not to be able to do without it, and so gallops along the picket line to rouse the foe to pop at him. Which reminds me of what Grant said (either by accident or on purpose). He had come out, with a great crowd of civilians, to ride round the lines. Someone proposed to go out and visit the pickets. "No," said Grant, innocently, "no; if I take a crowd of civilians, the enemy may fire and some of the soldiers might get hurt!"

November 14, 1864

If doctors and quartermasters had not quarrelled, *I* should not have come unto sorrow; thus, a hospital was placed nigh to a place on the railroad where the quartermasters would fain have a platform. "Move your tents," said the quartermasters. "We won't," said the doctors. "You shall," retorted the quartermasters. "We shan't," reiterated the M.D's. The strife waxed hot. Inspectors were called: they inspected much and shook their heads; that being a negative conclusion, the Major-General Commanding the Army of the Potomac was appealed to, and he rode out to enter a fiat. In riding out he took me, and *I* took a chill. So confusion to all doctors and quartermasters! But the former shall be forced to cure me and the latter to make me comfortable in mine house. There came over, for a visit, the Colonel Russell, of the funny turn, who commands now a brigade of negro troops. He has always something funny to relate of their manners and customs. It would appear that his nigs were once relieved by troops of the 2d Corps, and, as both parties had just been paid off, the ivory and the ebony sat down to play poker, wherein the ebony was rapidly getting the better of their opponents. The enemy meanwhile began to fire shells over the woods, but the players were too interested to leave off. At last one cute Yankee, who, despite his cuteness, had been entirely cleaned out, wandered off and found an empty shell, which he carefully filled with damp gunpowder, adding a paper fuse. Approaching the group that seemed to have most money on the board, he lighted the innocent combustible, screamed "Look out!" and threw it into the midst of them, following up himself, to secure the greenbacks left by the fugitives. Russell said when the recruits first come down they get into all sorts of snarls. As, for example, two of them found what they call "one er dese ere mortisses," by which they would say mortar shell. "Hullo, dar's er mortiss: s'pose dat ar'll 'splode?" "'Splode! 'corse it'll 'splode." "No, it wun't; how's gwine to 'splode, when's been shot out uv er cannon?" "Bet yer five dollars 'll 'splode." "Bet yer it wun't!" The next thing the Colonel knew was a tremendous report, and two or three bits of iron flying through his tent. He rushed forth and collared a handful of the darks, and demanded immediate explanation. Whereunto one replied, with the utmost simplicity: "Didn't mean nuphin, Kernul; all fault er dat ar stupid nigger — said er mortiss wouldn't 'splode!" This day was further remarkable by the erection of a stately flagstaff, which seemed to imply that General Williams thought we should stay some time; but I think it will doubtless make us move at once; just as building log huts has a similar effect.

November 16, 1864

They have made Sheridan a Major-General in the Regular Army. I think he deserves it for that remarkable battle of Cedar Creek. Those of Opequon and of Fisher's Hill were joyous occasions; but he *ought* to have won those, because his forces were probably at least as two to one, and his cavalry immeasurably superior; but this last battle was the thing that brought out his high merit. The language of the order is not to be commended, as it makes Sheridan a cat's-paw to give McClellan an insulting hit. It is hard on Meade, and I think he feels it; during a long campaign, in many respects unprecedented in military history for its difficulties and its grandeur, he has handled an army, which has at times considerably exceeded 100,-000 men; and that too under circumstances very trying to a man who has had a chief command; that is to say, obliged to take the orders and tactics of a superior, but made responsible for all the trying and difficult performance, which indeed is more than one half the game of war. I undertake to say that his handling of his troops, when a mistake would be the destruction of the entire plan, has been a wonder: without exaggeration, a wonder. His movements and those of Lee are only to be compared to two exquisite swordsmen, each perfectly instructed, and never erring a hair in attack or in defence. Of course, it is idle to tell such facts to people at large; they don't understand, or care, or believe anything about it. It is true, the army has played what seems its destined rôle, to kill and to be killed without decisive actions, until both sides pause from mere exhaustion; but do people reflect what a tremendous effect all this has on the Rebels? that by wearing ourselves, we have worn *them* down, until they are turning every teamster into the ranks and (of all things) are talking of arming the negroes. Suppose there had been no army capable of clinging thus for months in a death-grapple, and still clinging and meaning to cling; what would have become of Sherman and his great work?[1] The record of General Meade is a remarkably clear one. He

[1] Sherman was just leaving Atlanta in his march to the sea.

has risen from a brigadier of volunteers to all the higher commands, by hard fighting and an experience that dates from the first days of McClellan. He has done better with the Army of the Potomac than McClellan, Pope, Burnside, or Hooker; and — I will add boldly and without disparagement to the Lieutenant-General — better than Grant! and you would agree with me did you know what power and what men Grant has had to command. Meade's great virtue is, that he knows when to fight, and when *not* to fight. Taking up an army on the march, he fought and won the greatest battle of this war — Gettysburg — 100,-000 men against 110,000 — a battle that saved Baltimore, Washington, and Philadelphia, and nobody knows what besides. He wouldn't fight (assault) Lee at Williamsport, and immediately he was "timid, timid, timid!" Now look here: *we* assaulted at Spotsylvania, at Cool Arbor, at Petersburg, and were repulsed with perfect slaughter; *after* all that, if Lee had assaulted *us* in position what would, what would have become of him? Why, we would have used him up so, that he wouldn't have known himself. Just turn this about and apply it to Gettysburg and reflect how "the people" are frequently semi-idiotic! He followed Lee to the Rappahannock and got orders to stop. In September he was to move and attack Lee on the Rapid Ann; the day before this move they took 20,000 men from him and sent West: it couldn't be done to Grant. Then Lee marched on Centreville; Meade beat him and got there first; Lee wouldn't fight and retreated (he *also* knows when not to fight). It was in just such a move that Pope was smashed all to pieces and driven into Washington. Then Meade forced the Rappahannock, and drove Lee in haste over the Rapid Ann. The Mine Run expedition followed; we did not go fast enough — that was unfortunate; but it would have been more unfortunate to have left 10,000 men on the slopes there. If Meade had lacked the great moral courage to say "retreat," after having been called "timid" by the papers, and having been hounded on by Halleck and Stanton to "do something," he would not only have got a disastrous defeat, but would have destroyed the plan of re-enlistments by which we obtained the very backbone of our army for this campaign. His "timidity" lies in this, that he will not try to build a house without enough of tools and timber. Lately, they have turned round, 180 degrees, and now call him "butcher"; but that does just as well — blow hot, blow cold. This is a fair statement. I don't say he is Napoleon, Cæsar and Alexander in one; only that he can handle 100,-000 men and do it easy — a rare gift! Also, as Sherman and Sheridan, commanding the two other great armies, have been made regular Major-Generals, he too, who is doing his part, and has fought more than both of them put together, ought to have equal rank.[1] General Grant, as far as I can hear, thinks everything of General Meade, and it is said will have him promoted like the others. I believe it will turn out that Sherman is our first military genius, while Sheridan is most remarkable as a "field fighter," when the battle is actually engaged. Bless my soul! quelle lecture on my commanding General! Never mind, variety is the spice of life.

November 18, 1864

Warm it is this morning — too much so; I would prefer it frosty, but remember the farmer whom Jupiter allowed to regulate the weather for his own farm, and who made

[1] Meade was then a Major-General of Volunteers.

19

very poor crops in consequence. As Albert[1] came last night, I honorably discharged the ebony John this morning, giving him a character, an antique pair of trousers and a dollar or two extra wages, whereat John showed his ivory, but still remarked, standing on one leg: "Er ud like er pass." "What do you want a pass for?" asked I, in that fatherly voice that should always be used to a very black nig. "Go a Washington." "If you go to Washington they'll draft you, if you don't look out." "Oh," said John, with the grave air of a man of mundane experience, "dem fellers what ain't *travelled* none, dey gets picked up: but I's travelled a right smart lot!" Whereupon the traveller departed. It should be stated that his travels consist in having run away from his master, near Madison Court House, and in having since followed the army on the back of a spare horse. We were favored with a batch of two J. Bulls (lately they have taken to hunting about here, in couples and singly). These were a certain legation person, Kirkpatrick, and an extraordinary creature named H——, who is said to have been once in the British army and to be *now* in Oxford — rather a turning about. He had a sort of womanish voice and a manner of sweet sap; his principal observations were: "Ao, inde—ed"; "Ao, thank you"; and "Ao, I wish you a good morning." He had an unaccountable mania for getting shot through the head, and insisted on going to Fort Hell, and staring through embrasures; from which I judge he was more idiotic than he seemed. He was also, it would appear, very fond of fresh air, while his companion (who also disagreed with him on the shooting-through-the-head matter) rather liked a door shut. They were put in a log cabin to sleep, and H——

[1] The servant, whom he had brought from Brookline, who had been absent on sick leave.

secretly opened the door at night; whereupon it came to
rain and blow, and the Bulls awaked in the morning to
behold their shoes and stockings sailing about the room!
Really, General Hunt, to whom these creatures are usually billetted, ought to get board free from his many
former guests for the rest of his life.

In the evening we had a charge on the enemy under a
new form, or rather a very old one, for it was after the
fashion of Samson's foxes. A number of beef cattle, in a
pen near Yellow Tavern, were seized, in the night, with
one of those panics for which oxen are noted, and to which
the name "stampede" was originally applied. They burst
out of the enclosure and a body of them, forty strong,
went, at full gallop, up the Halifax road, towards Petersburg! What our pickets did does not appear; one thing
they did *not* do — stop the fugitive beef. On they went in
wild career through the dark, with no little clatter, we may
be sure. The Rebel videttes discharged their pieces and
fled; the picket sentries opened fire; the reserves advanced
in support, and fired too; heedless of killed and wounded,
the oxen went slap through the whole of them; and, the
last that was heard from that drove was the distant crash
of a volley of musketry from the enemy's breastworks!
When the gray morn lifted, the first sight that greeted our
disgusted pickets was a squad of grey-backs comfortably
cutting savory steaks from a fat beef, the quarry of their
bow and their spear! The evening brought us warm rain;
also, as toads fall in a shower, one military Englishman,
and one civilian Blue-nose. The Briton was a Major
Smyth, of the Royal Artillery — a really modest, gentlemanly man, with a red face, hooked nose, and that sure
mark of greatness, a bald head. The Blue-nose was modest also (the only one I ever saw) and was of the class of

well-to-do, honorable Common-Councilmen; his name was Lunn, suggestive of "Sally Lunns."

November 19, 1864

The rain continued, being cold, by way of variety, and from the northeast; whereby it happened that we got no mail. *Be*-cause what? as small Co says. Well, because the captain of that gallant ship went and ran her aground somewhere on a shoal which they told me the name of — whereat I was no wiser. The result to us was disastrous; when I say to *us*, I mean our mess; for the chef, Mercier, (no relation of French minister) was on board with many good eatables for us, but in the confusion, the knavish soldiery, who were on board as passengers, did break the boxes and did eat much and destroy and waste more. "Aussi," said little Mercier, "they broke many bottles; but," he continued, with the air of a good man, whom a higher power had protected, "that made no difference, for *they belonged to other people!*" In the night we were favored with quite a disturbance. The officer of the guard, who had possibly been storing his mind from some mediæval book on the ordering of warders in a walled town, suddenly conceived an idea that it was proper for the sentries to call the hours. So we were waked from the *prima quies* by loud nasal and otherwise discordant cries of: "Post number eight! Half-past twelve! All's well!" etc., etc. The factionaries evidently considered it a good joke, and, as they had to keep awake, determined no one else should sleep; and so roared often and loud. Some of the officers, hastily roused, fancied the camp was on fire; others conceived the sentinels were inebriated; others that Mosby was in the camp; and others again, like myself, didn't think anything about it, but growled and dropped off again to sleep. "What was that howling?" said the testy General, at breakfast. "Yes, what did the confounded fools mean?" added the pacific Humphreys. But the most indignant personage was Rosencrantz. "I do svear!" he exclaimed, "this whole night have I not a single vink slept. It is not enough that those sentry fellows should tell us vat time it is, but they must also be screaming to me a long speech besides! Vat do *I* care vat time it is; and if all is vell, vy can they not keep it to themselves, and not be howling it in my ears and vaking me up? This is the most fool tings I have seen!" You may be sure that was the first and last of the warders.

November 22, 1864

As it was fine, after three days' rain, General Humphreys bestirred himself to give rational entertainment to the two Englanders; and so General Meade ordered a couple of brigades of cavalry turned out and a horse-battery. We first rode along the rear line and went into a fort there. It made quite a cortège, for, besides the Generals and their officers and orderlies, there followed Mr. Lunn in a four-horse spring waggon, with General Hunt to bear him company; for Lunn had received the horseback proposition with mild horror. So he followed in a waggon, much as Mr. Pickwick was wheeled after the shooting party, when he finally turned up in the pound. In the fort was a company of soldiers that you might know beforehand were Germans, so dirty and especially so grimy — they have a great facility for looking grimy do the Germans. It was funny to see the different chaps among them: one, evidently a *ci-devant* Prussian soldier, was seized with rigidity in all his muscles on beholding a live brace of Generals. There was another who was an unmistakable student; he had a moustache, a poetically fierce air, a cap with the brim turned up, and a pair of spectacles. There he stood, a most out-of-place individual, with our uniform on, watching anxiously the progress of a pot, boiling on a fire. The cavalry looked what I have learned to consider as very well; that is, the men looked healthy, the horses in good flesh, and the arms and equipments in proper repair. To a European they must have been fearful; very likely so to Major Smyth, though he was silently polite — no polish, horses rough and woolly, and of all sizes and colors; men not sized at all, with all kinds of beards and every known species of hat; but as I know that men do not fight with their hats and beards, I was satisfied to see evidences of good discipline. Thereafter we called on General Gregg, where I had a treat in form of some Newton pippins, of which excellent apple there was a barrel on hand.

November 24, 1864

This was Thanksgiving, which is sloppy and snowy and haily with us, as a general thing, but here was sunny and pleasant. All day the waggons were distributing turkeys to the patriots, of whom I believe all got some, sooner or later. Flint, having seen that his squadron had their poultry, called a sergeant and asked him how much it made to each man. "Well," said the sergeant, "it makes about a quarter of a turkey, a piece of pie, and four apples." "Oh!" said Flint, "quite a meal." "Yes," said the sergeant dubiously, "yes, a *small* meal; I could eat half a turkey myself!" The turkeys were ready cooked and were a great treat to our ragamuffins. I took a ride in some woody spots within the lines, and it was pleasant, in the warm hollows, to hear the wee birds twittering and warbling, visitors from a northern climate, that have left you some weeks ago. Then there was a pileated woodpecker (not known with us), a great fowl, as big as a crow; black, with white feathers in his wings, an ivory beak and a gay scarlet cockade. He thought himself of great account, and pompously hopped up and round the trunks of trees, making a loud, chattering noise, which quite drowned the wee birds, like a roaring man in a choir. The pompous old thing was very much scared when I approached, and flew away, but soon began his noise on a distant tree.

November 27, 1864

I think I will occupy the remainder of this letter with an account of our picnic yesterday to Butlerdom. The day was further remarkable for the departure of my dear General Humphreys to take command of the 2d Army Corps. For Hancock has got a leave of absence, and will doubtless be put to recruiting fresh troops, while it is hoped that the President will permanently assign Humphreys to this Corps. He is in high glee at going, and will be in despair if a big fight is not got up for his special benefit. He was a great favorite and was escorted by some fifteen mounted officers of the Staff to his new quarters, at which compliment I think he was gratified. I regretted not to be with him, but had to go with the General, who started by the mail train, at 8 A.M., to be early at Grant's Headquarters, whence they were to start. We took our horses on a freight car. In the train we found Generals Warren and Crawford, who were invited to be of the party. Arrived at City Point, we discovered that the Lieutenant-General was still in bed, whereat Meade did laugh, but the three stars soon appeared and went to breakfast. After which meal, our horses were put on the boat and we put ourselves on, and off we started. The party was a big one. There were Generals Grant, Meade, Warren, Crawford and Ingalls, and several Staff officers. There were then the bourgeois: to wit, a great many "Turkeys" (gentlemen who had come down to distribute those Thanksgiving fowls); two men who wanted to sell a steamer; one Senator, viz., Nesmith of Oregon, and one political blackguard named H——, whose special business was to praise a certain Greek fire, of which more anon. This fellow's name is usually prefixed by "Pet." He has wild hair and beard and a face showing a certain ability; his distinguishing mark, I am told, is the absence of any sort of morality or principle. With him was his son, a small and old boy, of whom they said that, if papa could not get the best at a game of poker, son would come in and assist. Senator Nesmith is a child of the people, and was prepared for his congressional duties by a residence of twenty-five years among the Indians. When he first got to Washington, he had never before seen a railroad, a telegraph, or a gas-light. "Senator Fessenden asked me what I thought of things. 'Well,' says I, 'when I first came along I was full of the dignity of the position to which I had been elected; but *now* all I want to know is, who in thunder ever sent you fellers here!'" He has plenty of brains, this same, but is a very coarse man. The "Turkeys" were of various sorts: several of them were Club men, *e.g.*, Mr. Benson, a gentleman who seemed a middle-aged beau, with much politeness and no particular brains. He kept bowing and smiling and backing into persons, and offering his chair to everyone, from orderlies up to General Grant. He requested to know whether in my opinion he could be properly considered as having been "under fire; because," said he, "I stood on the Avery house and could see the shells explode in the air, you know!" All this motley crowd started at once for Deep

Bottom; nor should I omit to say that we had also on board a Secesh bishop — Leigh of Georgia — who was going by flag of truce to Richmond. He had remained in Atlanta, and Sherman had told him if he wished to get back, he must go via Richmond. From him they got a good deal of entertaining conversation. His opinion of Sherman was very high and complimentary. " The old Book tells us," he said, "that the race may not be to the swift, nor the battle to the strong, and we feel that Providence will not desert our righteous cause." "Yes," said General Meade, "but then *we* feel that Providence will not desert *our* cause; now how are you going to settle that question?" Whereat they both laughed. The bishop was a scholastic, quiet-looking man, and no great fire-eater, I fancy. The boat made fast at Aiken's landing, halfway between Deep Bottom and Dutch Gap. A Staff officer was there to receive us and conduct us, two miles, to General Butler's Headquarters. Some rode and some were in ambulances. The James Army people always take pretty good care of themselves, and here I found log houses, with board roofs, and high chimneys, for the accommodation of the gentlemen of the Staff. You might know it was Butler's Headquarters by the fact that, instead of the common ensign, he had a captured Reb battle-flag stuck up! This chieftain asked in the general officers and we were left to the care of the Staff, who were not behindhand in their civility. . . . Presently Butler climbed on his horse and led the way to see Fort Harrison, which was captured in the movements at the end of September. It was well worth seeing, for on our side of the river we have no hills: it is pretty much one plain with gullies. But here was a regular hill, of some size, dominating the whole country about. How they took the place, I hardly see, for the land is open for a mile in front of it, and the Rebs had artillery in position and a regular infantry running quite to the river. . . .

November 28, 1864

Let me see, I had got to Fort Harrison, had I not? Really I got so sleepy last night over the second sheet that I should not be surprised if it contains numerous absurdities. From the Fort you have an excellent view of the Rebs in their line opposite, their main fort being only 800 yards distant. I was surprised they did not fire upon us, as there was a great crowd and evidently several generals among us. But I believe they never shoot. The pickets, on either side, are within close musket-range but have no appearance of hostility. There was one very innocent "Turkey," who said to me: "Who are those men just over there?" When I told him they were Rebs, he exclaimed: "God bless me!" and popped down behind the parapet. . . .

Thence we all went to view the great canal. You will notice on the map, that the river at Dutch Gap makes a wide loop and comes back to nearly the same spot, and the canal is going through there. This cuts off five or six miles of river and avoids that much of navigation exposed to fire; and it may have strategic advantages if we can get iron-clads through and silence the Rebel batteries on the other bank. The canny Butler sent an aide to see if they were shelling the canal, who reported they were not; so we dismounted a little way off and walked to the place. It was very worth seeing. Fancy a narrow ridge of land, only 135 yards wide, separating the river, which flows on either side; a high ridge, making a bluff fifty feet high where it overhangs the water. Through this a great chasm has been cut, only leaving a narrow wall on the side next the enemy,

which wall is to be blown out with several thousand pounds
of gunpowder. We stood on the brink and looked down,
some seventy feet, at the men and the carts and the horses
at work on the bottom. Where we stood, and indeed all
over the ridge, was strewed thickly with pieces of shell,
while here and there lay a whole one, which had failed to
explode. Had the Rebs known that a Lieutenant-General
and two Major-Generals were there, they would hardly
have left us so quiet. . . .

Though we got off very nicely (I thought as I stood
there: "Now *that* line is the shortest one to our horses, and
you must walk it with dignity — not too fast when they
begin to shell"), there was a fat "Turkey" who came after
us and was treated to a huge projectile, which burst over
his head; he ran and picked up a piece and cried out: "Oh!
it's warm. Oh!! it smells of sulphur. Oh!!! let us go now."
He was delighted with this and all other adventures, and
was quite elated when his horse tumbled in a ditch and
muddied him greatly. After dark we were treated to an
exhibition of a "Greek fire." They burst a shell in a bunch
of bush and immediately the whole was in a roaring blaze.
"They've got the fuses to work well now," said Grant
calmly. "They tried the shells on three houses, the other
side of the river, and burnt them all without difficulty."
Good thing for the owners! Then they spirted the stuff
through a little hose and set the stream on fire. It was a
beautiful sight and like the hell of the poets, with an
unquenchable fire and columns of black smoke rolling up.
Owing to these pyrotechnics, we only got home at midnight. In my next I will tell more of the genius of Butler.
General Meade, you will be glad to learn, has been informed officially, that he will be appointed a Major-General
in the Regular Army, to rank General Sheridan!

November 29, 1864

I did not have room to tell you of the ingenious inventions of General Butler for the destruction of the enemy. He never is happy unless he has half a dozen contrivances on hand. One man has brought a fire-engine, wherewith he proposes to squirt on earthworks and wash them all down! An idea that Benjamin considered highly practicable. Then, with his Greek fire, he proposed to hold a redoubt with only five men and a small garden engine. "Certainly," said General Meade; "only your engine fires thirty feet, and a minié rifle 3000 yards, and I am afraid your five men might be killed, before they had a chance to burn up their adversaries!" Also he is going to get a gun that shoots seven miles and, taking direction by compass, burn the city of Richmond with shells of Greek fire. If that don't do, he has an auger that bores a tunnel five feet in diameter, and he is going to bore to Richmond, and suddenly pop up in somebody's basement, while the family are at breakfast! So you see he is ingenious. It is really summer warm to-day; there are swarms of flies, and I saw a bumble-bee and a grasshopper.

November 30, 1864

Did you hear how the Hon. Nesmith, whom I have mentioned, discovered the real cause of the defeat at the first Bull Run? He was in Washington at the time, and the military wiseacres, as soon as they got over the scare, were prolific in disquisitions on the topic. One evening Nesmith found a lot of them very verbose over a lot of maps and books. They talked wisely of flank movements and changes of front, and how we should have won a great victory if we had only done so and so; when he remarked solemnly: "Gentlemen, I have studied this matter and I have discovered the real reason of our defeat." They were all ears to hear. "Well," said Nesmith with immense gravity, "well, *it was them darned Rebels!*" . . .

Last night the 2d Corps picket line was relieved by the 9th — a delicate job in face of the enemy, who are pretty close up; but it all was done in entire quiet, to the relief of General Humphreys, who feels the new honor of the 2d Corps. That worthy officer stopped on his way to his new Headquarters and honored me by taking a piece of your plum cake. He was much tried by the noisy ways of Hancock's late Headquarters. "They whistle of mornings," said the fidgety little General, "and that Shaw, confound the fellow, amuses himself with imitating all the bugle-calls! Then the negroes turn out at four in the morning and chop wood, so that I am regularly waked up. But I shall stop it, *I* can tell you." And I have no doubt he will, as he is wont to have his own way or know the reason why. I rode out with him to his new Headquarters and followed the line afterwards, and was much amused to see them drilling some of the worthless German recruits, in a polyglot style: "Steady there! *Mehr heraus* — more to the front. Shoulder arms! *Eins, zwei!* One, two!" etc.

December 1, 1864

At daylight General Gregg made a start, with nearly his whole cavalry division, for Stony Creek station. For you must know that, since we have held the Weldon road, the enemy have been obliged to waggon much of their supplies from Stony Creek station, by cross roads to the Boydton plank and thus to Petersburg. Lately we have had reports that they were building a cross railroad from Stony Creek to the southside road. Gregg's object therefore was to go to the station, which is over twenty miles by the road from

our lines, find out if this railroad were really in progress or
not, and do as much damage as possible. Instead of going
straight down he, by advice of General Meade, bore a
little to the east and then suddenly swung round, when he
got a little below the station. The consequence was he
came on them where they didn't look for him. There were
two redoubts, with regular ditch, etc., intended to keep
off raiders; there was a thirty-pounder Parrott and a
twelve-pounder field-piece mounted in them, and a few
infantry as garrison. Their cavalry took to their heels,
prudently. The infantry got in the redoubts and fired
away with their cannon; but it got taken in a novel fashion. A regiment of cavalry charged to within 100 yards,
then tumbled off their horses and made a rush at the parapet, and ran right over the occupants. This gave them
possession of the station, and then there followed a scene
of general smashing, which, according to witnesses, was
highly amusing. The men, feeling like mischievous boys,
went at everything tooth and nail. They took several
hundred bales of hay and piled them against a stack of
short forage, which contained between 3000 and 5000 bags.
Then they set the whole on fire, and helped the blaze with
a lot of new tents. Next they tied down the safety-valve
of a locomotive, built a big fire under the boiler, and blew
her up by this scientific process. After distributing the
contents of a number of Rebel Thanksgiving boxes on the
principle of *spolia forti*, they ended by a display of fire-
works consisting of a shed full of ammunition, which was
fired and allowed to go off at its convenience. Then they
retreated, in great glee, taking with them 170 prisoners,
who were *not* in such great glee. One was a scamp named
Major Fitzhugh, who, when Captain Lazelle, of our cavalry,
was made prisoner, put a pistol to his head and made him

give him his *boots*. Captain Freikle told me he had a mind
to make the scoundrel march the twenty miles barefooted,
but couldn't bring his mind to anything so mean. *I* would
have made him do it.

December 3, 1864

At the end of each month, General Meade sends up his
pay-rolls, that is, a large printed sheet which each officer
fills up, stating what the Government owes him, and saying that he hasn't cheated Uncle Sam, and don't owe him
anything and is all right generally. The pay department
keeps this as a receipt and returns your money for the past
month. Lieutenant-Colonel Woodruff gets the General's
pay. One part he sends to Mrs. Meade and the rest he
sends to the General, who, the moment that he gets it,
sends violently for Mercier and John and everyone else to
whom he is indebted, and pays them all, in hot haste, as if
his last day were come. He is a thorough old soldier about
money and regards greenbacks in a weak and helpless sort
of way. "Once," said he, "Mrs. Meade said it was my
plain duty to go to market, as other gentlemen did: it
would be so satisfactory and saving. I went the next morning. We had a famous dinner — oysters, terrapin, and lots
of good things — the children were delighted; but, when
I came to look, I found I had spent the week's allowance
in one day! I wasn't allowed to go any more to market."
You would have laughed to see yesterday the crowd of
contrabands that came in with Gregg. Usually, wherever
they can, they cut and run, not showing that devotion to
their masters described by the Southrons. It is sometimes
rather remarkable the way they run off. Now in this lot
(mostly women) there was all the way from a newly born
baby to an old woman who, they told me, was over ninety,

and who, from her looks, might very likely have been a hundred and fifty. The young women had their mistresses' things on, if I know myself. There was one Christian Commission kuss who went whining about and saying: "Oh! you are free, free! Oh! thank God for it!" "Look here, my friend," said I, "if you want to show your Christian feeling, go and tell your commission to get these people something to eat; they have had nothing since yesterday." The pious party took this with an ill grace, but was fain to walk off "to see our agent," who, I hope, made some good soup for them.

December 5, 1864

The weather continues very fine and really warm of days, though the nights are provocative of blankets — weather, law! that isn't very interesting, is it? My head has indeed been singularly empty for letter-writing; when a man talks about weather to his own wife he must be pretty hard up. I heard a characteristic anecdote of Hancock which made me laugh, as I knew his ways. It appears that he had issued stringent orders against plundering, despite which the troops had fallen on a large flock of sheep and were making short work of them. Away went Hancock, followed by the inevitable Morgan, Mitchell, and Parker. Very soon all these three were sent spinning off at tangents, after distant delinquents, and the General went frothing along alone. Presently he catches sight of four men pursuing a poor sheep, bayonet in hand, and off he goes, full tilt, to arrest them; but, before he can get in, poor ba-ba is down and still. "You blank blank all-sorts-of-bad-things," roars Hancock, "how dare you? How dare you kill that sheep?" "Please, General, we didn't kill it," cried the terrified soldiers. "What! Didn't kill it!

WINFIELD SCOTT HANCOCK

You liars! You infernal, desperate liars! I saw you kill it, with my own eyes; and there it lies dead!" — when — *the sheep hopped up and ran away.*

December 6, 1864

There arrived Captain Alden, with 253 brevets, of all grades, for the Army of the Potomac. Do you know what a brevet is, and the force thereof? A brevet commission gives the dignity, but not always the pay or the authority, of the rank it confers. If, for example, a colonel is breveted general, he may wear the stars and may rank as general on courts-martial, but, unless he be specially *assigned* by the President, he has only the command of a colonel, just as before. A colonel brevetted general in the *regular* army draws the pay of a general when assigned to duty by the President; but a brevet in the *volunteers* can under no circumstances bring additional pay. Brevets, like other appointments by the President, must be confirmed by the Senate before they become permanent. At any rate, however, they last from the time of appointment to the time of their rejection by the Senate. The object of brevets is to pay compliments to meritorious officers without overburdening the army with officers of high rank.

As aforesaid, there came a grist of these papers in all grades, from 1st lieutenant up to major-general. All the Headquarters' Staff, with few exceptions, were brevetted one grade, in consequence of which I should not wonder if the Senate rejected the whole bundle! Barstow is Brevet Lieutenant-Colonel; Biddle, ditto; Duane has two brevets, which brings him to a full Colonel, and will give him a colonel's pay, if he can be assigned, as they are in the regular army. We are all very melancholy over General Williams, who, though one of the most deserving officers

20

in the whole army, could not be brevetted because that would make him rank the Adjutant-General of the whole army, Brigadier-General Thomas. They were not so careful to except Barnard, whom they formerly made a Major-General though *his* chief, Delafield, was only a Brigadier. It is to be considered, however, that Major-General Barnard had found leisure from his military duties to publish a criticism on the Peninsular Campaign, or, in other words, a campaign document against McClellan, which is a circumstance that alters cases. I should say, that the statement that General Meade was only a *Brevet* Major-General in the regular service was a mistake naturally arising from the confusion with the other letters of appointment. . . .

General Grant was at the Headquarters for about an hour. He brought with him Captain de Marivault, a French naval officer and a very gentlemanly man. I took him as far as Fort Wadsworth, and showed him it and the neighboring line. He has had great chances of seeing this war, as he was at New Orleans, and, later, Admiral Dahlgren allowed him to go into Charleston, where he even went about in the city. Oh! I forgot to mention, in particular, that Rosencrantz is brevetted a Major, at which he is much pleased. There followed much merriment in the camp over shoulder-straps, those who had been promoted giving theirs to the next grade below. Majors' straps were scarcest and were in great demand. The General was in high spirits (as he might well be, with a letter of appointment in his pocket) and stood in front of his tent, joking with his aides, a very rare performance with him. "Now here's Lyman,"[1] said he, looking like Mephistopheles in

---

[1] Lyman, being a volunteer aide, was not eligible for a brevet.

good humor, "he has no brevet, but I am going to write to
the Governor of Massachusetts to make him a Field Marshal." Whereat he rubbed the side of his long nose, as he
always does when he laughs.

December 8, 1864

There came down an elephant of a young Englishman,
who, if there be brains in his skull, they are so well concealed that nobody has found them hereabout. To entertain him is like rolling a barrel of potatoes up a steep hill.
Nevertheless, he is a Lieutenant of Engineers. I should
think he might construct an earthwork in, say, a century.
I fancy he has played out all his intellect in trying to spell
and pronounce his own name which is the euphonious one
of S-tt-rthw—t; you will find it gives you a cramp in your
tongue to pronounce it. Query — would it not be for the
best interests of the human race to drown all Englishmen?

Gibbon's division of the 2d Corps got in a towering
passion, because, having erected log huts just a little way
outside the line of parapet, they were ordered to pull them
all down and come inside, for of course these huts would
give cover to an attacking enemy. This was what I call a
stupid thing all round. Stupid in the infantry commanders to allow it; stupid in the inspectors not to see it; stupid
in the artillerists and engineers not to stop it — in fact,
stupid all round. Gibbon came over and pitched into
Duane, who received the attack with stolidity; so Gibbon
thought he would get good-natured. At evening I had the
greatest sight at a lot of stragglers that ever I did. It is
always customary, when possible, to sweep the path of a
column and gather up all stragglers, but I never before
had a chance to see the leavings of a large force, marching
by a single road. When Warren got to the Nottaway, he

took up his pontoons behind him, so that the laggards, who were toddling leisurely behind, as well as those who really had no intention of catching up till their rations were out, were all caught on the north side. General Warren sent back about 100 cavalry to sweep the whole road and bring the men back to the lines: and after dark, they arrived, looking, in the dusk, like a large brigade. Schuyler, the Provost-Marshal, put them in ranks, had them sorted and counted, and there proved to be 856! Their way was not made soft to them. They were marched three miles more, making twenty in all, and were then put out on picket in a right frosty night. This seems a large number, and it is more than it ought to be, a great deal; but, in reality it only made four and a half men out of every 100 in Warren's force. That they were able to go on is proved by the fact that they were able to come *back*, though some did limp merrily, and others were so stiff that, when once down, they could scarcely get up. A force of a few hundred cavalry was sent in the afternoon down the Vaughan road to reconnoitre, and see if they could see that any troops were moving against our rear, or against Warren. They got at dusk to Hatcher's Run, where the opposite bank was held by the enemy in a breastwork; and, after losing half a dozen men, our cavalry came back.

December 9, 1864

Miles's division of the 2d Corps was sent to aid the cavalry in forcing Hatcher's Run. They marched out early and found several regiments holding the crossing; a severe skirmish followed; our poor men went into the icy water up to their armpits and drove off the Rebels, though not without some loss to us. I know the cavalry Lieutenant, whom I saw bringing in all those stragglers last night, was killed there. Then Miles built a bridge and sent over the cavalry, which went as far as within sight of the Boydton plank, where they found the enemy in their works. They captured a Rebel mail-carrier and from him learned that A. P. Hill was yesterday at Dinwiddie. General Meade had to read all the letters, of course, and said there was one poor lover who promised to marry his sweetheart when the war was over, but "how could he support her *now*, on $12 a month?" We sent out another body of infantry and our own "red-legs" and the engineers, to support Miles, who we thought would be attacked. They all spent the night midst a wretched snow, sleet and rain, and raw wind.

December 10, 1864

Miles, with the troops which had been sent to reinforce him, maintained a threatening attitude near Hatcher's Run till afternoon, when he was ordered to withdraw again to our lines. The enemy undertook to follow up a little, but the rear guard faced about and drove them away. — There was I seized with a fearful sleepy fit last night and went to bed; thus missing a letter home to you. However, I have not before missed one in a very long time; and, if I followed Duane's advice, I should miss much oftener. "Lyman," says this ancient campaigner, "you are foolish to write so much. Now I write only once a week, so my letters are valued. You write every day, and probably Mrs. Lyman puts them in her pocket and pays no attention to them." Ah! I was speaking of Miles, and had got him with all his forces, and put him inside the works, all right. We had to pay farewell respects to Riddle, for his resignation has been accepted and he goes to-morrow. For a long time he has been in miserable health and, in warm weather, is seldom well enough for hard duty. He has been twice wounded, at Antietam and on the Peninsula, and was taken prisoner, but got away from Libby and arrived, after many hardships, within our lines. He is a very good officer and quite a superior person, whom we shall miss on our Staff. The kind-hearted Woolsey invited us all to take oysters in his honor (for you must know that there is a log house where one may have a "fancy roast," "plain stew," or "one fried," just across the road). We gathered in the greatest force, for oysters attracted, even if Riddle didn't, and had a high festival. We had songs, whereof I sang several, with large applause. "You don't drink," said Duane, "but it don't make any difference, because you *look* as if you had been drinking, and that's all that is necessary."

Before I finish this day I must go back to tell of the beginning and progress of the Weldon road expedition. Last Wednesday, General Warren, with his own Corps, Mott's division of the 2d Corps, and nearly the whole of Gregg's division of cavalry, started in the morning and marched down the Jerusalem plank road, striking across to the Nottoway River, at Freeman's Bridge, a distance of from fifteen to seventeen miles. There a pontoon bridge was thrown and the whole command got over before daybreak the next morning, the advance getting that night to Sussex Court House. Meantime the enemy, getting [wind] of the move, sent off A. P. Hill's Corps, that evening, twelve hours after Warren. Hill went to Dinwiddie Court House, but what became of him thereafter, I have not yet learned. Their place in the lines was taken, I presume, by some of Early's men, who were nearly all come down from the valley and are helping Lee now. On Thursday Warren continued his march and struck the Weldon road, a little

south of the Nottoway, in the afternoon, and immediately
went to destroying the track and burning the river bridge.
The work went on systematically: the line being halted on
the road, the men stacked arms, and went at the track.
Sleepers were torn up, and these, with fence-rails, made
great bonfires, on which the rails were laid. Soon the iron
would wax red-hot, when the weight of the ends would
bend the rails. Some of the men, however, were so enthusiastic as to take rails and twist them round trees,
which could be done while the ends were cool and the middle hot. As soon as a brigade had finished its work, it
marched down to a new piece, passing the other men who
were destroying; and so they kept on till midnight, when
they had got to Jarrott's station and there halted. Next
day, Friday, the column kept on, as before, the cavalry
preceding them, who, when they arrived at Meherrin
Bridge, found strong earthworks on the opposite side and
some ten guns, which immediately opened on them. . . .

This night was a very severe one, with its high wind and
snow, sleet and rain; but it was rendered tolerable by the
big fires that the soldiers lighted to heat rails with. General Warren did not deem proper to cross the Meherrin, as
it would take a day to flank the Rebels' works, and he
started with but six days' provisions. Next day, Saturday
to wit, he began his return march and the head of the column got as far as Sussex C.H. On this march the people
of the country had the bad judgment to "bushwhack" our
troops: that is, to kill any stragglers or small parties they
could catch. This is against the rules of war. I will not
say it is surprising, because the stragglers of an army always steal and plunder and exasperate the people. Colonel
Sergeant told me he himself saw five of our men shot and
stripped nearly naked. The troops were so enraged by such

cases, that they fired every house on their march, and, what made them worse, they found a great amount of apple-brandy in the country, a liquor that readily intoxicates. The superior officers destroyed a great deal of it, but the men got some and many were drunk. The people make this brandy on account of its great price. It sells for $1500 a barrel. Colonel Wainwright told me he found two tithing-bills in one house, one a year old, the other recent; in the old one wheat was valued at $10 a bushel, in the recent, at $40, showing that it has quadrupled in price within a year. It was on this day that a cavalry reconnaissance that pushed out on the Vaughan road reported heavy artillery firing in the direction of Jarrott's station. This made Grant so uneasy that he directed aid to be sent Warren. Accordingly Potter, with 9000 men, marched that night, and arrived next morning at five A.M. at the Nottoway, at Freeman's Bridge. A wretched march indeed! in slush and mud and a damp cold; but his men followed on very well and arrived with little straggling, which surprised me.

December 11, 1864

Weather as before — only a little more so. I suppose they have a good deal such in England. If so, don't want to live there. Pretty times for half the army, off and on, to be marching and reconnoitring and expeditionizing about the country, as if it were picnic season! And still stranger is it to be sitting quiet in my tent when so many people are running round loose. Our affairs are rather mixed up, you see. So are those of everybody. Sherman has disappeared in Georgia and nobody knows what awful strategy he contemplates. Not so Hood: he is poking about in a manner I don't at all like: jamming Thomas up

in Nashville, and now I fancy he is just marching round
the city and into Kentucky. That won't do! Old Lee
don't let us march round towns unless he chooses, or has
at least a hard fight for it. However, I can't think Hood
can do severe damage with so powerful an army as that of
Thomas in his neighborhood. Well, we will hope for a big
thing, of some sort, somewhere, for there are a number of
irons, small and great, in the fire, and as much activity
prevails as if we were not near the real winter. One thing
I am sure of, that, what with expeditions little and big,
threatenings and reconnaissances, the Rebels must be kept
in quite an active state of simmer. Poor General Potter!
He had a frightful night march and was doubtless buoyed
up by the feeling that he had a separate command and
could distinguish himself if there was a fight, and slam in
on Hill's left flank, and win a great name for himself.
What then was his disgust to see, about noon, the head of
Warren's column trudging peaceably back, on the other
side of the river! There were two decent-sized armies staring at each other, across the stream, each wondering what
the other meant by being there; and both wondering why
so many men were concentrated against nobody. General
Potter philosophically shrugged his shoulders, gave the
word to face about, and put his best leg forward for home,
where he arrived a little after dark. It was a terrible night
for a bivouac, with an intensely piercing cold wind and
everything frozen up. Warren crossed the river and spent
the night on this side of it.

December 12, 1864

Clear and cold we have had it this day, blowy this morning but still in the evening. Last night it blew in a tremendous manner. My tent flapped in a way that reminded

one of being at sea, and my chimney, for the first time got
mad and actually smoked. My only consolation was that
the General's smoked a great deal worse. He made quite
a *bon-mot* at breakfast, despite the smoke: "Grant says
the Confederates, in their endeavors to get men, have
robbed the cradle and the grave; if that *is* the case, I must
say their ghosts and babies fight very well!" I did not fail
to ride out and see the raiders come in. The head of the
column arrived about noon, or an hour before. I was much
amused by a battery, the first thing that I met; one of
the drivers was deeply intent on getting his pair of horses
over a bad bridge, but, midst all his anxiety and pains on
this head, he did not fail to keep tight hold of a very old
rush-bottomed chair, which he carefully held in one hand!
How far he had brought it or what he meant to do with it,
I know not, but his face wore an expression which said:
"You may take my life but you can't have this very old
rush-bottomed chair which I have been at much pains to
steal." Then came the infantry, with a good deal of weary
straggling, and looking pretty cold, poor fellows; then another battery spattered with mud; then a drove of beef
cattle, in the midst of which marched cows, calves, and
steers that never more will graze on Rebel farms. Finally a
posse of stragglers and ambulances and waggons, all putting the best speed on to get to a camping-place. I pitied
the poor bucks who, for six days, had endured every
fatigue and hardship.

December 13, 1864

As the Rebels have known the fact for some time, and as
the newspapers have hinted at it in unmistakable terms,
I conceive there is no impropriety in my saying that we
have now with us the 6th Corps once again. A week ago

Sunday night the first division came from City Point on the cars, having come straight from the neighborhood of Winchester by car and boat. The next morning we were treated to the sight of the familiar red crosses, and soon General Wheaton rode up, to see the General and report. . . . Very loath were the Sixth Corps bucks to leave the valley (where they had plenty of sheep and chickens and victories, and no fighting except in the regular battles), and come to a place with which they only connected more or less fighting, day and night (rather more than less), much dust, heat, and drought, and no particular victories. However, they find things better now, and will doubtless get contented in time. What must have gratified them was that they relieved Crawford's division of the 5th Corps, on the line, and took possession of their very nice log huts, which had been carefully constructed uniformly in all the brigades. Crawford's people by no means saw the thing in the same light. They took down their canvas roofs and rolled them up with dudgeon, and marched off to take a temporary camp, previous to the Weldon road expedition. I rode along the breastworks as the red crosses marched into the deserted camps, and observed the aspect of grim satisfaction with which the new comers went about, looking into the abandoned huts. The luxurious Crawford had his nice log cabin taken down and carted to his new locality. "However," said Wheaton, "I slept in Crawford's kitchen, and that was good enough for me." On Tuesday came the 3d division, also with a new commander, for brave General Ricketts lies at Washington, still suffering from his wound; and General Seymour, he who was taken the second day of the Wilderness, has the command. Seymour is a fiery and irrepressible sort of party, and enraged the inhabitants of Charlottesville beyond measure. When they told him they had had most extraordinary victories over Grant, he made them a speech, in which he said it didn't make any sort of difference how many victories they had, it wouldn't do them any sort of good; that in every battle we killed off a good many of them, and that we intended to keep piling up men indefinitely, until they knocked under, or were all shot! This enraged them much, and they invited him to air himself for sixteen miles on foot, after it. . . . It was only last Monday that the 2d division got here, under Getty, and with it came General Wright, commanding the corps. Good General Wright, though always pleasant, is, I think rather in low spirits. He has had poor luck, on numerous occasions, and it culminated at Cedar Creek, where he chanced to have command of the army when it was surprised. He had rallied it, when Sheridan arrived on the field; but of course Sheridan had the credit of the victory, and indeed he deserved it. All the officers say that Wright made prodigious exertions and rode along all parts of the line in the hottest fire.

December 14, 1864

General Winthrop [in speaking of Warren's operations] said his brigade bivouacked in a cornfield; it blew, snowed and sleeted all night, and when reveille beat in the morning, you could only see what seemed a field full of dead bodies, each covered with a rubber blanket and encased with ice. Some of the men had to kick and struggle, they were so hard frozen down. Yet, despite this, I have not learned that it has caused much sickness. How would you like to carry forty or fifty pounds all day, be wet through, have your feet soaked with mud and snow-water, and then go to sleep in a cornfield, with a drifting sleet coming down on you all night? This is what twenty-five thousand men

did, for more than one night, on that expedition. This is
what our poor slovenly ragamuffins can do; and this it is
to be a good soldier. The Rebels are still tougher, if anything. Being still in love with the new picket line, which
has been established in our rear, I again went down what is
called the Church road, until I struck the infantry pickets,
near a Colonel Wyatt's house. This once was a well-to-do
establishment. The house is large and a huge cornfield
testifies that he (or our cavalry) had gathered a good har-
vest that very year. There were the usual outbuildings
of a well-to-do southern farmer: little log barns, negro
huts, and odd things that might be large hencoops or
small pigstyes. The Virginians have a great passion for
putting up a great lot of diminutive structures as a kind
of foil to the main building, which, on the contrary, they
like to have as extensive as possible; just as the old painters
added importance to a big saint by making a number of
very small devotees, kneeling below him. A stout old gent,
in a shocking bad beaver, who was walking about in
the back yard was, I presume, the distinguished Colonel.
Having stared at the house and been in turn stared at by
a pretty little girl who threw up a window, to have a more
clear view of the Yank, I went, still along the Church road,
till I got to the Weldon road.

A picket line is always one of the most picturesque
sights in an army, when it runs through woods and fields.
You know it consists of a string of "posts," each of half a
dozen men, or so, and, in front of these, a chain of sentries
who are constantly on the alert. The squads of men make
to themselves a gipsy bough-house in front of which they
make a fire in cool weather. They must always have their
belts on and be ready to fight at a moment's notice. In
the woods, you follow along from one rustic shelter to an-

other, and see the sentries, out in front, each standing behind a good tree and keeping a sharp lookout for Rebel scouts, bushwhackers and cavalry. A short distance in the rear you from time to time come on a "reserve," which is a large body, perhaps of fifty or a hundred, who are concealed and who are ready to come to the assistance of the posts, if they are attacked. Picket duty is, of all others, that which requires most individual intelligence in the soldiers. A picket line, judiciously posted, in woods or swamps, will oppose a formidable resistance, even to a line of battle. There was careful Mr. Corps, officer of the day, with his crimson scarf across his shoulder, inspecting his outposts and reserves; each one falling in as he came along and standing at a shoulder.

VIII

THE END OF THE WAR

[As the Army of the Potomac was now settling down to winter quarters before Petersburg, Meade chaffingly remarked to Lyman one day toward the end of December: "I have a Christmas present for Mrs. Lyman — a certain worthless officer whom I shall send home to her." And that evening he gave him a 300-day leave, with the understanding that Lyman was to return with the opening of the active campaign in the spring.

Toward the end of February, Lyman became restless, and fearing that operations might start in his absence, turned up at Headquarters on March 1. On going into dinner, he was kindly greeted by General Meade, who, poor man, although he had just come back from burying his son, managed to say playfully that he would have Lyman court-martialed for returning without orders.

The Appomattox campaign opened in the spring, with the forces under Grant numbering 113,000, while those under Lee were only 49,000.[1] The resources of the North were unimpaired, those of the South were rapidly vanishing. On March 25, Lee made an energetic but unsuccessful sortie. On April 1, Sheridan won a brilliant victory at Five Forks. Grant followed this up by attacking all along the line the next day. The result of the engagement was that the Confederate Army was cut in halves, and Grant established himself between the two parts.

[1] T. L. Livermore, *Numbers and Losses in the Civil War in America*, 135–137. Lyman's estimate at the time was 122,000 and 50,000.

Lee's position was untenable; Richmond and Petersburg
were abandoned that night. Retreat was still open toward
the westward. Accordingly, Lee withdrew along the line
of the Richmond and Danville railroad, hoping to join
Johnston, who was opposing Sherman's advance from the
south. As a last resort, Lee planned to retreat to the
mountains of Virginia, where he thought he might continue
the war indefinitely. The Union Army followed close on
the heels of the retreating southerners. The chase was continued for eighty miles. In the neighborhood of Appomattox Court House, the cavalry under Sheridan got
across the railroad in front of the enemy. Lee was unable
to break through. Hemmed in, with his men worn out and
starved, Lee surrendered the remnant of his army, less
than 27,000 men,[1] on April 9. This virtually ended the
war.]

HEADQUARTERS ARMY OF POTOMAC
March 2, 1865

It was raw yesterday, or chilly rather, without being
cold, and to-day we are favored by a persistent northeast
rain, such as we had a month later than this at Culpeper.
The season, I should fancy, is earlier here than at Culpeper — very likely by two weeks or more. Indeed last
night the toads were whistling in the bog-holes, as they do
with us in the last of April; and Rosie had, on his mantel,
a bud of narcissus, or some such flower, he had found in a
swamp. You would not give us much credit for a chance
to move, could you see the country; the ground everywhere
saturated and rotten, and giving precarious tenure even to
single horses, or waggons. I did not believe very earnestly
that we should soon move, when I left, but only wanted
to be within all chances. I do really doubt whether any-

[1] Livermore, 137.

thing will be done before the 1st of April. I think the state of the country will hardly permit it to either party. When Sherman gets, say, in the latitude of Weldon, if he does so without check, he must, I think, strike the perfection of the mud zone; and must stick for a while; besides which he must establish a regular base, and, if he contemplates hard or protracted fighting, he must have a protected line for supplies. All these things take time, and take *season* also. Of course, it is not Lee's policy to let go his hold hereabout, till the very last moment. He has gone south in person, to gather up all possible forces and put them in the best order for resistance he can. The impression here seems to be, that the combined forces against Sherman are not very strong in the sum total, and are, of course, not so good in quality as Lee's own men. Then again, his very army, it is within bounds to say, never was so low in morale as now. During the twenty-eight days of February nearly 900 men deserted to the lines of this army alone, and a proportional number to those of the Army of the James. The remarkable point, also, is that these are *old* men — nearly all of them — and not the raw conscripts. In one day there came over 134 men, including also their non-commissioned officers, bringing their arms with them. Among the deserters have been four commissioned officers. During the time I have been with the army, I recall only two or three instances, besides these. Of course many more desert to the *rear* than to the enemy; so that I doubt not that Lee's losses from this cause during February were something between a large brigade and a small division. General Meade, after reviewing Lee's position and prospects, said: "I do not see what he is to do!" — which is a very strong speech for the cautious General. Well, as I have always said, he has the remaining chance, should everything work

21

precisely to favor him, of falling with fury and with all available troops, on a part of Sherman's army, or even on the whole of it, and dealing a stunning blow, whereby his evil day would be postponed; but how it could be averted seems to me inconceivable, save by a sort of miracle. If I am not mistaken, the forces now opposed to the Rebels in the east are at least as two to one. And again they have almost everything against them excepting the important advantage of interior lines.

Meantime all is very quiet with us. Last night I certainly heard not over half-a-dozen musket-shots, whereas in the autumn we had a real skirmish fire all the night through, not to speak of intermittent shelling. As I told you, Duane was on hand to welcome me. He looks very well and is better as to his eyes. Then Rosie — had he not, in my honor, caused constructed a new and very high hedge, or shelter, of pine branches, topped off with a tuft of cedar, and a triumphal arch of the same over the doorway! Within the tent were further improvements; andirons to wit (weak as to their legs, and frequently tumbling over on their sides at critical moments). Then a large Swedish flag, with the Union over my bed — a gift from some Scandinavian marines who visited the Headquarters, and upon whom Rosie quite ran himself aground in the matter of oysters, at the saloon over the way. Then, too, the middle tent-pole has been removed and the interior of the tent supported by a framework, a part of which takes the form of a shelf, running round the sides and very handy for any small articles. I must also give credit to that idiotic Frenchman, who waited at table, for having ingeniously burned down our mess tent, during my absence, whereby we now have a much improved hospital tent, very pleas-

ant, and we have got rid of the idiot and have a quite intelligent nig, who actually keeps the spoons clean.

March 3, 1865

Our evanescent Chief-of-Staff, General Webb, has gone
to Washington for a day or two, to see his wife. He insisted, before he went, that the Rebs were not going to
evacuate Petersburg at present, on any account. "Ah!"
said General Meade, "Webb is an anti-evacuationist, because he wants to go to see his wife, and so wants to prove
there isn't going to be any move at present." General
Webb is a good piece of luck, as successor to General Humphreys. He is very jolly and pleasant, while, at the same
time, he is a thorough soldier, wide-awake, quick and attentive to detail. In fact, I believe him much better for the
place than Gen. H. from the very circumstance that *he*
was such a very superior man, that General Meade would
take him as a confidential adviser, whereas the General does much better without any adviser at all. My only
objection to General Webb is that he continually has a way
of suddenly laughing in a convulsive manner, by drawing
in his breath, instead of letting it out — the which goes to
my bones.

It is not too much to say that yesterday was a day without striking events, as it was characterized by a more or
less steady rain, from the rising to the going down of the
sun. I wrote you a letter, I entertained the chronic Duane,
and I entertained — oh, I forgot to tell you about him.
I entertained the officer from Roumania, the one whom
General Meade could not make out because he had no map
of Europe. This Roumania, as I have ascertained by dili-
gent study, is what we call Wallachia and Moldavia, and

is a patch of territory lying north of the Danube, and running from its mouth, on the Black Sea, to the northwest, into the Carpathian mountains. As to the Roumanians themselves, they have the misfortune to be tremendously protected by everybody. *Imprimis*, they pay to the Porte an "honorary tribute" of 600,000 crowns, in return for which his word is pledged to protect them against all comers, which is a good joke, seeing he can't protect himself against any comer at all! Then the Emperor Nap considers them *"une nation Latine,"* and *so* he is to protect them. Then the British protect them for fear the Russians should invade Turkey on that side. Then the Russians protect them because they want their land as a high road to Constantinople; and finally, the Austrians and Italians protect them, just to keep in the mode. Meanwhile the Roumanians seem to dislike all their kind friends, but still keep smiling and bowing round at them, hoping these protectors will one day get into a shindy, when they, the protected, propose to discontinue the honorary tribute, grab Bulgaria from the Turks, Bessarabia from the Russians, the Banat and part of Transylvania from the Austrians, and make a grand pan-Roumanian empire, with no protectors at all. All of which we shall know when they do it. Captain Botiano (that's his name) informed me that his countrymen were descended from Roman colonists, led thither by Trajan. To judge from the gallant Cappy, as a specimen, the colonists must have intermarried considerably with various Gentiles; for his face denotes a combination of Greek, Italian, and Turk, with a dash of Tartar and a strain of some other barbarian, whose features are to me not familiar. On the whole, I felt like saying to him: "Oh, fiddle! don't come humbugging round here. Just put on a turban, and stick five silver-mounted pistols and seven

oriental daggers in your cashmere sash, and look like yourself!" For you must know he has received his education
in the French army, and now appears trussed in a modern
uniform, a cross between a British Grenadier Guard and a
Prussian Chasseur. He talks good French and is sufficiently intelligent, and apparently well educated. We
aired our Gallic for a long time together and discussed
many mighty topics. He, of course, like all those who have
the French way of thinking, was mildly horrified at the
want of central power in this country and thought the
political power delegated to the states was highly dangerous. They ought only to have power to look out for the
bien publique. All of which was edifying to me, as coming
from a descendant of a colonist of Trajan.

March 4, 1865

Yesterday the rain gave over partly, and so, in the afternoon, Rosie and I mounted and rode forth to see the new
line to the left. The mare knew me and greeted me, in her
characteristic way, by trying to kick and bite me. I felt
quite funny and odd at being once more on horseback, but
had a fine time, for the mare was in great spirits and
danced and hopped in a festive manner. Rosie was very
proud to show me all the last battle-ground, and to explain the new roads; for he has a high opinion of his ability
to find roads, at which, indeed, he is very capable. So we
jogged along, sometimes in danger of sticking in the mud,
and again, finding a sandy ridge where we could canter a
little. This last addition, which goes to Hatcher's Run,
makes our line of tremendous extent; perhaps a continuous
parapet of eighteen miles! The Rebs are obliged to draw
out proportionately, which is a hard task for them. As we
rode along the corduroy we met sixteen deserters from the

enemy, coming in under guard, of whom about a dozen had their muskets, a sight I never saw before! They bring them in, all loaded, and we pay them so much for each weapon. The new line is a very handsome one, with a tremendous sweep of artillery and small arms. To eke out this short letter I enclose the report of the Court of Enquiry on the "Mine." You see it gives fits to Burnside, Ledlie, Ferrero, and Willcox, while the last paragraph, though very obscure, is intended, I fancy, as a small snub on General Meade.

March 5, 1865

. . . Well, the rain held up and some blue sky began to show, and I mounted on what I shall have to call my Anne of Cleves — for, in the choice words of that first of gentlemen, Henry VIII, she is "a great Flanders mare" — and rode forth for a little exercise. Verily I conceived we should *rester en route*, sich was the mud in one or two places! She would keep going deeper and deeper, and I would strive to pick out a harder path and would by no means succeed. Nevertheless, I made out to find some terra firma, at last, and, by holding to the ridges got a very fair ride after all. I found not much new out there, towards the Jerusalem plank: some cavalry camped about, as usual, and a new railroad branch going to supply them, and called Gregg's branch. Gregg, by the way, has resigned. He is a loss to the service, and has commanded a cavalry division very successfully for a long time. I don't know why he went out, since he is a regular officer. Some say it is a pretty wife, which is likely, seeing the same had worked in that style with others. Then there is Major Sleeper, resigned too. He has served long and well, and been wounded; so I say, what a pity that he should not stick to the end. It is human nature to expect a full performance of duty,

David McMurtrie Gregg

when once a man has done decidedly well. These branch
railroads are like mushrooms, and go shooting out at the
shortest notice. The distinguished Botiano was entirely
taken down by the performances of this sort. Just at the
time of our new extension to the left, he went for a few
days to Washington. When he got back, he was whisked
over five miles of new railroad, including a number of
bridges! This upset him wholly, and it was hard to make
him believe that there hadn't been an old line there before. Now where do you suppose I went last night? Why,
to the theatre! Certainly, in my private carriage to the
theatre; that is to say, on horseback, for may high powers
forfend me from an ambulance over corduroys and these
mud-holes! Rather would I die a rather swifter death. To
explain, you must understand that good Colonel Spaulding
commands a regiment of engineers, a fine command of
some 1800 men. As they are nearly all mechanics, they
are very handy at building and have erected, among other
things, a large building, which is a church on Sundays, and
a theatre on secular occasions. Thither the goodly Flint
rode with me. On the outside was about half the regiment,
each man armed with a three-legged stool, and all waiting
to march into the theatre. We found the edifice quite a
rustic gem. Everything, except the nails, is furnished by
the surrounding woods and made by the men themselves.
The building has the form of a short cross and is all of
rustic work; the walls and floors of hewn slabs and the roof
covered with shingles nailed on beams, made with the bark
on. What corresponds to the left-side aisle was railed off
for officers only, while the rest was cram-full of men. The
illumination of the hall was furnished by a rustic chande-
lier, that of the stage by army lanterns, and by candles,
whose rays were elegantly reflected by tin plates bought

from the sutler. The entertainment was to be "minstrels"; and, to be sure, in walked an excellent counterpart of Morris, Pell, and Trowbridge, who immediately began an excellent overture, in which the tambourine gentleman, in particular, was most brilliant and quite convulsed the assembled engineers. The performances were, indeed, most creditable, and there was not a word of any sort of coarseness throughout. A grand speech on the state of the country, by a brother in a pair of gunny-bag trousers, was quite a gem. He had an umbrella, of extraordinary pattern, with which he emphasized his periods by huge whacks on the table. I think the jokes were as ingeniously ridiculous as could be got up, and that, you know, is the great thing in minstrels. Brudder Bones came a little of the professional by asking his friend: "What can yer play on dat banjo?" "Anyting," says the unwary friend. "Well, den, play a game o' billiards!" "Can't play no billiards! kin play a *tune*," cries the indignant friend. "Well den, if yer kin play a tune, jis play a pon-toon!" All to the inextinguishable delight of the engineers. After the play the good Colonel, who is one of the salt of the earth, insisted on my taking pigs' feet as a supper.

March 6, 1865

I think I must relate to you a small story which they have as a joke against Major-General Crawford. As the story will indicate, the Major-General has some reputation for possessing a decided admiration of the looks and figure of his own self. There came to the army a young artist, who was under a certain monied person. The young artist was to make models for bronze medallions, and the monied person was to sell the same and take the profits, if any. He proposed to model the commander of the army, and each of the corps commanders, and General Webb, but no one else. As the artist was modelling away at General Webb, he asked: "Isn't General Crawford rather an odd man?" "What makes you ask that?" says the Chief-of-Staff?" "Why, he waked me up in the middle of the night, and asked what I could make a *statuette of him for!* I told him $400 and he said he thought he would have it done!" Webb, who is a cruel wag, said naught, but, the next time he met C., asked him if he had seen the young sculptor who had come down. "Seen him!" quoth C. "My dear fellow, he has done nothing but follow me round, boring me to sit for a statuette!"

General Hunt was telling me an anecdote of Grant, which occurred during the Mexican War and which illustrates what men may look for in the way of fame. It was towards the last of the fighting, at the time when our troops took by assault the works immediately round the City of Mexico. Grant was regimental quartermaster of the regiment commanded by Colonel Garland; and, it appears, at the attack on the Campo Santo, he, with about a dozen men, got round the enemy's flank and was first in the work. Somewhat after, he came to the then Lieutenant Hunt and said: "Didn't you see me go first into that work the other day?" "Why, no," said Hunt, "it so happened I did not see you, though I don't doubt you were in first." "Well," replied Grant, "I *was* in first, and here Colonel Garland has made no mention of me! The war is nearly done; *so there goes the last chance I ever shall have of military distinction!*" The next time, but one, that Hunt saw him, was at Culpeper, just after he was made Lieutenant-General. "Well, sir!" cried our Chief-of-Artillery, "I am glad to find you with some chance yet left for military distinction!"

March 8, 1865

Yesterday, as I hinted in my last, we had a toot, of much duration. At ten A.M. the General got a telegraph (one of those charming City Point surprises) saying that a train was just then starting, holding a dozen of womenkind and a certain force of the male sex; that they would arrive in an hour or so, and that we would please rather to entertain them pretty well! We telegraphed to the 5th Corps to turn out some troops, and to General Wright, to say we were coming that way, and ordered out ambulances to go to the station, and turned out officers to go over also. Your hub, not without growls of a private sort, girded hisself with a sash and ordered the charger saddled. In due time they kim: Colonels Badeau and Babcock to guide them. As sort of chief of the honorable committee of reception, I took off my cap and was solemnly introduced to twelve distinct ladies, whose names I instantly forgot (ditto those of distinguished gentlemen accompanying), all except Mrs. General Grant, who was, of course, too well known to slip from memory. However, at the end of the day, I began to have a flickering and vague idea who some of them were. . . . Then Miss Stanton — of course I was brilliant about her. After I had more or less helped her over puddles and into ambulances for an hour or two, it occurred to me that the name of the Secretary of War was also Stanton. Then, after a period of rest, my mind roused itself to the brilliant hypothesis that this young lady might be the daughter of the Stanton who was Secretary of War. Once on this track, it did not take me over thirty minutes to satisfy myself that I actually had been rendering civilities to the offspring of him who holds the leash of the dogs of war! She is not a roarer, like her paternal, but very subdued and modest, and reminded me of the *ci-devant* New-

port belle, Miss L—— C——. . . . Likewise, may we
here mention Bradlee père, a dried-up lawyer of New
Jersey, after the fashion of the countenance of Professor
Rogers. He was valiant and stuffed his trousers in his
boots and clomb an exceeding tall horse, which so pleased
another old party, Judge Woodruff, that he did likewise,
and subsequently confessed to me that his last equestrian
excursion was in 1834; from which I infer, that, at this
present writing, Judge Woodruff's legs are more or less
totally useless to him as instruments of progression. He
had a complement, his daughter, to whom I did not say
much, as she had somebody, I forget who it was. Then we
must mention, in a front place, the Lady Patroness, Mrs.
H——, and the Noble Patron, Mr. H——. These two
seemed to take us all under their protection, and, so to
speak, to run the machine. Mrs. was plump, fair, and getting towards forty. Mr. was of suitable age, stout, looked
as if fond of good dinners, and apparently very tender on
Mrs., for he continually smiled sweetly at her. Also he
is a large legal gun and part proprietor of the Philadelphia
Enquirer. Then there was a pale, no-account couple, Dr.
and Mrs. G——. The Doctor's sister was Mrs. Smith, to
whom Rosie attached himself with devotion that threatened the tranquillity of the absent S. All these, and more,
were carted over to the Headquarters, where the General
bowed them into his tent and cried out very actively:
"Now Lyman, where are all my young men? I want all of
them." So I hunted all that were not already on hand,
and they were introduced and were expected to make
themselves as agreeable as possible. Without delay we
were again *en voyage* (I, being sharp, got on a horse, which
tended much to my physical comfort, prevented my conversation from being prematurely played out) and took

the party to see the glories of the engineer camp and the
chapel thereof; after which, to the model hospitals of the
6th Corps, of which Dr. Holman is the Medical Director,
who prides himself on doing everything without aid from
the Sanitary, which he doubtless can do, when in winter
quarters. It was like packing and unpacking so many
boxes, to "*aussteigen*" and "*einsteigen*" all the females.
We descended them, for the third time, at Fort Fisher,
whence we showed them the Reb line and the big guns, and
the signal tower of trestle work, 140 feet high. The next
pilgrimage was a long one, as far as the 5th Corps Headquarters, on the left of the line. General Warren issued
forth and welcomed the ladies to oranges, apples, grapes,
crackers, cheese, ale, and cider, into the which the visitors
walked with a vigor most commendable. By the time the
males had made a considerable vacuum in the barrel of ale,
Griffin's division was ready for review, and thither we all
went and found the gallant Humphreys, whom I carefully
introduced to the prettiest young lady there, and expect
to be remembered in his will for that same favor! A review
of Crawford's division followed, very beautiful, with the
setting sun on the bayonets; and so home to an evening
lunch, so to speak, whereat I opened my "pickles," to the
great delectation of both sexes. All this was dreamland
novelty concentrated to the visitors, who departed with
vehement thanks to us, well expressed by Mrs. Grant:
"General Meade, I would far rather command an army,
as you do, than live at City Point and have the position
of *Mr. Grant!*" They were to have a dance that night on
their boat at City Point, and politely and earnestly asked
me to go down with them; but the point was not noticed
by your loving hub.

March 10, 1865

What think you we did yesterday? We had a "Matinée Musicale," at the Chapel of the 50th New York Engineers. Nothing but high-toned amusements, now-a-day, you will perceive. In truth I was very glad to go to it, as good music always gives me pleasure. The band was the noted one of the New Jersey brigade, and consisted of over thirty pieces. But the great feature was Captain Halsted, aide-de-camp to General Wright, in capacity of Max Maretzek, Carl Bergmann, Muzio, or any other musical director you please. It appears that the Captain is a fine musician, and that his ears are straight, though his eyes are not. There was a large assemblage of the fashion and nobility of the environs of Petersburg, though most of the first families of Virginia were unavoidably detained in the city. We had a batch of ladies, who, by the way, seem suddenly to have gone mad on visiting this army. No petticoat is allowed to stay within our lines, but they run up from City Point and return in the afternoon. Poor little Mrs. Webb accompanied the General to our monkish encampment and tried, in a winning way, to hint to General Meade that she ought to remain a day or two; but the Chief, though of a tender disposition towards the opposite sex, hath a god higher than a hooped skirt, to wit, orders, and his hooked nose became as a polite bit of flint unto any such propositions. And so, poor little Mrs. Webb, aforesaid, had to bid her Andrew adieu. The batch of ladies above mentioned were to me unknown! I was told, however, there was a daughter of Simon Cameron, a great speck in money, to whom Crawford was very devoted. Then there was Miss Something of Kentucky, who was a perfect flying battery, and melted the hearts of the swains

in thim parts; particularly the heart of Lieutenant Wm.
Worth, our companion-in-arms, to whom she gave a ring,
before either was quite sure of the other's name! In fact,
I think her parents must have given her a three-week vaca-
tion and a porte-monnaie and said: "Go! Get a husband;
or give place to Maria Jane, your next younger sister."
The gallant Humphreys gave us a review of Miles's division, on top of the concert; whereat General Meade, followed by a bespattered crowd of generals, Staff officers and
orderlies, galloped wildly down the line, to my great
amusement, as the black mare could take care of herself,
but some of the more heavy-legged went perilously floun-
dering in mud-holes and soft sands.

March 11, 1865

From Grant we got a despatch that he would come up,
with some ladies and gentlemen, to see our left and to review a few troops. The General rode down to the termi-
nus of the railroad (which is not very far from Hatcher's
Run), and soon after came the train, with Grant and his
party. Among them was our old friend Daddy Washburn,
the same who came to the Rapid Ann, last May, to behold
Grant swallow Lee at a mouthful, and — didn't see it!
Two divisions of the 2d Corps were turned out under the
eye of the redoubtable Humphreys. They made a fine
appearance, marching past; but I could have cried to see
the Massachusetts 20th with only a hundred muskets or
so, and commanded by Lieutenant-Colonel Curtis, whom
I used to see at Culpeper with a lieutenant's shoulder-
straps. How changed from last spring, when they passed
in review with full ranks, and led by Abbot! . . .
That evening we were invited to City Point, to see a
medal given to General Grant. This medal had been voted

by Congress in honor of him and his soldiers, after the battle and capture of Vicksburg. And you now see the rationale of the Hon. Washburn's presence. *He* was to present it. The Corps commanders with a few aides, and some division commanders, were all the General took with him in the special train. We arrived about 8.30 P.M. and at 9 the ceremony began, in the upper saloon of the steamer Martyn, lying at the wharf. The solemnities were these: General Grant stood on one side of a small table, with an expression as if about to courageously have a large tooth out. On the other stood Washburn, with what seemed an ornamental cigar-box. Whereupon W., with few words, remarked that the Congress of the United States of Ameri-kay had resolved to present him a medal, and a copy of their resolutions engrossed on parchment. "General" (unrolling a scroll), "this is the copy of the resolutions, and I now hand it to you." (Grant looked at the parchment, as much as to say, "That seems all right," rolled it up, in a practical manner, and put it on the table.) "This, General" (opening the ornamental cigar-box, taking out a wooden bonbonnière and opening *that*), "is the medal, which I also hand to you, together with an autograph letter from President Lincoln." The "all-right" expression repeated itself on Grant's face, as he put down the bonbonnière beside the scroll. Then he looked very fixedly at Mr. Washburn and slowly drew a sheet of paper from his pocket. Everyone was hushed, and there then burst forth the following florid eloquence: "Sir! I accept the medal. I shall take an early opportunity of writing a proper reply to the President. I shall publish an order, containing these resolutions, to the troops that were under my command before Vicksburg." As he stopped, Major Pell drew a long breath and said: "I thought we were sure of a speech *this* time, but now we never shall get one out of him." The medal was of gold, three pounds in weight; on one side a bad likeness of Grant; on the reverse a goddess, in an impossible position, who, as General Meade remarked, "seemed to keep a general furnishing shop of guns and sabres." "What is the meaning of the allegory?" he enquired of the Lieutenant-General. "I don't know," replied Grant, with entire simplicity, "I don't know, but I am going to learn, *so as to be able to explain it to people!*" Then the distinguished militaries crowded round to gaze. Major-General Ord, who can't get over his Irish blood, said: "I believe, sir, you are the first man who medalled with his battalion." To which Grant, not taking the point in the faintest degree, replied gravely: "I don't know but I was." There was a heavy crowd of Hectors, I can tell you. Generals Meade, Warren, Wright, Parke, Humphreys, Ord, Gibbon, Ayres, Griffin, Rawlins, Ingalls, etc., etc. Very few ladies. After this a moderate collation, and so home to bed.

March 13, 1865

We have a long telegram from Sheridan, dated Columbia (a small place on the James, between Lynchburg and Richmond). His raid has been a complete surprise. After defeating Early utterly at Waynesboro', he met with no further opposition, but entered Charlottesville and destroyed the rail and bridges; then struck south and got to the James, where he destroyed all destructible parts of the Lynchburg canal, and continued the work as he marched down the river. If you will look at the map, you will see how important it is to break these routes, for they leave only the road via Burkeville Junction open to their great base, Lynchburg. The canal was especially important for

ULYSSES SIMPSON GRANT

transportation of supplies, just as the Erie Canal is so essential to bring to market the grain of the West. . . .

March 18, 1865

This morning I sent you a telegraph, which may be rather late, I fear, though I sent it at the earliest chance. It was to ask you to pay a day's visit here, and see the army, as a curiosity. Mrs. Meade is coming with a party in a special boat from Washington. . . .

You probably are aware that yesterday was the nativity of the Holy Patrick, in whose honor the Irish Brigade, of the 2d Corps, got up a grand race, with a printed programme and every luxury. The weather, which had been most evil the night before, unexpectedly cleared up and the day was fine, exceedingly. We found the course laid out near the Cummings house, in rear of what you remember as the noted Peeble house. There was a judge's stand, flaunting with trefoil flags, and a band beside the same, which had been accommodated with a couple of waggons, in lieu of orchestra. Then there were plenty of guards (there need be no lack of such) and a tent wherein were displayed plates of sandwiches. Alas! *this* was the weak point, the bitter drop in the Irish festa. The brigade, with an Irish generosity, had ordered a fine collation, but the steamer, bad luck to her, had gone and run herself aground somewhere, and poor Paddy was left to eat his feast the day after the fair. Nevertheless, we didn't allow such things to stand in the way, and the races proceeded under the august auspices of General Humphreys, who didn't look exactly like a turfman, and had a mild look of amusement, as he read out: "Captain Brady's grey mare." — Captain Brady bows. "Captain —, Hey? What is that name? I can't read the writing." "Murphy," suggests

22

General Miles. "Oh, dear me, of course, yes; Captain Murphy's bay gelding." "No! *red*," suggests Miles. "Ah, yes, to be sure — red." "Here," says the long-expectant Murphy. Then a bugler blows at a great rate and the horses are brought to the line; the bugler blows at a great rate some more, and away they go. There were a good many different races, some of which were rather tiresome, by reason of the long waiting and the fact that none of the horses were really racers, but only swift officers' steeds, which were not enough trained to go round regularly, but often would balk at the hurdles and refuse to go round at all. Wherefrom we had tragic consequences: for one, scared by the crowd and by the brush hurdle, bolted violently and knocked down a soldier; and Colonel von Schack, in another race, had his horse, which had overleaped, fall on him heavily. . . . Everything was extremely quiet and orderly, and no tipsy people about. . . .

[Mrs. Meade, with a large party, including Mrs. Lyman, arrived at City Point on the evening of March 22. The next two days were spent in visiting the front, and in excursions on the river. On the morning of the 25th, it was found that the Confederates had made an unexpected attack. The visitors were shipped back to Washington, and their hosts made for the front.]

March 25, 1865

We may indeed call this a many-sided field-day: a breakfast with a pleasure party, an assault and a recapture of an entrenched line, a review by the President of a division of infantry, and sharp fighting at sundry points of a front of eighteen miles! If that is not a mixed affair, I would like to know what is? It has been a lucky day, for us; and the 9th Corps, after patient waiting for eight months, have

played the game of the "Mine" against their antagonists.
The official despatches will give you the main facts very
well, but I can add some particulars. About daylight, the
enemy having massed three divisions and a part of a fourth,
made a sudden rush and carried Fort Stedman and about
half a mile of line commanded by it. The garrisons of the
forts on either side stood firm, however, and repelled a
severe attack with much injury to the enemy. Meantime,
General Parke had ordered that the works should be retaken, if it cost every man in the Corps; and all the scattered regiments immediately at hand were put in and
checked a further advance, until General Hartranft (I'm
not sure about the spelling of *his* name) brought up the 3d
division, which had been camped in reserve. He personally led in one brigade of it, with conspicuous gallantry,
retook the whole portion lost, and captured, at one swoop,
1800 Rebels. It was just the "Mine," turned the other way:
they got caught in there and could not get out. Their loss
also in killed and wounded must have been severe, not
only from musketry, but also from canister, which was
thrown into a ravine by which they retreated. Upwards of
a hundred Rebel dead lay in and round Fort Stedman alone.
Our own losses in the 9th Corps will be somewhat over 800,
half of whom may be reckoned prisoners, taken in the first
surprise. I should guess the loss of their opponents as not
less than 2600.

March 26, 1865

My letter of yesterday only gave a part of the day's
work. Our train went briskly up to the front and stopped
not far from the little rustic chapel you saw; for there was
General Parke with his Staff, waiting to receive the General and report the morning's work. . . . Brevet Brigadier McLaughlen got taken in trying to maintain his line

— a good officer. He was the one who had been five days in Boston and told me he was so tired that he thought he should go right back. A certain Major Miller was captured and sent, with a guard of four men, a little to the rear. They sat in a bomb-proof for protection and Miller did so describe the glories of Yankeedom to his captors, that, when we retook the work, they all deserted and came over with him! Then we kept on and got out at our own *domus*, where General Meade (it being then about 11.30 A.M.) telegraphed sundry orders to his generals; wherefrom resulted, at 12.15, the greatest *bang, bang, whang*, from good Duke Humphrey, who, spectacles on nose, rushed violently at the entrenched skirmish line of the enemy and captured the same, with the double view of making a reconnaissance and a diversion, and furthermore of showing the Johns that we were not going to be pitched into without hitting back.

Then there was a lull, filled by the arrival of a long grey procession of some 1500 prisoners from the 9th Corps. Really these men possess a capacity for looking "rough" beyond any people I ever saw, except the townsmen of Signor Fra Diavolo. They grew rougher and rougher. These looked brown and athletic, but had the most matted hair, tangled beards, and slouched hats, and the most astounding carpets, horse-sheets and transmogrified shelter-tents for blankets, that you ever imagined. One grim gentleman, of forbidding aspect, had tempered his ferocity by a black, broad-brimmed straw hat, such as country ministers sometimes wear—a head-dress which, as Whittier remarked, "rather forced the season!" Singularly enough, the train just then came up and the President and General Grant, followed by a small party, rode over to the Headquarters. "I have just now a despatch from General

Parke to show you," said General Meade. "Ah," quoth
the ready Abraham, pointing to the parade-ground of the
Provost-Marshal, "*there* is the best despatch you can show
me from General Parke!" The President is, I think, the
ugliest man I ever put my eyes on; there is also an expression of plebeian vulgarity in his face that is offensive (you
recognize the recounter of coarse stories). On the other
hand, he has the look of sense and wonderful shrewdness,
while the heavy eyelids give him a mark almost of genius.
He strikes me, too, as a very honest and kindly man; and,
with all his vulgarity, I see no trace of low passions in his
face. On the whole, he is such a mixture of all sorts, as
only America brings forth. He is as much like a highly
intellectual and benevolent Satyr as anything I can think
of. I never wish to see him again, but, as humanity runs,
I am well content to have him at the head of affairs. . . .

After which digression I will remark that the President
(who looks very fairly on a horse) reviewed the 3d division, 5th Corps, which had marched up there to support
the line, and were turned into a review. As the Chief Mag-
istrate rode down the ranks, plucking off his hat gracefully
by the hinder part of the brim, the troops cheered quite
loudly. Scarcely was the review done when, by way of
salute, all those guns you saw by Fort Fisher opened with
shells on the enemy's picket line, which you could see, entrenched, from where you stood. Part of the 6th Corps
then advanced and, after a sharp fight, which lasted, with
heavy skirmishing, till sunset, drove off the Rebels and
occupied their position, driving them towards their main
line. At four and at seven P.M. the enemy charged furiously
on Humphreys, to recover their picket line, but were repulsed with great loss; our men never behaved better.
Both Wright and Humphreys took several hundred

prisoners, swelling the total for the day to 2700, more than we have had since the noted 12th of May. Our total loss is from 1800 to 2000; while that of the enemy must be from 4000 to 5000 *plus* a great discouragement. Isn't it funny for you to think of the polite Humphreys riding round in an ambulance with you Friday, and, the next day, smashing fiercely about in a fight?

March 28, 1865

You must let me off with a few lines to-night, because I have some little packing yet to do and would like a good modicum of slumber; for to-morrow we are up and moving betimes in light order. I do not look for any grand action from this (taking the liberty of guessing where I am in the dark). I fancy a heavy infantry force will move to our left and rear, to mask and protect a great movement of cavalry with Sheridan at its head, directed at the South Side R. R. and other communications; all of which the enemy must be fully aware of; but I don't think he can have one half our force in cavalry. The amount of fighting will depend on the moves of the enemy; but I do not ever expect to see more than one such field-day as we used to have in the ever memorable campaign of the Wilderness and Spotsylvania — perhaps not even *one*. Meantime I will not recklessly run against bullets. It isn't my style; not exactly. Yesterday I rode about with the General, who confabbed with Wright, Warren, and the gay Humphreys. The latter is confirmed as the commander of the 2d Corps, at which we are glad, for he was only its commander *ad interim* before.

March 29, 1865

This has been a day of manœuvre and not much fighting. To-morrow may see something more serious. It seems like old times to be once more writing on my knee and sitting in a tent without a board floor. I prefer it; there is novelty in seeing a new bit of country. Yesterday we had an interesting trip to City Point. General Meade said to me, to my great surprise: "I am going down to-morrow to *see Sherman!*" Which, as I supposed Sherman to be at that moment somewhere near Goldsboro', seemed a rather preposterous idea! At an early hour we got to Grant's Headquarters and found *le monde* not yet up. Soon, however, they began to peer out of their log houses and General Meade marched in to visit the great Mogul. As I was looking in that direction, there suddenly issued from the house a tall figure who jerked himself forward, pulled suddenly up, and regarded the landscape with an inquisitive and very wrinkled expression. This was the redoubtable Sherman himself. He is a very remarkable-looking man, such as could not be grown out of America — the concentrated quintessence of Yankeedom. He is tall, spare, and sinewy, with a very long neck, and a big head at the end of the same. The said big head is a most unusual combination. I mean that, when a man is spare, with a high forehead, he usually has a contracted back to his head; but Sherman has a swelling "fighting" back to *his* head, and all his features express determination, particularly the mouth, which is wide and straight, with lips that shut tightly together. He is a very homely man, with a regular nest of wrinkles in his face, which play and twist as he eagerly talks on each subject; but his expression is pleasant and kindly. But he believes in hard war. I heard him say: "Columbia! — pretty much all burned; and burned *good!*" There too was "little Phil Sheridan," scarce five feet high, with his sun-browned face and sailor air. I saw Sherman, Grant, Meade, and Sheridan, all together. A thing to speak of in after years!

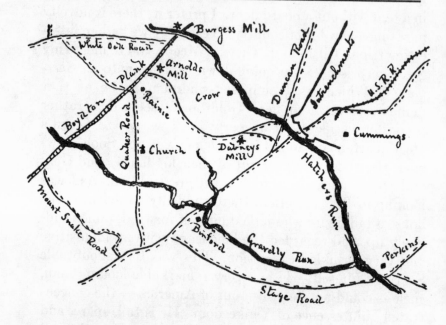

Note. From Cummings to Binford is 2½ miles

BOYDTON PLANK ROAD AND HATCHER'S RUN

March 30, 1865

I take advantage of a rainy morning to draw you a map and start a letter, to explain and recount the deeds of yesterday. . . . The day before, a part of the Army of the James had crossed to us, from Bermuda Hundred, and, under the sure conduct of Rosie, had relieved the 2d Corps in their part of the line. At daylight the 5th Corps moved from our extreme left, crossed the stream at the Perkins house and marched along the stage road. Somewhat later the 2d Corps crossed directly by the Vaughan road and marched down it as far as Gravelly Run, then faced to the right and formed from east to west. It was like to the

ruins of Carthage to behold those chimneys, which, since
October last, have been our comfort at Headquarters, now
left lonely and desolate, deprived of their tents, which
seemed to weep, as they were ruthlessly torn down and
thrown into waggons. At 7.30 A.M. we all got on the
chargers and wended toward the left. The fancy huts of
the 2d Corps were all roofless, and their Headquarters were
occupied by General Gibbon, of the other side of the river.
The 1st division was crossing the Hatcher's Run bridge,
as we got to it, the two others being already over. Near
Gravelly Run we came on the sturdy Humphreys, who was
gleaming through his spectacles with a fun-ahead sort of
expression and presently rode away to get his men "straightened out," as Pleasonton used to say. Bye-and-bye he
came jogging back, to say his Corps was now in position,
running from near Hatcher's Run, on the right, to near
Quaker Road Church on the left. Whereupon we rode off
to see General Warren, who had arrived at the Junction
of the Vaughan and Quaker roads. As soon as we got there,
Griffin's division was sent up the Quaker road, to join the
left of Humphreys', and to be followed by most of the rest
of the Corps. . . . At 1.30 P.M. we went up the Quaker
road to see General Griffin, being somewhat delayed by
Gravelly Run, a brook too deep for fording and whereof
the little bridge had been broken by the Rebs. The country is much more variegated over here. There are some
rocks and high ground, and the runs are quite picturesque,
with steep banks. One pretty sight was a deserted farmhouse quite surrounded by peach trees, loaded with blos-
soms. In the distance it seemed covered with pink clouds.
After starting Griffin's line forward, we rode along the line
of battle of Miles (who had the left of the 2d Corps), where
we found General Humphreys. The right of his line had

sent out a party which took possession of Dabney's Mill, driving out a few Rebels. The whole force from one end to another was ordered to go forward at once, Griffin being, from the nature of the ground, somewhat in advance. All went on without anything more than scattered skirmishing till near five P.M., when Griffin was struck by a part, or the whole, of two Rebel divisions. But G. is a rough man to handle, and, after a sharp fight, drove them back and followed them up, taking a hundred prisoners. Our losses were some 400 altogether in this affair. Of the enemy we buried 126; so that their total loss, including prisoners, must be, say, 800. The Griffin was in great spirits at this affair and vowed he could drive the enemy wherever he found them. Their object in attacking us was to delay our advance, and to get time to man their works. As soon as Warren got up the rest of his Corps, he pushed on the attack, but John had got enough and had fallen back to his parapets, and thus the day ended. Riding back to the Vaughan road, we found General Grant, who had come up with his Staff, and who camped near us last night, 29th. . . .

[To-day] nothing to note, but that there was a steady and drenching rain the whole livelong day, which reduced these sandy, clayey roads to a pudding or porridge, as the case might be. The chief Quartermaster told me it was the worst day for moving trains he ever had had in all his experience. A train of 600 waggons, with the aid of 1000 engineer troops, was fifty-six hours in going five miles!

March 31, 1865

The rain held up about ten A.M. and the sun once more shone. By this time our lines, running east and west, had been moved due north, till they rested their right on

Hatcher's Run, north of the Crow house, and their left on the Boydton plank, near the entrance of the Quaker road. For this purpose Ayres's and Crawford's divisions were pushed forward and Griffin held in reserve. We rode out, towards the left (our Headquarters were near the Vaughan road close to Gravelly Run), stopping some time to consult with Grant. About 10.30 we heard a brief fusillade on the right of our line (a demonstration to divert our attention), followed by heavy musketry towards the White Oak road. As we came to Warren's old Headquarters, high up on the Quaker road, I could see something had gone wrong. A cavalry officer galloped up and said: "I must have more men to stop these stragglers! the road is full of them." And indeed there were those infernal drummers, and pack-mules, and not a few armed men, training sulkily to the rear. I required no one to tell me what *that meant*. The enemy had tried on Griffin, two days since, without success, but this time they had repeated the game on Ayres and Crawford, with a different result. As these two divisions were moving through the thick woods, they were suddenly charged, broken, and driven back towards the Boydton plank road; but some batteries being brought to their aid, the men were rallied behind a branch of Gravelly Run. Griffin took up a rear line, to ensure the position. General Meade at once ordered Miles to go in, to the right of the 5th Corps, and Griffin to advance likewise. The General rode out in person to give Humphreys the necessary orders about Miles's division, and found him at Mrs. Rainie's, at the junction of the Quaker road and the plank. There was a wide open in front, and I could see, not far off, the great tree where we got such an awful shelling, at the first Hatcher's Run fight. Miles was in the open, forming his troops for the attack. Just then the enemy opened a battery on us, with solid shot, several of which came ricocheting round us. I recollect I turned just then and saw Charlie Mills sitting on horseback, near General Humphreys. He nodded and smiled at me. Immediately after, General Meade rode to a rising ground a couple of hundred yards from the house, while General Humphreys went a short distance to the front, in the field. Almost at that instant a round shot passed through Humphreys' Staff and struck Mills in the side, and he fell dead from his horse. He was indeed an excellent and spirited young man and beloved by us all. . . . When I rode that evening to the hospital, and saw the poor boy lying there on the ground, it made me think of Abbot, a year ago. It is the same thing over and over again. And strange too, this seeing a young man in full flush of robust health, and the next moment nothing that we can make out but the broken machine that the soul once put in motion. Yet this is better than that end in which the faculties, once brilliant, gradually fade, month after month.

About noon, Miles and Griffin went in, with sharp firing, drove the enemy back, and made a lodgment on the White Oak road. Meantime, Sheridan, after all sorts of mud toils, got north of Dinwiddie, where he was attacked by a heavy force of infantry and cavalry and forced back nearly to that place. Not to forgo our advantage on the northwest, we immediately sent the whole 5th Corps by night to Dinwiddie to report to General Sheridan and attack the enemy next morning — a hard march after the two days' fighting in the storm!

April 1, 1865

You will see the April Fool was on the Rebels; for they did not know that, the night before, we had sent down an entire corps of infantry (the 5th) to aid the worsted Sheridan. Their infantry had contented itself with retiring from Sheridan's front, half-way to the White Oak road, and going into camp with a precautionary breastwork in their front. As they lay there, resting, Warren struck them in the flank and swung round, even into their rear, while the cavalry charged their front. After a brief but determined resistance, the enemy broke and fled in wild confusion; 4000 and over were captured and a large part of the rest hopelessly scattered in the woods. Thus our movement, which had begun in simple advantage, now grew to brilliant success, and was destined to culminate, within twenty-four hours, in complete victory.

We were up pretty early, as usual, and at 6.30 A.M. were already at Grant's Headquarters. These were close to Dabney's Mill, now marked only by a huge pile of sawdust — a veteran battle-ground, marked by two considerable actions and many minor skirmishes. Indeed that whole tract is a network of picket-pits and hasty breastworks. After visiting Humphreys, on the Quaker road, we returned to the Lieutenant-General's, and here it was that a note from Sheridan told that he was driving the enemy. Grant folded the slip of paper, and, looking at Meade, said, very quietly: "Very well, then I want Wright and Parke to assault to-morrow morning at four o'clock." These dozen words settled the fate of Petersburg and of Richmond! It was midnight when General Warren suddenly came into our camp, followed by only one Staff officer. I got him something to eat, but was surprised to see no look of gratification at his victory to-day. Poor man! he had been relieved from command of his Corps. I don't know the details, but I have told you of the difficulties he has had with the General, from his tendency to substitute his own judgment for that of his commanding officer. It seems that Grant was much moved against him by this. The General had nothing to do with it. I am sorry, for I like Warren.

April 2, 1865

Last night was a busy one and a noisy. Some battery or other was playing the whole time, and, now and then, they would all wake up at once; while the skirmishers kept rushing at each other and firing, sometimes almost by volleys. All of which did good, because it wore out the enemy and made them uncertain where the main attack might come. At a quarter past four in the morning, Wright, having massed his three divisions in columns of attack, near Fort Fisher, just before daylight charged their works, burst through four lines of abattis, and poured a perfect torrent of men over the parapet. He then swept to the right and left, bearing down all the attempts of the enemy's reserves to check him; a part also of his force went straight forward, crossed the Boydton plank and tore up the track of the South Side Railroad. The assault was, in reality, the death-blow to Lee's army. His centre was thus destroyed, his left wing driven into the interior line of Petersburg, and his right taken in flank and left quite isolated. At the same moment Parke attacked the powerful works in his front, somewhat to the right of the Jerusalem plank road, and carried the strong outer line, with three batteries, containing twelve guns; but the fire was so hot from the inner line that his men could get no further, but continued to hold on, with great obstinacy, for the rest of the day, while the Rebels made desperate sorties to dislodge them. In this attack General Potter received a wound which still keeps him in an extremely critical condition. You may well believe that the musketry, which had spattered pretty well during the night, now broke out with redoubled noise in all directions.

Under the excitement of getting at my valise and having some fresh paper, I am moved to write you some more about the great Sunday, which I so irreverently broke off.[1] I was saying that the musketry broke out pretty freely from all quarters. Do you understand the position of the troops? Here is a rough diagram.[2] On the right Parke, from the river to west of the Jerusalem road; then Wright and Ord, stretching to Hatcher's Run; then Humphreys, forming the left wing. To the left and rear were Sheridan and Griffin, making a detached left wing. Humphreys' left rested somewhat west of the Boydton plank. Ord and Humphreys were now crowding in their skirmishers, trying for openings in the slashings to put in a column. Ord tried to carry the line, but could not get through; but the 2d division of the 2d Corps got a chance for a rush, and, about 7.30 in the morning, stormed a Rebel fort, taking four guns and several hundred Rebels; in this attack the 19th and 20th Massachusetts were very prominent. About nine o'clock the General rode off towards the left, from our Headquarters near the crossing of the Vaughan road, over Hatcher's Run. He overtook and consulted a moment with Grant, and then continued along our old line of battle, with no "intelligent orderly" except myself. So that is the way I came to be Chief-of-Staff, Aide-de-camp, Adjutant-General, and all else; for presently the Chief took to giving orders at a great rate, and I had to get out my "manifold writer" and go at it. I ordered Benham to rush up from City Point and reinforce Parke, and I managed to send something to pretty much everybody, so as

---

[1] Actually written April 13.

[2] No diagram is found with the letter.

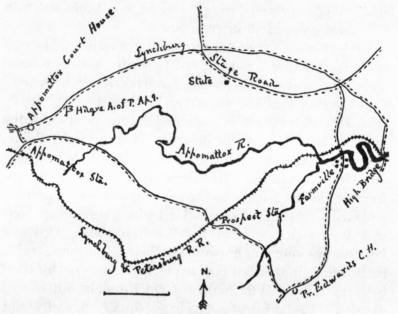

HIGH BRIDGE TO APPOMATTOX COURT HOUSE

to keep them brisk and lively. In fact, I completely went ahead of the fly that helped the coach up the hill by bearing down on the spokes of the wheels!

And now came the notice that the enemy were going at the double-quick towards their own right, having abandoned the whole of Ord's front and some of Humphreys'. We were not quite sure whether they might not contemplate an attack in mass on Humphreys' left, and so this part of our line was pushed forward with caution while Humphreys' right was more rapidly advanced. We met sundry squads of prisoners coming across the fields, among them a forlorn band, with their instruments. "Did you not see that band?" said Rosie to me that evening, in great glee. "Ah! I did see them. I did them ask for to

play Yan — kay Doodle; but they vould not!" About 9
o'clock we got to General Humphreys on the Boydton
plank road, by Mrs. Rainie's. It was now definitely known
that the enemy had given up his whole line in this front
and was retreating northwesterly, towards Sutherland's
Station. He was reported, however, as forming line of battle a mile or two beyond us. Immediately Miles's division
marched up the Claiborne road, while Mott, followed by
Hays (2d division, 2d Corps), took the Boydton plank.
Still more to our left, the cavalry and the 5th Corps were
moving also in a northerly direction. Meanwhile, Wright
had faced his Corps about and was marching *down* the
Boydton plank, that is to say *towards* the 2d Corps, which
was going *up;* on his left was the 24th Corps, which
had formed there by Grant's orders; so you will see, by the
map, that the jaws of the pincers were coming together,
and the enemy hastened to slip from between them! As
soon as Wright found that this part of the field was swept,
he *again* faced about, as did the 24th Corps (now forming
his right), and marched directly up the Boydton plank to
the inner line of Petersburg defences, rested his left on the
river, swung the 24th round to join Parke, on the right,
and *voila* the city invested on east, south, and west. I am
afraid this double manœuvre will rather confuse you, so
here are two diagrams, with the corps numbered, in their
first and second positions.

By eleven o'clock the General had got all his troops in
motion and properly placed, and the Staff had come from
the camp. We all started up the plank road, straight towards the town. It was a strange sensation, to ride briskly
past the great oak, near Arnold's Mill, where we got so
awfully cannonaded at the first Hatcher's Run; then on till
we came to the earthwork, on this side of the Run, whence

23

came the shot that killed Charlie Mills; then across the Run itself, passing their line with its abattis and heavy parapet, and so up the road, on the other side, marked by deep ruts of the Rebel supply-trains. As we got to the top of the rise, we struck the open country that surrounds the town, for several miles, and here the road was full of troops, who, catching sight of the General trotting briskly by, began to cheer and wave their caps enthusiastically! This continued all along the column, each regiment taking it up in turn. It was a goodly ride, I can tell you! Presently we spied General Grant, seated on the porch of an old house, by the wayside, and there we too halted. It seemed a deserted building and had been occupied by a Rebel ordnance sergeant, whose papers and returns were lying about in admirable confusion. A moral man was this sergeant, and had left behind a diary, in one page of which he lamented the vice and profanity of his fellow soldiers. He was not, however, cleanly, but quite untidy in his domestic arrangements. From this spot we had an admirable view of *our own works*, as the Rebels had, for months, been used to look at them. There was that tall signal tower, over against us, and the bastions of Fort Fisher, and here, near at hand, the Rebel line, with its huts and its defenders sorely beleagured over there in the inner lines, against which our batteries were even now playing; and presently Gibbon assaults these two outlying redoubts, and takes them after a fierce fight, losing heavily. In one was a Rebel captain, who told his men to surrender to nobody. He himself fought to the last, and was killed with the butt end of a musket, and most of his command were slain in the work. But we carried the works: neither ditches nor abattis could keep our men out that day! You may be sure Miles had not been idle all this time. Following up the

Claiborne road, he came on the enemy at Sutherland's
Station, entrenched and holding on to cover the escape of
their train. Though quite without support, he attacked
them fiercely, and, at the second or third charge, stormed
their breastwork, routed them and took three guns and
near 1000 prisoners. With this gallant feat the day ended,
gloriously, as it had begun. We went into camp at the Wall
house and all preparations were made to cross the river
next morning and completely shut in the town.

[The preceding letter like many others, was written
several days after the events described. The victory was
so overwhelming that all Lyman actually wrote home that
night was:]

HEADQUARTERS ARMY OF THE POTOMAC
Sunday, April 2, 1865
11 P.M.

MY DEAR MIMI: —

THE
REBELLION
HAS
GONE UP!

THEODORE LYMAN
LT.-COL. & VOL. A.D.C.

April 3, 1865

We began our day early, for, about light, I heard Duane
say, outside my tent: "They have evacuated Petersburg."
Sure enough, they were gone, across the river, and, at that
very moment, their troops at Richmond, and all along the
river, with their artillery and trains, were marching in all
haste, hoping to join each other and get to Burkeville
Junction, *en route* for Danville. How they succeeded will

be seen in the sequel. General Meade, to my great satisfaction, said he would ride in and take a look at the place
we so long had seen the steeples of. Passing a series of
heavy entrenchments and redoubts, we entered the place
about eight in the morning. The outskirts are very poor,
consisting chiefly of the houses of negroes, who collected,
with broad grins, to gaze on the triumphant Yanks; while
here and there a squalid family of poor whites would lower
at us from broken windows, with an air of lazy dislike.
The main part of the town resembles Salem, very much,
plus the southern shiftlessness and *minus* the Yankee
thrift. Even in this we may except Market Street, where
dwell the *haute noblesse*, and where there are just square
brick houses and gardens about them, as you see in Salem,
all very well kept and with nice trees. Near the river, here
large enough to carry large steamers, the same closely
built business streets, the lower parts of which had suffered
severely from our shells; here and there an entire building
had been burnt, and everywhere you saw corners knocked
off, and shops with all the glass shattered by a shell exploding within.

We then returned a little and took a road up the hill
towards the famous cemetery ridge. Petersburg, you must
understand, lies in a hollow, at the foot of a sort of bluff.
In fact, this country, is a dead, sandy level, but the water-
courses have cut trenches in it, more or less deep according to their volume of water. Thus the Appomattox is in
a deep trench, while the tributary "runs" that come in are
in more shallow trenches; so that the country near the
banks looks hilly; when, however, you get on top of these
bluffs, you find yourself on a plain, which is more or less
worn by water-courses into a succession of rolls. Therefore, from our lines you could only see the spires, because

the town was in a gully. The road we took was very steep and was no less than the Jerusalem plank, whose other end I was so familiar with. Turning to the left, on top of the crest, we passed a large cemetery, with an old ruined chapel, and, descending a little, we stood on the famous scene of the "Mine." It was this cemetery that our infantry should have gained that day. Thence the town is commanded. How changed these entrenchments! Not a soul was there, and the few abandoned tents and cannon gave an additional air of solitude. Upon these parapets, whence the rifle-men have shot at each other, for nine long months, in heat and cold, by day and by night, you might now stand with impunity and overlook miles of deserted breastworks and covered ways! It was a sight only to be appreciated by those who have known the depression of waiting through summer, autumn and winter for so goodly an event! Returning through the town, we stopped at the handsome house of Mr. Wallace, where was Grant and his Staff, and where we learned the death of Lieutenant-General A. P. Hill, who was killed by one of our stragglers whom he tried to capture. Crowds of nigs came about us to sell Confederate money, for which they would take anything we chose to give. At noon we left the town, and, going on the river road, camped that night near Sutherland's Station.

April 4, 1865

We had camped last night round about Sutherland's Station, as I told you. The fields there were covered with waggons that had parked ready to follow the army. Here too was the scene of Miles's fight of the 2d, and the Rebel breastworks, with scattered ammunition and dead artillery horses, still marked the spot. Grant had camped

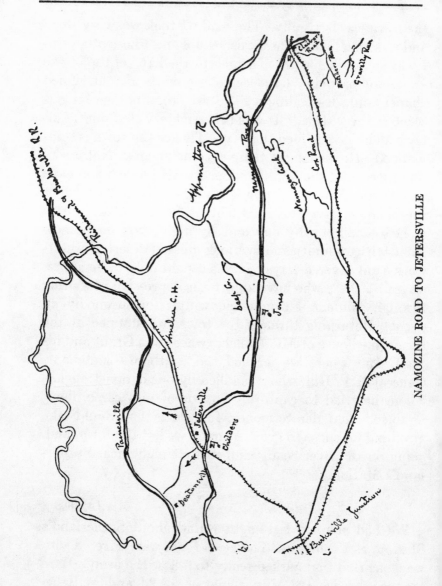

NAMOZINE ROAD TO JETERSVILLE

there, too, and had confirmed the rumor that Richmond
was in our hands; also had stated that Sheridan, in his
pursuit towards Amelia Court House, reported much
abandoned property by the way, and the capture of prisoners and guns. Everybody was in great spirits, especially
the 6th Corps, which cheered Meade vociferously, wherever he showed himself. It would take too much time to
tell all the queer remarks that were made; but I was
amused at two boys in Petersburg, one of whom was telling
the officers, rather officially, that he was not a Rebel at all.
"Oh!" said the other sturdily, "you've changed your
tune since yesterday, and I can lick you, whatever you
are!"

This morning the whole army was fairly marching in
pursuit. . . . It was a hard march, for two poor roads
are not half enough for a great army and its waggon trains,
and yet we took nothing on wheels but the absolute essen-
tials for three or four days. We were up at four o'clock,
to be ready for an early start; all the roads were well
blocked with waggons toiling slowly towards the front.
Riding ahead, we came upon General Wright, halted near
a place called Mt. Pleasant Church. The bands were playing and the troops were cheering for the fall of Richmond,
which, as the jocose Barnard (Captain on Wheaton's
Staff) said, "Would knock gold, so that it wouldn't be
worth more than seventy-five cents on the dollar!" Suddenly we heard renewed cheers, while the band played
"Hail to the Chief." We looked up the road, and, seeing a
body of cavalry, supposed the Lieutenant-General was
coming. But lo! as they drew nearer, we recognized the
features of Colonel Mike Walsh (erst a sergeant of cavalry),
who, with an admirable Irish impudence, was acknowl-
edging the shouts of the crowd that mistook him for Grant!

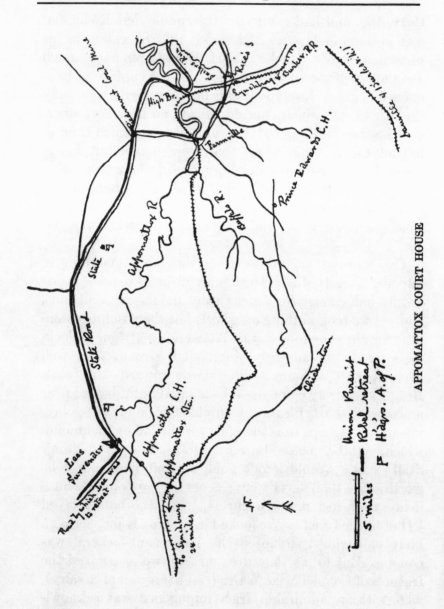

APPOMATTOX COURT HOUSE

We continued our ride. This country, from Gravelly Run up, is no longer the flat sand of Petersburg, but like Culpeper, undulating, with quartz and sandstone, and a red soil. About five we halted at Mrs. Jones's, a little east of Deep Creek, and prepared to go supperless to bed on the floor or on the grass, for our waggons were hopelessly in the rear. General Humphreys was across the Run, whither General Meade went, and came back with him at dusk. The General was very sick; he had been poorly since Friday night, and now was seized with a chill, followed by a violent fever, which excited him greatly, though it did not impair the clearness of his head. Good Humphreys got us something to eat and so we all took to our hoped-for rest.

April 5, 1865

Last night, at 9.30, came a note from Sheridan, dated at Jetersville, saying that he was there, entrenched, with the 5th Corps and a part of the cavalry; that the whole Rebel army was in his front trying to get off its trains; that he expected to be attacked, but, if the remaining infantry could be hurried up, there was a chance of taking the whole of the enemy. Although the 2d Corps had only gone into bivouac at eight in the morning, and had no rations at that moment, General Meade issued orders for them to move at one at night and push on for Jetersville, followed by the 6th Corps, which lay just behind. The distance was fifteen or sixteen miles. I was sleeping on the floor, in the same room with the General, to look out for him in case he needed anything; for he had a distressing cough and a high fever, but would not give in, for he has a tremendous nervous system that holds him up through everything. General Webb was worn out with want of sleep, so I was up most of the night, writing and copying and receiving the despatches. The General talked a great deal and was very excited in his thoughts, though his head was perfectly clear. General Humphreys had slept, I don't know when — but there he was, as sturdy as ever, issuing orders for the advance, with his eyes wide open, as much as to say; "Sleep — don't mention it!" At one in the morning, sure enough, he moved; but had not got a mile, when, behold the whole of Merritt's division of cavalry, filing in from a side road, and completely closing the way! That's the way with those cavalry bucks: they bother and howl about infantry not being up to support them, and they are precisely the people who always are blocking up the way; it was so at Todd's Tavern, and here again, a year after. They are arrant boasters, and, to hear Sheridan's Staff talk, you would suppose his ten thousand mounted carbineers had crushed the entire Rebellion. Whereas they are immediately cleaned out, the moment they strike a good force of foot-men, and then they cry wolf merrily. The plain truth is, they are useful and energetic fellows, but commit the error of thinking they *can* do everything and that no one else *does* do anything. Well, Humphreys could not stir a step till seven next morning, but, meantime, his men got rest by the roadside and his rations were, with incredible exertions, gotten up to him, over fearful roads. At about nine o'clock we put the General in his four-horse waggon, wherein he can lie down, and followed the column, first along the main Namozine road, and then, striking off to the right, across the fields to Jetersville. At ten, we got word that the enemy were still near Amelia Court House, and the infantry were continually ordered to press on, the General stirring up the halting brigades, as he rode past. Some four miles this side of Childer's house (where Sheridan was) we came upon General Humphreys, at a large

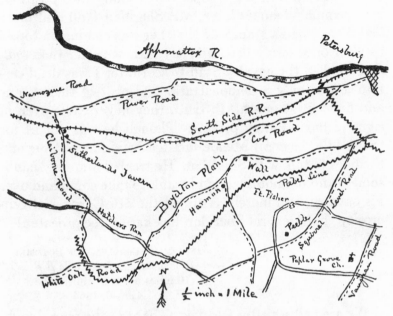

BOYDTON PLANK ROAD

house of one Perkinson. Near by were several hundred
Rebel prisoners, looking pretty gaunt, for we had nothing
to give, and but little food for our own troops. I think
that we have been obliged to give mule meat to some of our
prisoners, during this campaign, to keep them alive till
they could get to supplies; and some of our own men have
gone very hungry, because, in the haste of pursuit, they
marched straight away from the waggons. . . . At 1.30
we found General Sheridan at the house, which was perhaps a mile south of Jetersville. Along the front was the
5th Corps, strongly entrenched, while the cavalry covered
the flanks. A little before three, Sheridan rode off to the
left, to help in Davies whom the enemy's infantry was
trying to cut off. Before this, at two, the head of the 2d

Corps was up and the troops went rapidly into position; for, a couple of hours later, Mr. Sheridan (and still more his officers) had a stampede that Lee was coming on top of us. For once in my life I will say I knew better than *that*, and laughed the cavalry Staff to scorn; for I was dead certain it was only a demonstration, to protect their trains and find our strength. In truth they never came even in sight of our infantry pickets. Though he was not fit for the saddle, General Meade insisted on riding out beyond the lines to talk with Sheridan. He treated him very handsomely and did not avail of his rank to take command over his cavalry, but merely resumed the 5th Corps — a generosity that General Sheridan has hardly reciprocated!

HEADQUARTERS ARMY OF POTOMAC
Richmond and *Burkeville R.R.*
10 miles north of Burkeville
April 6, 1865

We are pelting after Old Lee as hard as the poor doughboys' legs can go. I estimate our prisoners at 16,000, with lots of guns and colors. At six A.M. the three infantry corps advanced in line of battle, on Amelia Court House; 2d on the left; 5th in the centre; and 6th on the right. Sheridan's cavalry, meantime, struck off to the left, to head off their waggon-trains in the direction of the Appomattox River. We did not know just then, you perceive, in what precise direction the enemy was moving. Following the railroad directly towards Amelia C.H., General Meade received distinct intelligence, at nine o'clock, that the enemy was moving on Deatonsville, intending probably to cross the Appomattox at High Bridge. Instantly General Meade gave orders for the 6th Corps to face about and move by the left flank and seek roads in the direction of High Bridge, with the idea of supporting the cavalry in their attempt to head off the enemy; the 2d Corps were turned into the left-hand road nearest Jetersville, and directed to push on and strike the enemy wherever they could. At nine we got to the left-hand road lying some way beyond Jetersville, and here the 5th Corps was turned in, with orders to follow the road through Paineville and attack whatever they found. These prompt dispositions ensured the grand success of the day, which the newspapers have gracefully handed over to General Sheridan!

Here I may as well say that Lee was trying to escape with his large artillery and waggon trains. At first he thought to move directly along the railroad, through Burkeville, to Danville. Cut off by the 5th Corps and the cavalry, he *now* was trying to march "cross lots" and get to the Danville road, somewhere below us. . . . At ten, we got back to Jetersville, a collection of half-a-dozen houses with a country church. From the second story of a house I witnessed a most curious spectacle — a fight, four miles off in a straight line! At that point was a bare ridge, a little above Deatonsville, and there, with my good glass, I could see a single man very well. It was just like a play of marionettes! and the surrounding woods made side scenes to this stage. At first, I saw only the Rebel train, moving along the ridge towards Deatonsville, in all haste: there now goes a pigmy ambulance drawn by mouse-like horses, at a trot. Here come more ambulances and many waggons from the woods, and disappear, in a continuous procession, over the ridge. Suddenly — *boom! boom!* and the distant smoke of Humphreys' batteries curls above the pine trees. At this stimulus the Lilliputian procession redoubles its speed (I am on the point of crying "bravo!" at this brilliant stroke of the gentleman who is pulling the wires). But now enter from the woods, in some confusion,

a good number of Rebel cavalry; they form on the crest —
but, *boom! boom!* go the cannon, and they disappear. Ah!
here come the infantry! Now for a fight! Yes, a line of
battle in retreat, and covering the rear. There are mounted
officers; they gallop about, waving their tiny swords.
Halt! The infantry form a good line on the crest; you
can't scare *them*. What are they carrying? Spears? No,
rails; that's what it is, rails for to revet a breastwork.
They scramble about like ants. You had better hurry up,
Yanks, if you want to carry that crest! (The stage manager informs me the Yanks *are* hurrying and the next act
will be — Enter Duke Humphrey, in haste.) Hullo!
There come six fleet mice dragging something, followed by
more: yes, a battery. They unlimber: a pause: Flash! —
(count twenty-two seconds by Captain Barrows's watch)
then, *bang!* — flash! flash! *bang! bang!* There come in their
skirmishers! running for their lives; certainly the Yanks
are in those woods. Now they turn their guns more to the
left; they are getting flanked. Their officers gallop wildly.
You seem to hear them shout, "Change front to the rear!"
anyhow they do so, at a double-quick. Then one volley of
musketry, and they are gone, guns and all! The next
moment our skirmishers go swarming up the hill; up goes
a battery, and down goes the curtain.

There is no rest for the wicked. All day long the peppery
Humphreys, glaring through those spectacles, presses
hotly in their rear; the active Sheridan is felling trees
across their front; on their right is the Appomattox, im-
passible; and now, as the afternoon closes, here comes the
inevitable Wright, grimly on their left flank, at Sailor's
Creek. The 6th Corps charges; they can't be stopped —
result, five Rebel generals; 8600 prisoners, 14 cannon; the
Rebel rear-guard annihilated! As we get to our camp, be-

yond Deatonsville, there comes a Staff officer with a despatch. "*I* attacked with two divisions of the 6th Corps.
I captured many thousand prisoners, etc., etc. P. H. Sheridan." "Oh," said Meade, "so *General Wright wasn't
there.*" "Oh, yes!" cried the Staff officer, as if speaking of
some worthy man who had commanded a battalion, "Oh,
yes, General Wright *was* there." Meade turned on his heel
without a word, and Cavalry Sheridan's despatch proceeded — to the newspapers!

April 7, 1865

The country about Deatonsville (a cluster of half-a-
dozen brick farmhouses) is a great improvement, full of
hills, not high but steep, with a nice brook in every hollow;
the air begins too to sniff of the distant mountains, one
or two of whose outlying spurs may hence be seen. We
started from camp about eight in the morning, and, on
the ridge, just beyond Sailor's Run, we came on the 5th
Corps, moving from right to left, in rear of the 2d and 6th
Corps, and taking the road towards Prince Edward Court
House. Sailor's Run is a considerable brook in the bottom
of a deep, precipitous hollow, where the Rebel train, closely
followed by Humphreys, had come to a hopeless deadlock.
The road thither, for several miles, showed that their animals were giving out. The way was completely strewed
with tents, ammunition, officers' baggage, and, above all,
little Dutch ovens — such a riches of little Dutch ovens
never was seen! I suppose they bake hoe-cakes in them.
You saw them lying about, with their little legs kicked up
in the air, in a piteous manner! But, when we got to the
Run, there was a complete mess! Waggons, ambulances,
cannon filled the hollow near the bridge! The hillside was
white with Adjutant-General's papers scattered from sev-

eral waggons of that department; here and there lay a
wounded Rebel, while everywhere lay broken boxes, trunks,
ammunition-cases and barrels. It was strange to see the
marks on the waggons, denoting the various brigades,
once so redoubtable! At 10.30 the 2d Corps, after some
firing, crossed the Appomattox, at High Bridge, where we
too arrived at eleven. Nothing can more surprise one than
a sudden view of this great viaduct, in a country like Virginia, where public works are almost unknown. It is a rail-
way bridge, nearly 2500 feet long, over the valley of the
Appomattox, and is supported by great brick piers, of
which the central ones are about 140 feet high. The river
itself is very narrow, perhaps seventy-five feet wide, but it
runs in a fertile valley, a mile in width, part of which is
subject to overflow. At either end the Rebels had powerful
earthworks (on which they were still laboring the day before). In these they abandoned eighteen pieces of artillery,
and, in one, they blew up the magazine, which made a sad
scene of rubbish. . . .

At four P.M. we heard heavy firing across the river from
Humphreys, who had gone towards the Lynchburg stage
road and had there struck the whole of Lee's army, entrenched and covering his trains. Nothing daunted, he
crowded close up and attempted to assault one point with
a brigade, but was repulsed with heavy loss. A despatch
was sent in haste to Wright, to push on to Farmville, cross
the river and attack the enemy in rear; but, when he got
there, behold the 24th Corps before, the bridges burnt and
everything at a standstill. A division of cavalry forded and
attacked, but the Rebel infantry sent *them* to the right-
about in short order. And so we got to camp at nine P.M.,
at Rice's Station.

April 8, 1865

We have been making our usual little picnic to-day —
say nineteen miles — and have got about half-way between
Burkeville Junction and Lynchburg. Did you ever see
that Washburn, Colonel in Louis Cabot's regiment,
rather a well-looking young man? He was sent the day before yesterday, by Ord, from Burkeville Junction, with a
small infantry and cavalry force, to destroy the Farmville bridges, to keep back the Rebels and head them off;
but he found the enemy there before him; they attacked
him, got him in the forks·of two runs and killed or took
most of his command, after a really desperate fight; Washburn getting a bullet through the cheeks and a sabre cut
in the head. Then the Rebels crossed from Farmville to
the other side and *then* they burnt the bridges in *our* faces.

Last night was a white frost, as my toes, under the
blankets, suggested to me in the morning. We left betimes, before six, to wit; for we had to get all the way back
to High Bridge and then begin our march thence. After
crossing the river beside the bridge (whereof the last three
spans had been burnt by the enemy), we bore to the right,
into the pine woods, then kept to the left, through a poor
wood road, and emerged on the main road, about a mile
east of the Piedmont coal mine, just as Humphreys's rear
guard were marching on. As they had supposed, the enemy
had retreated during the night and now we looked forward
to a day's stern chase. At the coal mine we found General
Humphreys, wearing much the expression of an irascible
pointer, he having been out on several roads, ahead of his
column, and getting down on his knees and peering at foot-
tracks, through his spectacles, to determine by which the
main body had retreated. Here we got a great excitement,

24

on learning that, last night, General Williams had conveyed a note from Grant to Lee, demanding his surrender. That, furthermore, Lee had made a reply, and that *now* General Williams had just gone forward, with a flag, to send an answer. All this looked favorable and gave a new aspect to the whole question! The original idea of sending a note came from the language used by Ewell and his Staff, captured on the 6th. These officers had stated that their position was hopeless and that Lee might surrender, if summoned. The good Williams's mission came near being fatal to the messenger of peace; for, as he got in sight of the rear Rebel videttes and was waving away, to attract their attention, they shot at him and wounded his orderly. However, he persevered, and, with a little care, got his note delivered.

We now trotted along what had been, years since, a fine stage road; but the present condition was not exactly favorable to waggons with delicate springs — the road at present being playfully variegated with boulders, three feet high, which had inconvenienced the Rebel trains, as many a burnt waggon testified. Toiling along past the trains in rear of the Second Corps, we were caught by General Grant, who was in high spirits, and addressed General Meade as "Old Fellow." Both Staffs halted for the night at Stute's house, and, as Grant's waggons could not get up, we fed him and his officers and lent them blankets. Grant had one of his sick headaches, which are rare, but cause him fearful pain, such as almost overcomes even his iron stoicism. To show how really amiable he is, he let the officers drum on the family piano a long while before he even would hint he didn't like it. Towards sundown we could hear rapid artillery from direction of Appomattox

SETH WILLIAMS

Station, which made us anxious; for we knew it was Sheridan, and could not know the result.

April 9, 1865

We all were up, according to habit, about daylight, with horses saddled, having staid near Stute's house for the night. In reply to a summons from Grant, Lee has sent in a note to say that he would meet Grant at ten A.M. to confer on measures for *peace*. The Lieutenant-General answered that he had no authority in the premises and refused the interview; but repeated his offer to accept the army's surrender on parole. Indeed, we suspected his affairs were from bad to worse, for last night we could hear, just at sunset, the distant cannon of Sheridan. He, with his cavalry, had made a forced march on Appomattox Station, where he encountered the head of the Rebel column (consisting, apparently, for the most part of artillery), charged furiously on it, and took twenty cannon and 1000 prisoners; and checked its progress for that night, during which time the 24th and 5th Corps, by strenuous marching, came up and formed line of battle quite across the Lynchburg road, west of Appomattox C.H. Betimes this morning, the enemy, thinking that nothing but cavalry was in their front, advanced to cut their way through, and were met by the artillery and musketry of two corps in position — (Ah! there goes a band playing "Dixie" in mockery. It is a real carnival!) This seems to have struck them with despair. Their only road blocked in front, and Humphreys's skirmishers dogging their footsteps! Well, we laid the General in his ambulance (he has been sick during the whole week, though now much better) and at 6.30 A.M. the whole Staff was off, at a round trot — (90 miles have I trotted and galloped after that Lee, and worn holes in my pantaloons, before I could get him to surrender!). An hour after, we came on the 6th Corps streaming into the main road from the upper one. A little ahead of this we halted to talk with General Wright. At 10.30 came, one after the other, two negroes, who said that some of our troops entered Lynchburg yesterday; and that Lee was now cut off near Appomattox Court House. This gave us new wings! An aide-de-camp galloped on, to urge Humphreys to press the pursuit, and all waggons were ordered out of the road, that the 6th Corps might close in immediately on his rear. Away went the General again, full tilt, along the road crowded by the infantry, every man of whom was footing it, as if a lottery prize lay just ahead! A bugler trotted ahead, blowing to call the attention of the troops, while General Webb followed, crying, "Give way to the right! Give way to the right!" Thus we ingeniously worked our way, amid much pleasantry. "Fish for sale!" roared one doughboy. "Yes," joined in a pithy comrade, "and a tarnation big one, too!" The comments on the General were endless. "That's Meade." "Yes, that's him." "Is he sick?" "I expect he is; he looks kinder wild!" "Guess the old man hain't had much sleep lately."

The heavy artillery firing we had earlier heard, now had suddenly ceased, and there was a perfect stillness — a suspicious circumstance that gave us new hope. Somewhat before noon we got to General Humphreys, some five miles east of the Court House and at the very head of his men. He reported that he had just struck the enemy's skirmish line, and was preparing to drive them back. At that moment an officer rode up and said the enemy were out with a white flag. "They shan't stop *me!*" retorted the fiery H.; "receive the message but push on the skirmishers!" Back came the officer speedily, with a note. General Lee stated that General Ord had agreed to a suspension of hostilities, and he should ask for the same on this *end* of the line. "Hey! what!" cried General Meade, in his harsh, suspicious voice, "I have no sort of authority to grant such suspension. General Lee has already refused the terms of General Grant. Advance your skirmishers, Humphreys, and bring up your troops. We will pitch into them at once!" But lo! here comes now General Forsyth, who had ridden through the Rebel army, from General Sheridan (under a flag), and who now urged a brief suspension. "Well," said the General, "in order that you may get back to Sheridan, I will wait till two o'clock, and then, if I get no communication from General Lee, I shall attack!" So back went Forsyth, with a variety of notes and despatches. We waited, not without excitement, for the appointed hour. Meantime, negroes came in and said the Rebel pickets had thrown down their muskets and gone leisurely to their main body; also that the Rebels were "done gone give up." Presently, the General pulled out his watch and said: "Two o'clock — no answer — go forward." But they had not advanced far, before we saw a Rebel and a Union officer coming in. They bore an order from General Grant to halt the troops. Major Wingate, of General Lee's Staff, was a military-looking man, dressed in a handsome grey suit with gold lace, and a gold star upon the collar. He was courageous, but plainly mortified to the heart. "We had done better to have burnt our whole train three days ago"; he said bitterly. "In trying to save a train, we have lost an army!" And there he struck the pith of the thing. And so we continued to wait till about five, during which time General Humphreys amused us with presents of Confederate notes, of which we found a barrel full (!) in the Rebel waggons. It was a strange spectacle, to see the officers laughing and giving each other $500 notes of a government that has been considered as firmly established by our English friends!

About five came Major Pease. "The Army of Northern Virginia has surrendered!" Headed by General Webb, we gave three cheers, and three more for General Meade. Then he mounted and rode through the 2d and 6th Corps. Such a scene followed as I can never see again. The soldiers rushed, perfectly crazy, to the roadside, and there crowding in dense masses, shouted, screamed, yelled, threw up their hats and hopped madly up and down! The batteries were run out and began firing, the bands played, the flags waved. The noise of the cheering was such that my very ears rang. And there was General Meade galloping about and waving his cap with the best of them! Poor old Robert Lee! His punishment is too heavy — to hear those cheers, and to remember what he once was! My little share of this work is done. God willing, before many weeks, or even days, I shall be at home, to campaign no more!

April 17, 1865

How wicked we are in this world! — Now, when I should be only overflowing with joy and thankfulness at these great results, I keep finding myself boiling and fuming over the personal neglect of General Meade and the totally undeserved prominence given to Sheridan. Yet Meade is really of no more consequence in this vast question of all time, than a sailor, who pulls a good oar, compared with the Atlantic Ocean. The truth will stand out in sober history, even for him — in the future Motleys and Prescotts. The plain truth about Meade is, first, that he is an abrupt, harsh man, even to his own officers, when in active cam-

paign; and secondly, that he, as a rule, will not even speak
to any person connected with the press. They do not dare
to address him. With other generals, how different: at
Grant's Headquarters there is a fellow named Cadwalader,
a *Herald* man, and you see the Lieutenant-General's Staff
officers calling, "Oh, Cad; come here a minute!" That is
the style! With two or three exceptions, Grant is surrounded by the most ordinary set of plebeians you ever
saw. I think he has them on purpose (to avoid advice), for
he is a man who does everything with a specific reason; he
is eminently a *wise* man. He knows very well Meade's
precise capacity and strong points. For example, if Meade
says a certain movement of troops should be made, Grant
makes it, almost as a matter of course, because he is so
wise as to know that there is one of Meade's strong points.

ON BOARD RIVER QUEEN IN POTOMAC RIVER
April 23, 1865

I think I must write you a letter, though it may get to
you not much before the winter, to tell of the end of our
campaign. Monday April 10 is a day worthy of description, because I saw the remains of our great opponent, the
Army of Northern Virginia. The General proposed to ride
through the Rebel lines to General Grant, who was at
Appomattox Court House; and he took George and myself
as aides; a great chance! for the rest were not allowed to go,
no communication being permitted between the armies.
At 10.30 we rode off, and, passing along the stage road,
soon got to the picket line, where a row of our men were
talking comfortably with an opposite row of theirs. There
the General sent me ahead to see some general of theirs
who might give us a guide through the lines. I rode a little
beyond a wood, and came on several regiments, camped

there. The arms were neatly stacked and the well-known
battle-flags were planted by the arms. The men, looking
tired and indifferent, were grouped here and there. I
judged they had nothing to eat, for there was no cooking
going on. A mounted officer was shown me as General
Field, and to him I applied. He looked something like
Captain Sleeper, but was extremely moody, though he at
once said he would ride back himself to General Meade, by
whom he was courteously received, which caused him to
thaw out considerably. We rode about a mile and then
turned off to General Lee's Headquarters, which consisted
in one fly with a camp-fire in front. I believe he had lost
most of his baggage in some of the trains, though his establishment is at all times modest. He had ridden out, but,
as we turned down the road again, we met him coming up,
with three or four Staff officers. As he rode up General
Meade took off his cap and said: "Good-morning, General." Lee, however, did not recognize him, and, when he
found who it was, said: "But what are you doing with all
that grey in your beard?" To which Meade promptly replied: "You have to answer for most of it!" Lee is, as all
agree, a stately-looking man; tall, erect and strongly built,
with a full chest. His hair and closely trimmed beard,
though thick, are now nearly white. He has a large and
well-shaped head, with a brown, clear eye, of unusual
depth. His face is sunburnt and rather florid. In manner
he is exceedingly grave and dignified — this, I believe, he
always has; but there was evidently added an extreme depression, which gave him the air of a man who kept up
his pride to the last, but who was entirely overwhelmed.
From his speech I judge he was inclined to wander in his
thoughts. You would not have recognized a Confederate

officer from his dress, which was a blue military overcoat, a high grey hat, and well-brushed riding boots.

As General Meade introduced his two aides, Lee put out his hand and saluted us with all the air of the oldest blood in the world. I did not think, when I left, in '63, for Germantown, that I should ever shake the hand of Robert E. Lee, prisoner of war! He held a long conference with General Meade, while I stood over a fire, with his officers, in the rain. Colonel Marshall, one of his aides, was a very sensible and gentlemanly man, and seemed in good spirits. He told me that, at one time during the retreat, he got no sleep for seventy-two hours, the consequence of which was that his brain did not work at all, or worked all wrong. A quartermaster came up to him and asked by what route he should move his train: to which Marshall replied, in a lucid manner: "Tell the Captain that I *should* have sent that cane as a present to his baby; but I could not, because the baby turned out to be a girl instead of a boy!" We were talking there together, when there appeared a great oddity — an old man, with an angular, much-wrinkled face, and long, thick white hair, brushed *à la* Calhoun; a pair of silver spectacles and a high felt hat further set off the countenance, while the legs kept up their claim of eccentricity by encasing themselves in grey blankets, tied somewhat in a bandit fashion. The whole made up no less a person than Henry A. Wise, once Governor of the loyal state of Virginia, now Brigadier-General and prisoner of war. By his first wife he is Meade's brother-in-law, and had been sent for to see him. I think *he* is punished already enough: old, sick, impoverished, a prisoner, with nothing to live for, not even his son, who was killed at Roanoke Island, he stood there in his old, wet, grey blanket, glad

to accept at our hands a pittance of biscuit and coffee, to
save him and his Staff from starvation! While they too
talked, I asked General Lee after his son "Roonie,"[1] who
was about there somewhere. It was the "Last Ditch"
indeed! He too is punished enough: living at this moment at Richmond, on the food doled out to him by our
government, he gets his ration just like the poorest negro
in the place! We left Lee, and kept on through the sad
remnants of an army that has its place in history. It would
have looked a mighty host, if the ghosts of all its soldiers
that now sleep between Gettysburg and Lynchburg could
have stood there in the lines, beside the living.

BURKEVILLE, VA.
Headquarters Army of Potomac
April 19, 1865

LT.-COL. THEO. LYMAN, A. D. C.

COLONEL: — In parting with you after an association of
over twenty months, during which time you have served
on my Staff, I feel it due to you to express my high sense of
the assistance I have received from you, and to bear testimony to the zeal, energy, and gallantry you have displayed in the discharge of your duties. Be assured I shall
ever preserve the liveliest reminiscences of our intercourse,
and wherever our separate fortunes may take us, I shall
ever have a deep interest in your welfare and happiness,
which, by the blessing of God, I trust may be long continued.

Most Truly Your Friend
GEO. G. MEADE
Maj.-Genl. U. S. A.

[1] He was at Harvard with Lyman.

INDEX

INDEX

Abbot, Henry Livermore, 76, 318, 332; death, 95, 97.
Adams, Charles Francis, Jr., 104.
Agassiz, Louis, iii.
Aide-de-camp, qualities of, 121.
Aiken house, 219, 220.
Alden, Algernon Sidney, 257, 289.
Alexandria, Va., 4.
Anderson, ——, 265.
Anderson house, 115, 128.
Annoy, use of word, 247.
Appleton, Nathan, 72, 127, 169.
Appomattox campaign, 303; High Bridge, 352.
Armistice, 154, 170, 201.
Armstrong house, 114.
Army, on the march, 29, 55; reinforcing, 31, 177; intercourse with enemy, 106, 153, 181; formation of, 263.
Assaults, effect of too many, 148n.
Atlanta, capture of, 228.
Atlanta, iron-clad, 161, 163.
Avery, Martin P., 171.
Ayres, Romeyn Beck, 234, 236, 242, 331.

Babcock, Orville Elias, 161, 314.
Bache, ——, 204.
Badajos, English at, 207.
Badeau, Adam, 314.
Baldwin, Briscoe G., 125.
Barlow, Francis Channing, 109, 117, 135, 157, 215, 216; described, 107, 158, 189; at Cold Harbor, 144; at Petersburg, 186.
Barnard, Daniel P., 343.
Barnard, George, 91n.
Barnard, John Gross, 248, 290.
Barnes, Joseph K., 248.
Barney, Hiram, 249.
Barrows, William Eliot, 350.
Barstow, Simon Forrester, 7, 48, 64, 232, 289.
Bartlett, Joseph Jackson, 72.
Battle, a great, 101.
Beauregard, Pierre Gustave Toutant, 173n, 201, 222.
Benham, Henry Washington, 23, 335; described, 241.
Benson, ——, 280.
Bethesda Church, 140.

Biddle, James Cornell, 24, 48, 69, 70, 122, 168, 204, 228, 249, 265, 289; on leave of absence, 59; camp commandant, 67; Meade and, 176; early hours, 239; excitement, 241; cigar incident, 249.
Bingham, Henry Harrison, 253.
Birney, David Bell, 77, 82, 92, 94, 114, 117, 121, 135, 137, 150, 233; described, 107, 188; at Cold Harbor, 146; at Petersburg, 165, 170, 174; death of, 266.
Blake, Peleg W., 169.
Blunt, ——, Miss., 76.
Boissac, ,—— de, 254.
Boleslaski, ——, Austrian officer, 20.
Bonaparte, Napoleon, 114.
Bootekoff, ——, 62.
Botiano, ——, 308, 311.
Botts, John Minor, 46, 82.
Boydton plank road, 293, 347.
Bradley, Joseph P., 315.
Breckinridge, John Cabell, 136.
Brevets, distribution of, 257, 289.
Briscoe, James C., 82.
Brockenbrough, Mrs., 131.
Brooks, William Thomas Harbaugh, 148.
Buford, John, 15, 40, 50; described, 21; advice to a volunteer aide, 35.
Bullets, explosive, 102.
Burnside, Ambrose Everett, 87, 91, 93, 94, 96, 97, 106, 108, 110, 114, 128, 134, 140, 211; at church, 120; corps incorporated, 127; at Smith's, 149; at Petersburg, 164, 167, 168, 197; mine, 199, 200, 310.
Bushwhacking, 295.
Butler, Benjamin Franklin, 118; orders demonstration, 68; Petersburg and, 160; described, 192; Smith and, 192; visit to, 193, 204, 279; sharpshooters and, 205; Dutch Gap canal, 213, 282; stampeded, 237; cabinet rumor, 266; devices, 284.

Cabot, Louis, 353.
Cadwalader, Charles E., 69, 130, 210.
Cadwalader, S., 359.
Calling the hours, 276.
Cameron, Simon, 317.
Cannon, management of, 202; wooden, 242.

Index

Mott, Gershom, 92, 93, 95, 108, 109, 217, 337.
Mott's division, misconduct, 92, 93, 95, 109, 110n, 114, 208, 252, 294.
Mt. Carmel Church, 122.

NAMOZINE ROAD, 342, 346.
Negro, Virginia, 67; free and slave, 74; troops, 102, 162, 180, 256, 262; "aunty," 183; Petersburg mine, 199, 214; burying Rebel dead, 203n; arming southern, 245; poker game, 269.
Nesmith, James Willis, 280; on Bull Run, 284.
New London, Conn., 223.
Newspapers, errors of, 100.
Newton, John, 33, 56, 60, 80; visited, 9.
Newton, *Mrs.*, 131.
North Anna, 122, 126.

O'CONNOR, W. ULICK, Viscount Castle-Cuffe, 49.
Officers, good quality, 11; promotion, 78; qualities of good, 121, 266; bearing of Rebel,152.
Ord, Edward Otho Cresap, 200, 233, 266, 320, 335, 357.
Ordinary, in Virginia, 119.
Otto, William Tod, 212.
Ovens, Dutch, 351.

PALFREY, FRANCIS WINTHROP, 65.
Parke, John Grubb, 233, 234, 236, 323, 334; described, 213; engineer, 246.
Parker, Isaac Brown, 288.
Parker, Theodore, 260.
Patrick, Marsena Rudolph, 74.
Patten, Henry Lyman, 208.
Pease, Charles Elliott, 358.
Peeble house, 235, 254, 321.
Peel, Cecil Lennox, *captain*, 49.
Pell, Duncan Archibald, 212, 312, 319.
Pemberton, John Clifford, 102.
Perkins house, 328.
Perkinson, ——, 347.
Petersburg, manœuvres about, 160; mine, 195, 310, 341; taken, 333, 339.
Phillips, Charles Appleton, 169.
Picket line, described, 301.
Piney Branch church, 122.
Platt, Edward Russell, 123.
Pleasonton, Alfred, 75, 79, 80; Lyman with, 14; for command, 60.
Pleasants, Henry, 195, 198.
Plunder, demoralizing effect, 40; Hancock and, 288.
Point of Rocks, Appomattox River, 193.

Pontoon bridge, 130, 159.
Po-Ny, 119.
Pope, John, 60.
Poplar Grove church, 234.
Porter, David Dixon, 249.
Porter, Georgia Ann (Patterson), 249.
Porter, Horace, 142.
Potter, Alonzo, 167.
Potter, Robert Barnwell, 166, 212, 219, 234, 237, 296, 297, 334.
Pourtalès, Louis Auguste de, 212.
Pratt, Mary, 26.
Prisoners, provost, 13; Rebel, 32, 45, 324, 336, 347.
Punishments, 243.

RACCOON FORD, 19, 68, 69.
Races, horse, 321.
Railroad construction, 311.
Rapidan River, 51.
Rawlins, John Aaron, 91n, 114n.
Reams' station, 224, 234.
Rebels, fighting qualities, 87, 99, 100, 208; privations, 132; valuable qualities, 186; wearing down, 245, 271; deserters, 305, 310; appearance, 324, 360.
Revere, Paul Joseph, 34.
Review of troops, 9, 316, 318; 2d corps, 75; 9th corps, 261.
Rice, James Clay, 109, 180.
Rice's station, 352.
Richmond, fall of, 343.
Ricketts, James Brewerton, 98, 139, 144, 174, 176, 177, 184, 208, 232, 299.
Riddle, William, 293.
Ring, ——, 172.
Robertson's Tavern, 53, 54, 58.
Robinson, John Cleveland, 104.
Rockwell, ——, *Rev.*, 74.
Roebling, John Augustus, 240.
Roebling, Washington Augustus, 56, 168, 253; described, 240.
Rogers, William Barton, 315.
Rosencrantz, Frederick, 63, 64, 177, 183, 193, 202, 204, 210, 232, 244, 249, 277, 304, 306, 309, 315, 336; first meeting, 6; on the English, 268; major, 290.
Roumania, 307.
Rowley, William Reuben, 84, 164.
Rush's Lancers, 130.
Russell, David Allen, 128, 144, 177.
Russell, Elizabeth, iii.
Russell, George Robert, iii.
Russell, Henry Sturgis, 161, 164, 165, 269.
Russians on horse, 61.